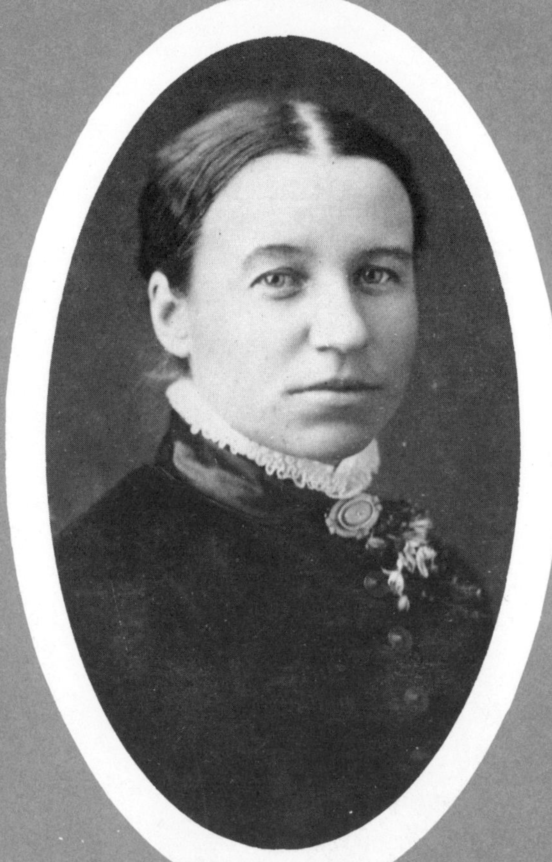

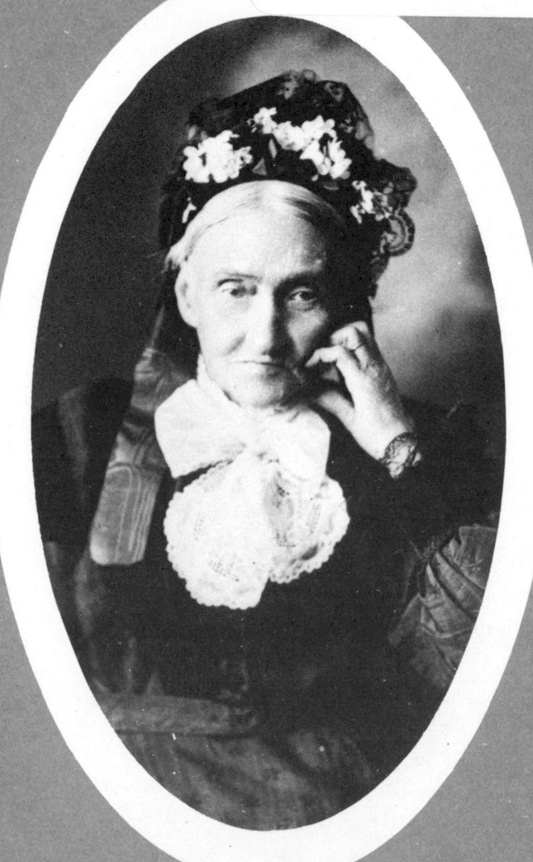

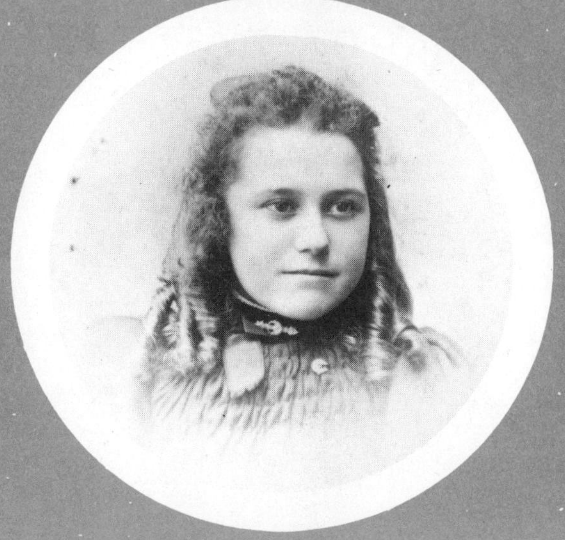

Far left: Ellen Blomfield (seated) with Bessie, Reggie, Tom, Nellie and Mary (standing)

Above left: Ellen Blomfield (née Wild)

Above right: Elizabeth Emily Blomfield, aged 95

Left: Bessie Blomfield

CHARLES
BLOMFIELD

CHARLES BLOMFIELD

HIS LIFE AND TIMES

Muriel Williams

HODDER AND STOUGHTON
AUCKLAND LONDON SYDNEY

The publishers make acknowledgement of the permission to reproduce the following paintings from the Maurice Lennard Collection: 'Wanganui River' (front cover), 'Atiamuri' (p. 50), 'Mud Valley, Rotomahana' (p. 50), 'Pararahi Logging Mill' (p. 57) and 'Mount Ruapehu' (p. 119).

The author wishes to thank all friends and relatives who so kindly granted permission to reproduce the paintings in their possession.

Designed by John Booth
Typeset by Typemasters (N.Z.) Ltd., Auckland. Printed and bound in Hong Kong for Hodder and Stoughton Ltd., 44-46 View Road, Glenfield, Auckland. New Zealand.

Contents

To my mother
Without whose memories I could not
have written this book

"I have never ceased to be thankful for two things. One is that I was born
with an intense love for the beautiful in Nature, and the other that I came
to New Zealand before the hand of man had spoiled most of its natural
beauty."

— Charles Blomfield

❧ ❦ ❧

"The lordly Kauri, King of the Forest, and his graceful consort the Rimu,
hold sway over a numerous court of stately trees. The sturdy Puriri grows
side by side with the handsome Tawa, throwing out its dark tapering
branches in picturesque abandon; the ornamental Puketea with its
buttressed root and the Kohe with its broad canopy of large delicate
leaves; the Kahikatea and the Matai struggle upwards to get a glimpse of
sun and air, while the Hinau, close attendant on the king, is content to
dwell in the shade. The court jester is not wanting, for just look at that
giant Rata, its uncouth form leaving under it a mass of creepers and
parasites that completely hide its shaggy trunk, while the forest vines like
ropes and cordage, wanton from tree to tree hang in graceful festoons
gently swaying in the summer breeze. The court ladies are there too;
here, there, and everywhere the tall tree ferns lift their feathery fronds,
their slender shafts decorated with an exquisite mantle of moss and lichen;
and the little ones gambol about the feet of their elders while the floor is
carpeted with the softest of moss."

— Charles Blomfield

❧ ❦ ❧

Preface

Charles Blomfield is known to many as the painter of the Pink and White Terraces of New Zealand's thermal region, the extraordinary formations of siliceous rock once hailed as the Eighth Wonder of the World. The destruction of these terraces in the 1886 eruption of nearby Mount Tarawera led to the sudden rise in importance of all representations of them; and Blomfield's terrace paintings, because they were among the most beautiful ever done, and were perhaps the most faithful to their subject, shot to instant fame. His habit of making sketches and painting his subjects from many different angles and in different lights to provide models for later copies, meant that for years after the eruption Blomfield could depend upon his steady stream of terrace paintings to bring him a modest income and recognition both in New Zealand and abroad.

Yet although the Pink and White Terraces proved to be Blomfield's favourite subjects, they were by no means his only ones. He was a zealous traveller and exhibitor for the more than sixty years between 1862 and 1926, constantly exploring the countryside for new and exciting subject matter. "A waterfall on the Mangawhero, unvisited and almost unknown," he once wrote, "virgin ground to the artist and photographer! This was quite enough to induce me to start on a sketching tour up the Mangawhero." He was prepared to tramp great distances, negotiate rivers and lakes in rowboats, and endure all kinds of discomforts to find scenes that would inspire him. If his destination required a journey too difficult to allow him to take along large canvases, he would make small sketches and watercolours, then create his paintings when he returned. His dedication was enormous. His travels took him the length and breadth of New Zealand and over to Australia, at a time when such travelling was by no means easy. He would hold exhibitions as he went, often earning just enough from his picture sales to support his family back in Auckland, and to enable him to continue on his way.

Nor are Blomfield's terrace paintings, despite being his most popular and widely recognised works, necessarily his best. There is quite as much variety in the standard of his painting as there is in subject matter. Some of the results of his forays into the wild New Zealand landscape are little more than bland pictorial records; others, however, are fine, beautifully executed paintings that rank with the work of New Zealand's best colonial painters. Charles Blomfield cannot be ignored as an important early artist.

Blomfield's most notable characteristic, however, must be his highly developed aesthetic sense. It is apparent in his painting, his writing, and his way of life. Completely self-taught, he began to paint while very young and spent the rest of his life struggling to make a livelihood out of painting the countryside he loved so much. He could perceive beauty in all landscapes, all skies and weathers; his variety of approach led one contemporary critic to comment: "Mr Blomfield . . . is evidently in love with Nature in all her moods." His efforts to faithfully portray nature can also be found in his letters to his wife, Ellen, and in the many articles he wrote for local newspapers; he would describe each new impression with much enthusiasm and in careful detail, taking as many pains with his pen as he would with his brush. In his writings he also revealed himself to be one of New Zealand's first conservationists, showing an advanced awareness of the threat civilisation was imposing on the previously untouched landscape.

But sadly, and as so often happens, Charles Blomfield outlived his own popularity. Just as he was reaching what he himself considered to be the heights of his technical ability and awareness, the public of the 1920s began to reject his Victorian mode. His last years were spent in disappointment and disbelief: "I paint nature as I see it," he would say. "Surely there is some virtue in that." His paintings were to take a further plunge in popularity for many years after his death; coinciding with the inevitable drop in prices due to the Depression, even his larger works fetched as little as £1 each in the 1930s. But now, fifty years later, the value of some of his paintings soars into the thousands of dollars. More importantly, his work is now being recognised for what it is: a loving portrait of a virgin country, by one of its pioneers.

— H.R.S.

1

Emigration
1862 - 1874

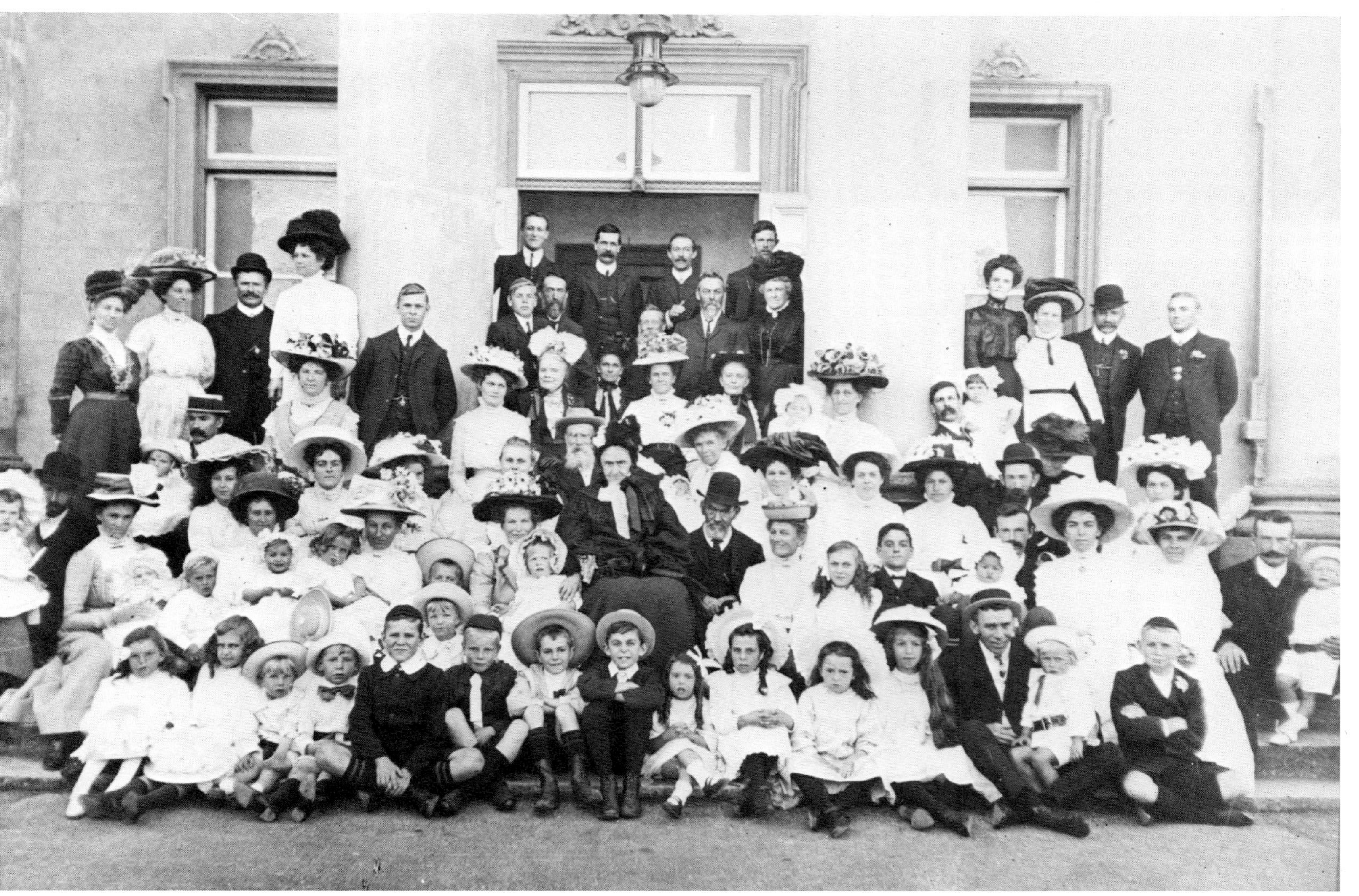

The Blomfield family, 1909. Elizabeth Emily Blomfield in centre, Charles Blomfield second to left, second back row.

1. The Albertlanders

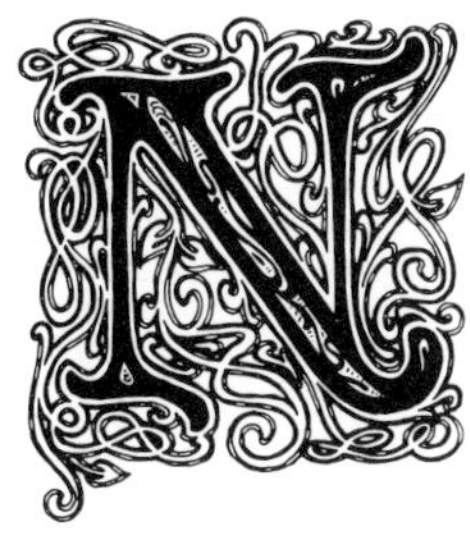

OVEMBER 20TH, 1909 dawned bright and fair, and at that early hour there was unusual activity in homes across Auckland and beyond, for this was the day that Elizabeth Emily Blomfield was to celebrate her ninety-fifth birthday. As many of her family as possible were to attend a reunion lunch to pay court to the grand old lady known to everyone as "Grandma Blom". Watching all her offspring arrive, Elizabeth felt very proud; she had a hundred and one living descendants by this time, of whom eighty were here at her party. If children were riches, then she was truly a wealthy woman!

After a magnificent lunch several of the men made speeches, telling the gathering about their adventures on the goldfields, in the kauri forests, and on their camping trips throughout the country. Last to speak was Elizabeth's youngest son Fred, now in his fifties, who described the experience of coming out to New Zealand as perceived by a five-year-old boy. He remembered the large gathering at Bow Church in London, where men and women were openly weeping and sobbing as their friends and relatives prepared to emigrate to a savage country at the other end of the world. He remembered the Minister calling all the men and boys to the altar and giving to each an axe to clear the forest, a spade to till the ground, and a Bible to convert the Maori savages to Christianity.

Elizabeth Blomfield decided to emigrate in 1862. In England, her family had been fervent Baptists, attending the Metropolitan Tabernacle in London of the well-known Baptist Evangelist, the Reverend Charles Haddon Spurgeon. When Elizabeth's husband William died, leaving her a widow with a large family to care for, she began to attend the meetings of the Albertland Settlement Association, so-called in memory of the Prince Consort who had died a few months earlier. At these meetings she heard many speakers, including the Rev. Spurgeon, urging interested persons to join in establishing a nonconformist settlement in New Zealand.

To Elizabeth Blomfield the idea sounded exciting. They were to found a settlement in New Zealand similar to the one started by the Pilgrim Fathers when they emigrated to America two hundred years earlier. On reaching New Zealand, each man would be given forty acres, with another forty for his wife and twenty for each child, on the condition that they lived on the land for five years. Reasonably priced passage would also be provided — about £16 each — on ships specially chartered through Shaw Savill.

The Albertland block to be used for this settlement consisted of thirty thousand acres situated on the upper reaches of the Kaipara Harbour,

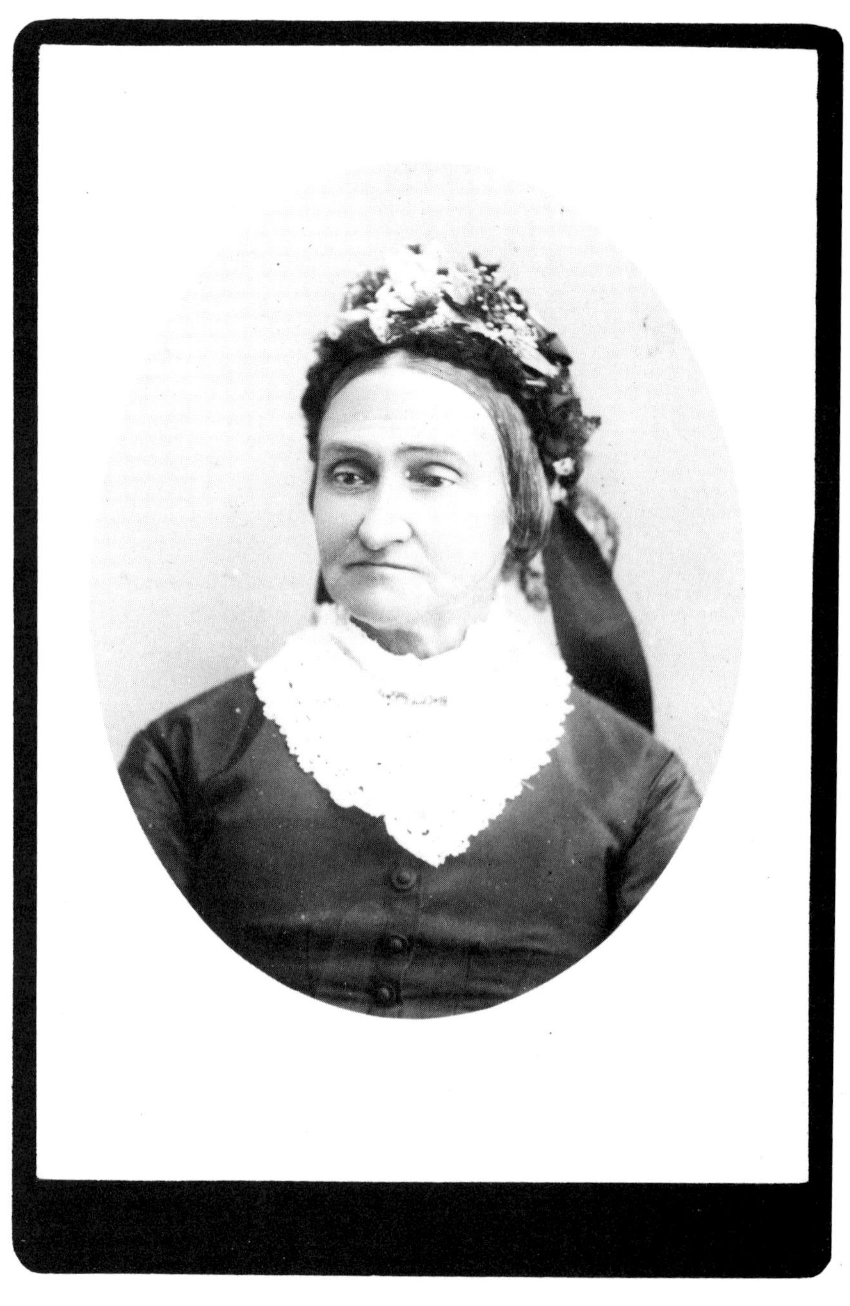

The proud matriarch, Elizabeth Emily Blomfield.

only about eighty miles north of the Port of Auckland. There would be plenty of space and clean air, with opportunities for the young people. What a wonderful chance to get away from the dirt, grime and crowded conditions of over-populated London!

After much discussion with her eldest son, Samuel, who was already married with two children, Elizabeth Blomfield decided to join the Albertlanders and emigrate to New Zealand.

Shaw Savill's contract ticket for the Blomfield family, 1862.

SPECIAL SETTLEMENT OF NONCONFORMISTS AND OTHERS.

SHAW, SAVILL & Co., 34, LEADENHALL STREET.

No. 85   PASSENGERS' CONTRACT TICKET.

1.—A Contract Ticket in this form must be given to every Passenger engaging a passage from the United Kingdom to any place out of Europe, and not being within the Mediterranean Sea.

2.—The Victualling Scale for the voyage must be printed in the body of the Ticket.

3.—All the Blanks must be correctly filled in, and the Ticket must be legibly signed with the Christian names and surname and address in full of the party issuing the same.

4.—The day of the month on which the Ship is to sail must be inserted in words and not in figures.

5.—When once issued, this Ticket must not be withdrawn from the Passenger, nor any alteration, addition, or erasure made in it.

Ship _Gertrude_ of _1300_ Tons Register, to take in Passengers at _London_ for _Auckland_ on the _thirtieth_ day of _October_ 186_2_

I engage that the person named in the margin hereof shall be provided with a { Second Cabin / Steerage } Passage to, and shall be Landed at, the Port of _Auckland_ in _New Zealand_ in the Ship _Gertrude_ with not less than { Thirty / Twenty }* Cubic Feet for Luggage for each Statute Adult, and shall be victualled during the voyage and the time of detention at any place before its termination, according to the subjoined Scale, for the sum of £ _112.10_ including Government dues before embarkation, and head money, if any, at the place of landing, and every other charge † except Freight for excess of Luggage beyond the quantity above specified, and I hereby acknowledge to have received the sum of £ _66 . 0 . 0_ in { part / full } payment.

The following quantities, at least, of Water and Provisions (to be issued daily) will be supplied by the Master of the Ship, as required by Law, viz.: to each Statute Adult Three Quarts of Water daily, exclusive of what is necessary for cooking the articles required by the Passenger Act, to be issued in a cooked state, and a Weekly Allowance of Provisions according to the following Scale:—

NAMES.		AGES.	Equal to Statute Adult.
Eliz. E. Blomfield		46	1
Frances	do	19	1
Mary A.	do	17	1
Charles	do	14	1
Ellen	do	11	1/2
Fred.	do	5	1/2
Samuel	do	27	1
Emma	do	22	1
Alice	do	2	1/2
Grace	do	9/12	—

Signature in full _Walter Smith_

Scale of Dietary for each Adult Passenger per Week.

ARTICLES.	Second Cabin.	Third Cabin or Intermedte.	ARTICLES.	Second Cabin.	Third Cabin or Intermedte.
Preserved Meats	2 lb.	1 lb.	Tea	2 oz.	1½ oz.
Soup and Bouilli	½ lb.	½ lb.	Coffee	3 oz.	2 oz.
York Ham	½ lb.	—	Butter	½ lb.	¼ lb.
Fish	½ lb.	—	Molasses	½ lb.	½ lb.
Salt Beef	1 lb.	1¼ lb.	Cheese	½ lb.	—
Salt Pork	1¼ lb.	1 lb.	Currants, or	¼ lb.	—
Biscuit	3½ lb.	2¼ lb.	Raisins, Valentia	¼ lb.	¼ lb.
Flour	4¾ lb.	3½ lb.	Suet	6 oz.	6 oz.
Rice	1 lb.	1 lb.	Pickles	¼ pint	¼ pint
Barley	½ lb.	—	Mustard	½ oz.	½ oz.
Peas	½ pint	½ pint	Pepper	¼ oz.	¼ oz.
Sugar, raw	1 lb.	1 lb.	Salt	2 oz.	2 oz.
Sugar, Lump	6 oz.	—	Potatoes, fresh, or	3½ lb.	2 lb.
Lime Juice	6 oz.	6 oz.	Preserved ditto	½ lb.	½ lb.
Carrots	4 oz.	4 oz.	Water	21 quarts	21 quarts
Lard	4 oz.	4 oz.			

Substitutions, at the following rates, may, at the option of the Master, be made in the above Dietary Scale:—

1 lb. of Preserved Meat	FOR	1 lb. of Salt Pork or Beef.
1 lb. of Flour, or Bread or Biscuit or }	„	{ 1¼ lb. of Oatmeal or
½ lb. of Beef or Pork }	„	{ 1 lb. of Rice or Peas.
1 lb. of Rice	„	1¼ lb. of Oatmeal, or *vice versa*.
½ lb. of Preserved Potatoes	„	1 lb. of Potatoes.
10 oz. of Currants	„	8 oz. of Raisins.
3½ oz. of Cocoa or Coffee, Roasted and Ground	„	2 oz. of Tea.
½ lb. of Treacle	„	½ lb. of Sugar.
1 gill of Mixed Pickles	„	1 gill of Vinegar.

34, LEADENHALL STREET.

LONDON, _October 10th_ 186_2_

‡ Deposit ...... £ _66 . 0 . 0_   £31-5/-

Balance ...... £ _46 . 10 . 0_ to be paid at 34, Leadenh. St., London, prior to Embarkation.

Total ...... £ _112 . 10 . 0_

Shaw Savill & Co
T.H.H. Sutherland

NOTICES TO PASSENGERS.

1.—If Passengers, through no default of their own, are not received on board on the day named in their Contract Tickets, or fail to obtain a passage in the Ship, they should apply to the Government Emigration Officer at the Port, who will assist them in obtaining redress under the Passenger Act.

2.—Passengers should carefully keep this part of their Contract Ticket till after the end of the voyage. If lost, no second Ticket will be issued.

N.B.—If Passengers are not maintained on Board after the above named date, they will be paid Subsistence Money after the rate of 1s. 6d. per day for each Statute Adult.

N.B.—This Contract Ticket is exempt from Stamp Duty.

* SHAW, SAVILL and Co. will not undertake to land more than the above quantity of Luggage.

† All charges on board the vessel between embarkation and disembarkation.

‡ It is understood that this Deposit will be absolutely forfeited in case the parties named herein fail to embark in a fit state of health for the voyage, at the above-mentioned place and date.

Her decision was received with mixed feelings by her children. Emily, already in her twenties, stubbornly refused to go. "My work is here," she said, "with the needy people of London."

Frances on the other hand, not quite twenty, could see all the young men in the party travelling to the colonies. Maybe she would find a nice beau — either on the ship, or in that faraway land.

Seventeen-year-old Mary Ann was thrilled at the prospect of the long sea voyage. She loved children, and looked forward to the months on board ship when she would be able to teach her small brother Fred, and help Sam's wife Emma with their two little girls, Alice and Grace. She derived great joy from gathering young children around her and telling them stories. Unlike Frances, she was not interested in young men, being very conscious of her deformed hand with two fingers where the thumb should be, and she tucked this hand into the front of her blouse as she said, "Oh yes, Mother, I think it would be a wonderful idea for all of us."

Young Charles Blomfield was deeply religious, even at fourteen, and he wanted to go to New Zealand in order to help "sow the seeds of perfect religious equality in that far-off region", as he had been exhorted to do at the meetings the family had attended. But little Ellen and Fred were too young to voice their opinions, and just went along quite happily wherever the family took them.

Sam Blomfield and his mother made all the final arrangements with the Albertland Settlement Association and Shaw Savill, and booked to travel on the *Gertrude*, a fine roomy ship of thirteen hundred tons, due to sail on October 31st, 1862. It was to cost a total sum of £112.0.0, but after some discussion Sam was able to work his passage, and the fare was reduced by £15.5.0. The deposit was paid on the 10th October, leaving the family only three weeks to pack up their belongings and prepare to say goodbye to their home country.

2. Sea Journey

At last the great day arrived. Charles Blomfield discovered that his quarters for the journey were to be a large open cabin, in which there were twenty hammocks for the single young men. But Charles did not take long to become acquainted with the other youths, some of whom, like William Haszard, were to be close and life-long friends.

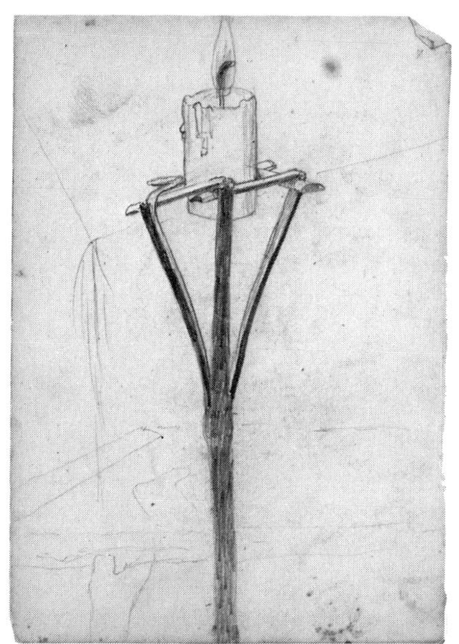

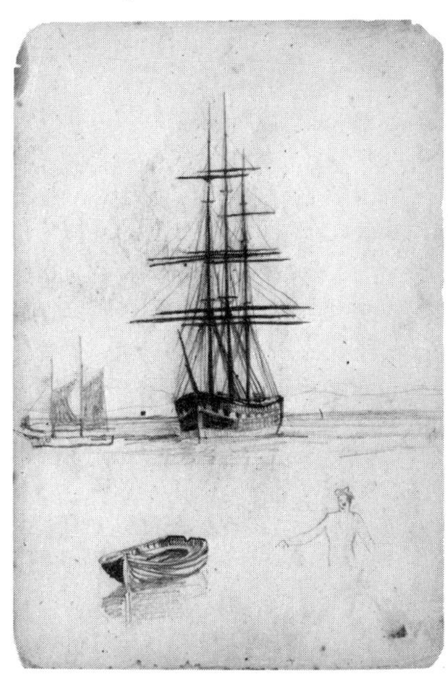

One of the young men in this cabin, Robert Smith, filled in the slow hours aboard ship by writing a long letter to his father in England:

We were towed out of the East India Docks on Saturday 1st, about 9 a.m. amidst great cheering from a concourse of people who had assembled to witness the departure. We went smoothly down the Thames, and although the day was rather dull and threatening rain, yet we had a beautiful view of the surrounding scenery as we passed. We arrived at Gravesend, cast anchor, there to undergo the inspection of the Government Commission agents. We all lined up on the poop and had to pass one by one showing our "contract tickets" which constituted the Government inspection of the passengers. The ship had yet to undergo a search by these gentlemen, and as there was a great deal of luggage lying in among the tables and seats in a sort of topsy-turvy fashion, they concluded that she had too much cargo on board, and that some of it must come off and be sent by another vessel. This created a great deal of discontent among the passengers as everyone was afraid of losing some of their belongings for a time. However it was

getting dark and nothing could be done that night, so we amused
ourselves a little with music of various kinds until bed-time, and then
retired for the night. About 7 a.m. I was awakened by the noise of
passengers running to and fro, shouting in all tones about their luggage
as a lighter was alongside, and the men of the ship were already actively
putting off some of the cargo. While this was going on I went to breakfast and at 11 a.m. went to Divine Service which was well attended,
hearing a very good sermon. I could scarcely realise that it was Sabbath,
seeing some collected in a group in one part of the ship praising God,
and in another part of the ship men busy discharging cargo in a very
unbecoming manner, tearing and swearing at their work, so you may
guess what sort of Sabbath we had for the first — very different from
what you see in Scotland; but it appears to concord with the feelings
of the English. I judge they can be praying very earnestly at one time
and immediately after be singing and whistling all the various tunes
in existence.

I almost forgot! We even had vendors of apples and nuts from
Gravesend pressing the passengers to purchase from them and I have
no doubt they did a good stroke of business although it was Sunday.
However, the day was spent. In the evening we formed into groups
singing hymns and church music, and then went to bed. I slept tolerably
well getting up next morning (Monday) at 7 a.m. After a wash and
stroll on deck there was breakfast, then orders were given out that we
would get our weekly rations served out after breakfast, which caused
a great hubbub. You must first know that there are two different kinds
of passengers, namely two hundred nonconformists, and the others
composed of any persons sent by the ship-brokers to fill up. Consequently we had two scales of rations — one inferior to the other.
The ship was going to serve us all on the inferior scale, which we
resented. Fortunately the government agent was on board the second
time, so ten of us went to him and presented our contract tickets and
ventilated our grievances. He immediately gave orders that we were
to get no less than what was on our tickets, whatever more. So we had
all to show our tickets before we got our rations — consequently we
were fed at one pitch while the other party were fed at one much less.
However we got matters corrected and spent the rest of the day feeling
rather idle and discontented — everyone complaining at being kept so
long and anxiously enquiring when we were going to start. Many reports
were made — some that we were going to start immediately, some that
we were going to start two or three days hence, while others were that
the ship was condemned and that we would be required to go back to
London and join another. However we were a little pacified when we
were informed by the Mate that we would start early next morning. At
that stage everyone drew towards his evening's amusement of
various sorts — music was struck up and dancing was entered into with
great spirits. Gradually they retired to rest and by ten o'clock most of
them were in the arms of Morpheus. I myself remained on deck till near
twelve o'clock, then went to bed and slept well till six a.m., when I

was awakened by the tremendous cheering of those who had got up before me. I hurried on deck along with many others in shirt and trousers to join the crowd in cheering, as we were actually leaving the place, which seeded a release to our detention of three days and three nights.

The tug came alongside, lines were made fast, and the impatient paddles, after a hesitating splash or two, moved steadily on; the three days' familiarised scenery gradually glided away. We were no sooner off than we were proceeding with moderate speed down the long avenue of ships stretching towards the sea. Looking around us as we ploughed the centre of the river, what a fine view we obtained of the surrounding scenery. Although the country on both sides was very flat and comparatively uninteresting, it was not without charm, however, and very fitting for an English landscape. Rich alluvial plains on either side stretched far around, and although the river was very wide and the land pretty distant from us, yet we could easily discern fine hedgerows and belts of planting, with here and there an elegant mansion or a snug little farmhouse beautifully studded round about with clumps of trees, and on every elevated and prominent part we could see windmills busily at work. The river now grew so wide that we could scarcely discern anything at all. The passengers left off looking at the land, their attention now turned in amusement towards the sailors, who were spreading the sails, singing their merry songs as they did so, which was something new to those who had never been to sea. Our tug was about to leave us, and darkness was setting in, so the passengers were gradually going below and turning towards their evening's amusement. We had had a great deal of music in the evenings so far, but tonight a few of the young men had a meeting for the purpose of forming a class for mutual improvement, and it was decided that we shall have meetings each Tuesday and Friday evening at seven-thirty p.m. Our first subject for discussion is to be "Who are the heroes of the day?"

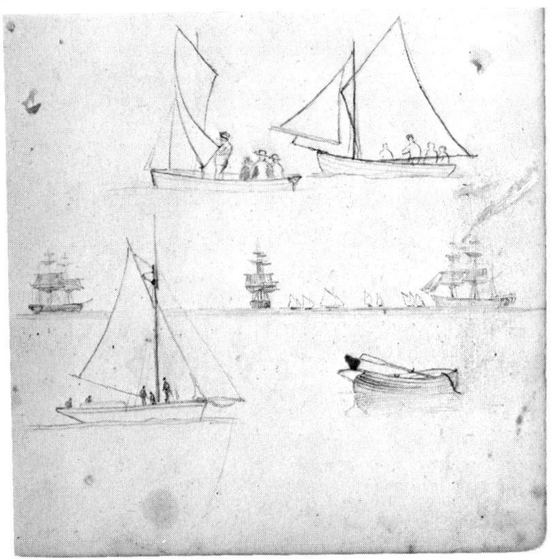

Wednesday, November 5th. Got up at 6.30 a.m., feeling rather sickly, and learned that we had made no progress during the night — a head wind still very strong so they have thought fit to cast anchor. We are lying off Deal not far from Dover; we are very near land and a magnificent place it is. About a mile along the shore is a beautiful white chalk rock falling almost perpendicularly into the sea with lovely rising ground behind and windmills flying in all directions. The town of Deal lies to the right, Dover is round the corner. We have men coming from Deal in small boats selling apples and gingerbread, nuts and onions at an exorbitant price and offering to take letters on shore for sixpence each, but we were warned against doing so, as they would very likely take off the stamp.

We had a prayer meeting at 6.30 and sang a great many hymns. We also had a meeting for the purpose of electing watchmen to go about all night to see that all lights were put out at the specified time, and to see that no fire originated anywhere. It was agreed that a married and a single gentleman go together each night, everyone taking their respective nights in succession which means that the duty will only fall to each one once or thereabouts during the voyage.

Thursday November 6th. We were again pestered with men from Deal selling new loaves a good deal smaller than those 3d loaves at home, for the sum of 7d. Today we had a very busy day making dumplings and puddings. It is rather laughable to see a great many unpractised hands all busily employed baking in whatever quiet corner they can find — dough to the elbows and flour all over and all as earnest as if it were for a wager — then you can see them all running to the galley, each with his bag of flour and raisins to get them cooked for dinner. We however consider ourselves aggrieved in some things, for instance in the matter of coffee — in place of giving us two ounces of coffee in a prepared state, they are giving us two ounces of raw berries, which when roasted and ground is one third less — and several other things. However, if we don't get an amendment there will be disturbances amongst us.

We have had dinner and our dumplings were delightful — perhaps there is a little partiality because being made by ourselves. Our seamen are again very busy weighing anchor and spreading sail preparatory to starting. In the midst of the bustle, the *John Duncan*, a vessel that lay close to us in the East India Docks, passed us about fifty yards distant, bound for Otago with five hundred passengers on board — we have three hundred and sixty-five on board our ship. You may guess we were a little cheered but had some reason to murmur when we saw a ship that was two days later in sailing, pass us briskly and us standing still and idle as a painted ship on a painted ocean.

We got round the cliffs of Dover when the breeze freshened and became more favourable, giving us a speed of eight knots. It was dark when we passed Dover so that I cannot give you any description of it, only we could see rows of lights along the sea coast and the rising ground behind studded all over with a whole host of lights which was altogether

a charming scene. We could also see on the opposite side a few lights
which were at Calais, but too far away to distinguish anything but the
signal lights. We had our usual time dancing, then retired to bed to
sleep away the time and wait the results of another day.

Friday, November 7th. There was a great hubbub on board as it was found
that we had a little stowaway on board. Everyone was anxious to see
the little urchin which caused some great crowding in different parts of
the ship. There was also the matter of an Irishman on board whose
passage had been paid by his brother in New Zealand, but through
some default or other had not received a contract ticket; consequently
the Captain ordered him to go on shore. Both went ashore with the
pilot at midday when we were off the Isle of Wight. A fresh breeze was
blowing and in the evening we had a meeting of our "Mutual Improvement Class", which saw some very able discussion. We had two meetings
in the afternoon. One for the purpose of forming a music class, as we
have a professor of music on board from whom eighteen of us have
bought music books at a shilling each, and we get taught free on
Monday, Wednesday and Friday evenings. The other meeting was for
the purpose of having an amateur social concert once a week, and I
have been elected President of the committee for this.

By this time the ship was beginning to roll very much, and as we had
not yet got our sea-legs, it was rather laughable to see those trying to
walk, gripping whatever came within their reach. Matters were still
getting worse as most of us were gripping our way towards our hammocks. There were twenty in our berth and all sick but one. It was a
terrible storm and the ship was rolling tremendously. Persons could not
stand without having a firm hold of something fast, nor could they sit
or lie without a firm hold. Casks, pig-pens and dog-houses were knocked
loose and sent flying.

I and a few other young men were stuck upon some large casks that
were firmly tied under the quarter deck, witnessing the dreadful scenes,
and expecting every roll of the ship to be the last. The sea was breaking
over at intervals, making altogether a horrid spectacle. A large box
came skipping along smashing the poop steps and part of the cabin front
— two of the sails were torn to rags — there was scarce a female face to
be seen and only a few males — all were so ill they could not get out of
their berths, in fact they did not come out until the Mate and the
Doctor compelled them to do so on Monday evening when the weather
moderated. A great deal of water came through the decks on to the
bunks, some of them being saturated, but fortunately mine was comparatively dry. The experience was totally different to the few days previous, and something that none of us expected. Perhaps you may think
that I have exaggerated a little on this experience, but I should have
very little interest in doing so. In fact I wish you to understand that I
have sat down innumerable times and risen as often, feeling it impossible
to write. On the same table we have some baking, some mending chests,
some doing a bit of tinkering among our tinware, as the pitching of the
ship has made a few wrinkles in most of them — so among all this

turmoil and the rolling of the ship you may guess what sort of conveniences we have for writing.

Friday, November 14th. Have been very busy today baking as this falls to be my week of being Captain of the Mess. There are ten of us in our Mess, each taking week about being Captain, who has an assistant. The Captain's duty is to bake, carve the meat, and divide all other sundries while the assistant carries all the food to and from the galley, assists in washing the dishes, etc. So I have been unfortunate enough in having the sick week, which is not very pleasant for a sick person. In the evening we had our Mutual Improvement Class, the subject being "New Zealand, its comforts and capabilities", which was very freely discussed for an hour. I then went on to the poop where I remained until about 11 p.m. I was very much interested in the strange appearance of the surface of the water. All round the vessel seemed to be a mass of fires sending forth sparks in all directions as if it were at war with us.

Saturday, November 15th. When I got up this morning I felt all right again. A ship was in sight right ahead of us — spoke to her about midday — found she was from Liverpool bound for Calcutta. They speak by hoisting various kinds of flags, which I do not fully understand, therefore won't attempt to describe.

Sunday, November 16th. Got up pretty early, and as the weather had improved all seemed anxious to have a more cleanly appearance than usual — no doubt on account of their expecting to attend Divine Service, which took place at 10.30. The Reverend delivered a very appropriate discourse from St. John's Gospel. Distance run since noon of the previous day, one hundred and ninety-six miles.

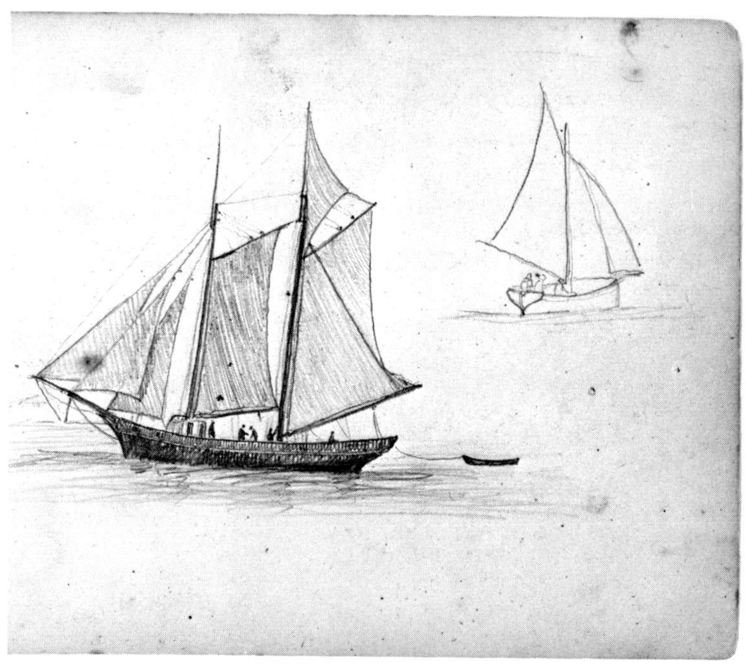

Early sketches by the young Charles Blomfield.

Wednesday, November 19th. Today has been remarkably warm, fully as warm as the hottest day ever I felt at home, and so calm that I believe we are not going as fast as a donkey and cart. While the passengers were spread out all over the ship apparently enjoying the heat of the day, for my part I preferred being in the shade with Goldsmith in my hands to assist in whiling away the tedious hours, for I can't help saying that they are tedious. No matter what you set your mind to, or what you endeavour to study you are always disturbed in some way or other by some who have got nothing else to do. I assisted in throwing overboard one of the cows and a couple of pigs that died through the effect of the storm previously referred to. It being my night to go on watch, instead of going to bed I was left to pace the deck alone all night, conscious of the blissful snoring of my friends.

In the evening I had a great time fiddling on the poop while the cabin passengers were dancing, which was carried on till a late hour. We have not got our position these last two days, the progress being too small to record. Very warm — was obliged to put off my flannels and put on lighter clothing. We had some good sport today, the boxing gloves being introduced, besides leap-frog, high-jumping and various other amusements.

We have had a good deal of confusion and noise regarding the sanitary condition of the ship in certain quarters, consequently we had a meeting and passed resolutions for betterment in this respect.

I now want you to understand that it is very difficult for me to describe one day from another — they are all so much alike. Every morning has the same appearance — nothing but water to be seen all round.

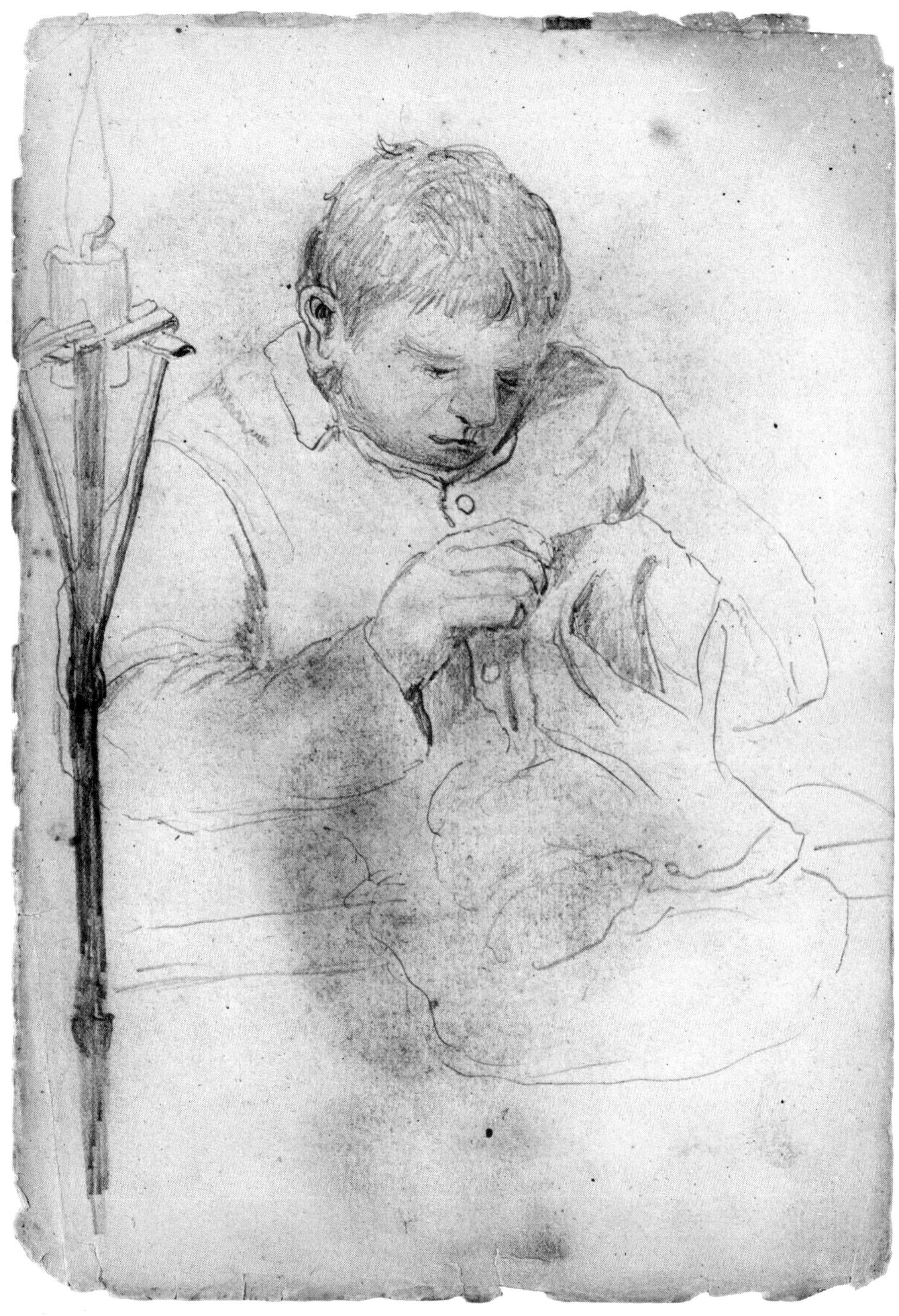

3. The New Country

While Robert filled in his days with writing his diary, Charles Blomfield whiled away the hours trying his hand at drawing what he could see on the ship, from a fellow passenger trying to mend his clothes, to the candle in the corner which was their only source of light.

Meanwhile, Robert continued his story:

In the meantime I shall try to give you a little advice which will be of some service to you if you come out. In the first place, if you desire to make a little money on the voyage bring the following articles — a box of eggs (to preserve them grease them well with sweet oil and pack them in salt, seeing that they are properly covered), cheese, baking powder, ham, apples, jellies, and so on. Firstly you will appreciate these things for your own use and secondly many will want to buy them as they are considered luxuries on board. We had an auction sale today of a general assortment of goods included in which were pistols, guns, books, concertinas, flutes, ironmongery, besides various lots of provisions and delicacies which were highly competed for and brought a great price. In the evening we had a public supper to celebrate the birthday of one of our friends. We had a first class supper, several toasts and songs, which was kept up till the hour appointed for extinguishing lights.

Thursday, November 27th. Hearing the cry of 'Land Ahoy' I got up pretty early this morning and on reaching deck I could easily see, though at a great distance, a very lofty hill, the middle of which was covered by a cloud that hung around it, but the top stood out clearly to view. It was Cape Verde Islands. We sighted a vessel — the *City of Delhi* from Glasgow — between us and the Islands. Distance run two hundred and fourteen miles.

Friday, November 28th. On awakening this morning I learned that we had had a birth on board during the night, which was the subject of conversation for a while, various questions being asked as to what the name should be, the name of the parish and so on. We had a death on board last night, that of a child one year old. The wind turned right ahead of us, coming on as a dreadful squall, with rain such as I have never seen the like — one pitiless persevering sheet of water interspersed with lightning, drenching most of us almost as properly as the "wife-beater" the night previous. So sudden was its approach that before half of us got below we were thoroughly drenched. However, we gained something by it, as we caught a lot of fresh water. A ship came in sight, and it was rumoured homeward bound. A good many hastened to get a letter written, but before we managed to write many lines we found out our mistake as the ship was on the same course as ourselves. In the evening another homeward vessel was in sight, but as a squall was seen to be coming the Captain said it would be on us before the vessels would be in reach of each other, consequently no boat was lowered. This terminates the first month of my voyage.

The Captain's report mentions that they caught the North East trade wind on November 27th; it was a moderate wind and carried the *Gertrude* outside the Cape de Verde and across the Equator on December 7th. Robert's account continues:

A vessel came into sight close by our stern, words were exchanged by the Captains such as two deaths, one birth etc. She was the *Cornwallis* from Madras, seventy-two days out, bound for London. To our great disappointment no boat was lowered to take our letters, for what reason I don't know, but there have been a great many grievances on board and I came to the conclusion that the Captain was afraid of complaints being sent too early. We exchanged hearty cheers, then turned to our course and were soon a great way off.

Wednesday, December 10th. In the evening we had another death, that of a child.

Thursday, December 11th. We have three vessels in sight, all apparently bound in the same course as ourselves. . . . On referring to the map you will see that we are not far from the coast of South America.

Tuesday, December 23rd. Today our Volunteer Company had drill going through gun exercises. All those who had guns of their own brought them into use. The Captain gave us the loan of the ship's muskets which gave us quite a decent number — some with muskets, some with old blunders, some with rifles, and some with fowling-pieces. I had my double-barrel gun among the rest. We made a line of thirty-four.

Wednesday, December 24th. Today was a remarkably busy day getting plumduffs, pies, and tarts ready for the noted Christmas feast. At the request of the Captain our music class went on the poop and sang a few anthems, duets, etc., which was well appreciated. It being Christmas Eve, something more was to be done. Almost all got a bottle or two of beer, which elevated their spirits while comic songs and speeches were struck up and kept going until 12 o'clock when the entertainment came to an end and the greater portion retired to their bunks.

Thursday, December 25th. At dinner there was a display of eating propensities in various degrees, and there being an abundance of beer, many became elevated, a few intoxicated, and one or two mortally drunk. The evening was conducted much in the same style as the previous one.

Friday, December 26th. In the evening we had a grand moonlight masquerade ball, that is all those that took part were dressed up in fancy costumes with masks on their faces, which rendered them wholly unrecognisable to the onlooker. A great many Cape pigeons and albatrosses are flying around the ship. The pigeons frequently come and sit on the end of the yards and fall asleep, and can then be caught.

Wednesday, December 31st, New Year's Eve. This is the last day in the closing year. How many at this time are reminded of the changes each succeeding year has witnessed, the gaps in the little world they have created — for life is measured not by its duration but by its events, and as their lost friends rise up in memory around them, many a dormant chord is wakened that tells of a dreary blank in their affections time can never replace. We ought not to regret too much the past or depend too much upon the future, but rely more upon the present.

In the evening ten of Scotland's sons and daughters met to have a little jollification in memory of our friends at home. Tea was served out at 8 p.m. The table was covered with a great variety of fancy breads of our own manufacture such that a nobleman's board would have been proud of. Thinking we had equally as good a right to hold New Year's Eve as our English friends had to hold Christmas, we treated ourselves after tea to a little brandy-punch to comfort our hearts and enliven the soul. We had a variety of Scottish songs, sung with great glee till the bell struck 12 o'clock and New Year was cheered in all over the ship, then we sang "Auld Lang Syne" which was no sooner finished, when the ship gave a great roll sending the most of us on our beam ends and the contents of the table on top of us. Thus ends the second month of my journey.

However, not all the passengers of the *Gertrude* were as cheerful as Charles and his friend Robert, and described the storm on New Year's Eve as making a noise as if the ship would fall apart, and told how a tub of beef rolled over, and pigs and dogs were let loose and started to fight. These passengers complained bitterly, considering the ship unsafe for the bad weather. By this time they hated their food and the cramped conditions. Some of them had left the niceties of English living and now had to do their own cooking and cleaning, and sleep in a very small space; they were tired of their rations of salt meat and butter, and of making their own bread.

But Robert Smith and the other young men continued to enjoy their adventure, and he wrote home:

Thursday, January 1st, 1863. We are now supposed to have turned another page — a blank spotless leaf, and what is to fill this leaf no man can tell.

Friday, January 2nd. Today we learn that we had made the best run, being two hundred and sixty-two miles. We are now round the Cape of Good Hope, and may expect a little stormy weather.

Monday, January 5th. Today is piercingly cold — something like some of those days I have experienced at home.

Tuesday, January 6th. One of the young men in our cabin had an experience, but was fortunate enough in escaping what might have been a serious accident. He was sitting on the bulwarks when one of the sails that was hanging loosely was suddenly filled with a breeze and, extending toward one side, caught him and pitched him overboard. Fortunately for him a rope ran along the outside of the ship, which he managed to grasp and hang on until he was relieved.

Trursday, January 15th. Today is fine, which gladdens us all. Another little "Gertruder" made its appearance this morning in the shape of a son. In the evening our Mutual Improvement Class was favoured with a lecture from a passenger returning to New Zealand, giving an outline of his experience and the prevailing conditions, with amusing anecdotes regarding the natives and their customs.

Wednesday, January 21st. I have been busy these few days past, drawing plans for farmsteadings, and have already got two finished of different construction, but whether I may ever work to them or not, I can't tell.

Saturday, January 24th. This morning was ushered in with the announcement of the death of another child aged three years.

Monday, January 26th. Still very cold. We are drawing towards Van Diemen's Land, but whether we will sight it or not we can't tell. We had a meeting of the Albertlanders convened by the Minister, for the purpose of discussing and arranging the best methods to adopt for the transit of passengers and goods en route for Albertland. Several plans and opinions were discussed, to be further considered when drawing towards the end of our voyage. There was the death of another child today, this being the fifth.

Friday, January 30th. We are now past Van Diemen's Land or Tasmania and making North. Consequently it is getting warmer. A weighing apparatus was erected to settle some wagers after which there was the weighing of all and sundry. I found that I had increased two pounds since being weighed in Leith, being twelve stone two pounds.

Thursday, February 5th. The ship I referred to yesterday is well in sight now. We began signalling, and learned that she was the ship *Dawson* from Melbourne bound for Callao, fourteen days out — all well. She passed close by our stern when her Captain called out to us, saying if we lowered a boat he would give us some papers, which was immediately done, and about a dozen of the latest English papers were taken to her for which we got in return a quantity of Melbourne and New Zealand news. The rest of the evening was spent in forming groups around a reader, listening attentively to the news.

Friday, February 6th. This morning about eight o'clock I had the honour of being first to discover land! The news soon spread through the ship, and all came on deck to catch a glimpse of the long looked-for island. By midday we got sufficiently close to distinguish trees and large tracts of a yellowish sandy colour. After sunset we could see several fires quite distinctly. There was a great deal of speculation among the passengers. Some thought that settlers had seen us during the day and had lit fires for our guidance; others that they were war signals among the natives; others thought it was simply the burning of bush, or perhaps a native camp, and so on. Many remained on deck until the early hours of the morning, eagerly watching the coast by moonlight.

Saturday, February 7th. This morning a different landscape presented itself to us, but as it was rather misty we could not see so clearly. We received intimation of the death of the mother of the last child born.

Her body was consigned to the deep at seven a.m. off the North Cape. By midday, we were close to the land and could see it pretty clearly. It is rather a romantic-looking coast, neither high hills nor extensive plains, but rather a sort of jaggy broken outline, with here and there massive towering rocks studded with little bushes and furze, like nature's wildest grandeur, the monotony of which is broken every here and there with columns of white curling smoke, apparently rising from a hut or bonfire, but neither a human soul, animal, or hut can yet be seen.

Sunday, February 8th. This morning many rocky islands are seen, but as we are a great way off, they can only be seen very faintly. We have a head wind, consequently we are tacking about, one time with our bow towards the land, then turning round and leaving it astern. In the evening the Captain considered it prudent to "lay-to" all night, no doubt considering it safer to have daylight to wend his way among the islands. Meanwhile the beauties of the day were followed at night by a phosphorescent scene of unrivalled splendour and sublimity. We have often before observed luminous pin-like sparks of fire floating here and there in the furrow of our vessel, but now the whole ocean is literally bespangled with them. Notwithstanding the smoothness of the surface, there is a considerable swell of the sea, and sparkling on every part as with fire, the mighty heaving of its bosom is indescribably magnificent— it seems as if the sky had fallen to a level with the ship, and all its stars in tenfold numbers and brilliancy were rolling about with the undulations of the billows.

Monday, February 9th. We started off again this morning at daylight — passed several pretty large lofty islands and lots of smaller ones standing like pinnacles all alone in the water. All on board were eagerly watching the new islands as they came in view. The pilot came on board at seven-thirty p.m., when we gave him a hearty cheer. Shortly after, he told us that a frigate and two hundred and six lives were lost on Saturday, not far from where we were. At length the lights of the town appeared, and every face on board seemed to be beaming with joy. We cast anchor a short distance from the pier, and in a few minutes paper reporters, likewise friends of passengers, were alongside in boats.

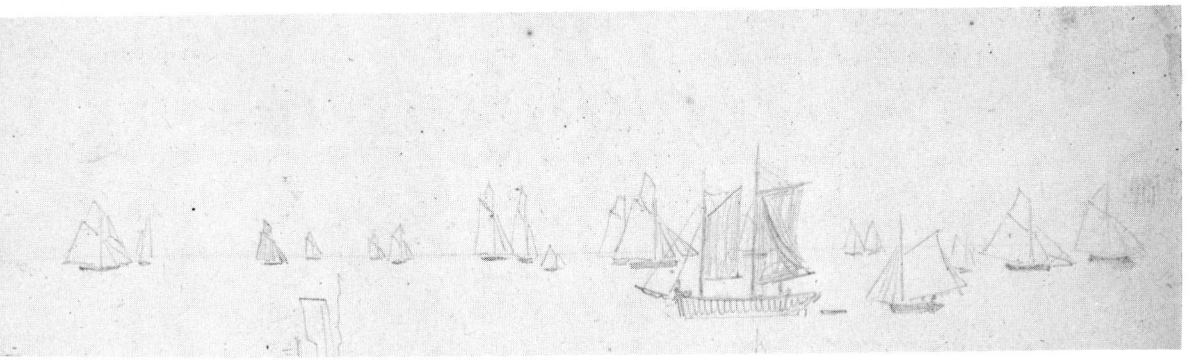

So on February 11th, 1863, after ninety-seven days at sea, the passengers of the *Gertrude* set foot on New Zealand soil. They were immediately confronted with a problem. They found there was a great scarcity of accommodation in Auckland at the time, a large fire having recently ravaged the town. Many of the *Gertrude*'s passengers were required to go to the Immigration Barracks, a large building especially provided for immigration purposes — the charges being free for the first week, 1/- per week for the next four weeks, and after that according to the ordinary rates of the day.

Robert Smith extended his letter to his father to include his impressions of this new town in a new land.

I went for a stroll through the town, and was rather astonished at its grandeur. The shops are extensive and well stocked, and can be favourably compared with any in Argyle Street, Glasgow. The people in town are very stylish, especially the ladies, I think surpassing those at home. A word or two about the natives. The natives go about in great numbers. Mostly all, male and female, are tattooed very neatly — the lips, in place of being red, are all daubed with blue. They have large holes in their ears, with a long massive ribbon through, attached to which is a kind of greenstone hanging over their shoulders. Some of the males look tolerably well, the females are very indifferent. All smoke tobacco. It is quite common to see the young on their mother's back, take the pipe out of their mother's mouth and put it in their own. They squat in the street, gibbering away in their own dialect. Lots of them go about selling peaches, onions, potatoes, honey and fish, in baskets of their own make, made of flax resembling in shape and material a joiner's basket at home. Some are dressed well, others have only a kind of blanket around their waist. Some of the females are lady-like, while others have on only a cloak made of native grass, the outside of which resembles a piece of thatch-work. In their merchandise, they are very shrewd, and give you no more than they have a mind to. Almost everything they sell they want a shilling for. Apparently it is their standard value. They abhor coppers, neither do they like small silver. They walk about bare-footed. After dark they can be heard in all directions, howling at the utmost pitch of their voice, which I understand is looked upon by themselves as a musical expression, although to strangers it is rather alarming. Their reputation for honesty is very high, but they are fond of begging old clothes. A few of them can speak English, but they are so good at signs and gestures that you can easily understand them.

The climate here is good. Comparing it with home, it is a little hotter in the sun, but in the shade, I don't notice any difference. During the day there is a perpetual sound caused by a locust which resembles very much the chirping of a flock of sparrows. This noise of the daytime is followed at night by the noise of the cricket resembling very much the continuous sound of a policeman's whistle.

Sunday, February 14th. In place of going to church, I took a ramble out in the country where I visited Mount Eden, which is an extinct volcano.

It is a great height, and its sides are strewn with stones and ashes with here and there patches of fern and teatree. On the top of the mountain is a large crater, resembling in shape a bottle filler about one hundred and fifty feet deep, and about two hundred feet across the top. From the top of this hill I had a commanding view of the country. There is no forest land near, the only native tree predominating the scene being the cabbage tree which grows about twenty feet high with a bare trunk and a cluster of long leaves at the top. The weeping willow seems to grow profusely, and it is seen in every direction.

The country in general has rather a black appearance, being mostly covered with short teatree or fern, or perhaps large blocks of it newly burnt. What is free of that is of a brown colour in place of green, on account of the summer heat and shortage of rain which has been lately experienced.

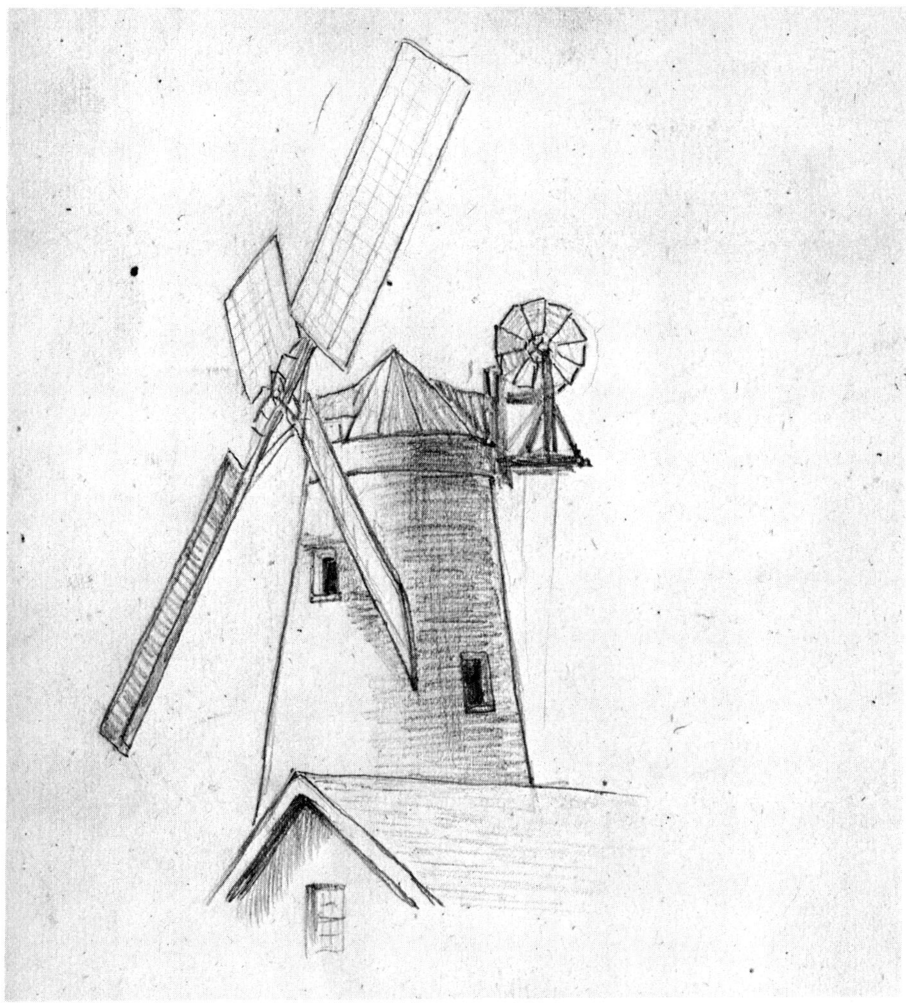

Partington's Mill, Auckland, 1863.

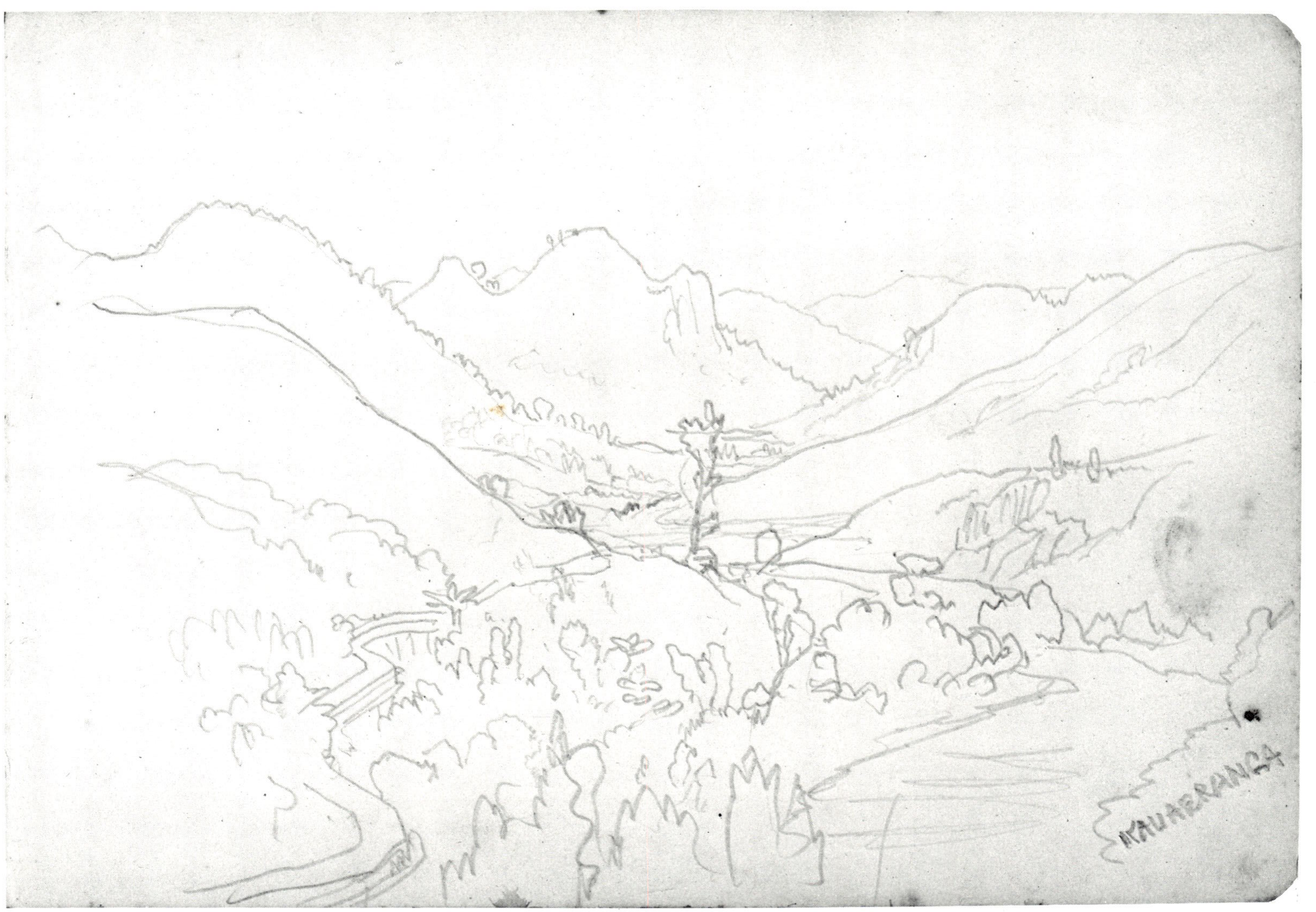
KAUAERANGA

4. Gold Rush

The Blomfields found on their arrival in New Zealand that the Maori Wars were in progress in the Waikato and around Auckland. In the eyes of five-year-old Fred, the highlight of the whole trip was the presentation to every immigrant arriving in Auckland of a rifle and bayonet side-arm with which to fight the Maoris. But war or no war, after three months on a sailing vessel, Auckland looked peaceful, pretty and prosperous.

"I've come far enough," Mrs Blomfield announced to her children. "Let us settle in Auckland."

The children agreed unanimously.

"Wonderful idea, mother," said Sam. "I've heard terrible stories about those who have travelled on looking for Albertland. No-one arrives in less than two weeks, and some take much longer. There are no roads, and even taking a boat up to the upper reaches of the harbour at Riverhead, and by dray to Helensville, has been taking weeks and is very hard uncomfortable travelling. I am sure I can get a job here as a carpenter, starting right away."

The girls also approved. "Let's stay here — the ladies are so smart, and the shops are full of such beautiful things."

So the Blomfield family settled in Auckland. True to his word, Sam immediately got work as a carpenter and Elizabeth set herself up as a midwife, while Mary Ann became governess to the children of Mr Buddle, a leading Auckland lawyer, who lived at Dunholm House in Remuera Road. Charles signed on as an apprentice to a house painter and decorator, where he very quickly learned the art of mixing colours, and painting intricate and artistic designs for interior decoration, including various types of wood graining, and also an imitation marble finish. The whole family immediately involved themselves with the Baptist Church in Chancery Street, and one of Sam's first jobs was helping to build the new Baptist Chapel in Wellesley Street.

Meanwhile Robert Smith had fallen in love with one of his fellow passengers, Grace Lamberton. He obtained work as a building contractor, but after a few years he married Grace and they travelled to Thames, where he and his brother were commissioned to build the water-race from the top of the Kauaeranga Valley to the Thames township.

Although Auckland looked peaceful, there was soon a scare that the Maoris would come from the north to attack the town. Provision was made by a strict order that on the ringing of the warning bell from the Barrack Hill (Albert Park) every citizen, man, woman and child, should hurry to the barracks, where, after a certain period, the gates would be shut.

At this time Sam Blomfield was working on the shingling on the chapel roof. Being very deaf, he would work on, not noticing the others. One day, thinking it was about lunchtime, he looked around and saw nothing and nobody. Then looking down Wellesley Street, he spied people; men, women and children running for their lives with all sorts of bundles. He knew then that the alarm had been sounded! He scrambled down off the roof, and ran to his home in Graham's Road, to find Emma and her children with their bundles, sobbing and crying in fear. He rushed them to the barracks, only to meet the people coming back. It had been a false alarm — to give the people practice! It was an uneasy time for all.

On June 7th, 1863, just four months after the Blomfields arrived in New Zealand, another, much smaller ship, the *Aloa* sailed up the Waitemata Harbour. On board was another pioneer family, Mr Alfred Edward Wild, with his wife Sarah, and six children.

But tragedy soon befell this group. Sarah, being 'great with child' during the trip, contracted typhoid fever, and although she was able to give birth to her seventh child, Anne, about two weeks after their arrival in the new country, she died on July 23rd of typhoid fever and exhaustion. Alfred had set up a boot shop in Franklin Road, and here his eleven-year-old daughter, Ellen, had to help him bring up the younger members of the family. The eldest boy, Fred, was immediately put to work at Partington's Mill, but was fired from this position 'for throwing the dough about' and he was conscripted into the army and sent to the Waikato. The second son, Harry, was then sent to the Mill, where he stayed for some time. Ellen used to sit sewing clothes for the younger sisters, and occasionally was allowed to play hopscotch, but often did so with the new baby on her hip. Poor little Anne, she was weak from birth, and without a true mother to look after her, also died when only a few months old.

One of Ellen's friends invited her to attend the Baptist Sunday School, instead of the Church of England where her father was a member. It was there that she first met the tall dark Charles Blomfield, who some years later was to become her husband, but at the time she merely thought he looked funny, trying to grow a beard!

By 1865 Mrs Blomfield was able to have her own house built in Ponsonby Road, paying £135.0.0 for the cottage, and an extra £3.0.0 for 'the Closet'. From there Charles walked across Newton Gully every Sunday to teach singing to the Mt. Eden Baptist Sunday School. He remembered the lessons he had received on the *Gertrude,* and was one of the first to teach the Tonic Solfa method in New Zealand. The gully was steep in those days, and often the track very muddy, but he never missed a Sunday through bad weather.

Although Auckland had been prosperous in 1863, by 1867 jobs were very hard to get. So when gold was discovered in Thames, most of the young men rushed down to 'make their fortune'. Sam Blomfield packed up and took his wife and three children to live in Thames. He obtained a miner's licence in November 1867, and stayed in the district for many years, also taking on building work.

Charles also went to the gold field, and later told his own story:

No one at the present day can have any idea of the hard times in Auckland just before the Thames 'broke out'. Empty houses everywhere, scores of unemployed, people leaving every day like rats from a sinking ship.

The news of gold found at the Thames was like a lifebuoy to a drowning mariner. The first reports of the find were so extravagant that few believed them; but when solid bars of the real metal were exhibited in a jeweller's shop in Queen Street, Auckland, citizens took the fever, and all who could possibly get away went down to try their luck. I was then a young fellow of nineteen, and, having nothing to do, went with two bosom friends. Our hopes ran high, for had we not heard of how the stampers in the Golden Crown Battery had jammed because of the richness of the quartz, how the Shotover people had taken out £27,000.0.0 of gold by merely scratching the surface, and had not one of our leading ministers, the Rev. P. H. Cornford, come to see us off and hoped we should come back and pay off the church debt! We knew nothing at all about gold mining and very little about camping, but managed to pitch our tent on a vacant spot between the Hape and Karaka Creeks.

One day soon after our arrival we noticed a crowd surrounding a man on horseback in what is now Pollen Street. He had a butcher's basket on his arm, just like a butcher-boy delivering meat, but when we came near we found he had a mass of gold in the basket, thirty pounds or forty pounds weight. It looked very remarkable to us, all rough and porous at the top and round and smooth underneath! It turned out to be the last return from the Golden Crown, and had just been turned out of the retort. That was the way gold was sent to the bank in those days.

After a lot of prospecting we found a sort of reef on the Hape Creek, pegged out our claim, built a little hut of teatree, using our tent for a roof, fixed up bunks, chimney, and table, and made ourselves comfortable. Times were hard. We lived mostly on damper and biscuits, with a pound of dripping once a week for a treat. While the dripping lasted we had pancakes for breakfast. Sometimes we treated ourselves to a pound of mutton chops. These were always stewed; we wanted all the virtue.

In spite of all we were very happy. The open-air life, exercise and hard living all conduced to robust health. We were all fond of singing. One of the party, a handsome young Welshman named Williams, had a fine tenor voice. We had a good stock of glees and part-songs, and after every meal we had half an hour's part-singing for dessert.

Then there was the charm of novelty, the lovely surroundings, the song of the tuis and bell-birds, the flutter of the friendly fantails, the call of the morepork. I don't think it would be possible to exaggerate the exquisite beauty of the native bush. We see nothing like it now. Such a wealth of luxurious and varied growth! Tall kauris and rimus lifted their massive shafts among spreading cedars and picturesque tawas, while great tree-ferns and nikaus added grace and beauty to the scene. Every stump was decorated with moss and creeper, and every vacant inch of ground carpeted with crepe and kidney ferns.There was only one drawback — mosquitoes. They simply swarmed every-where. Day and night they gave us no rest. We tried every remedy, but to no purpose. Sometimes in despair we carried our blankets to the top of the ridge, but they followed us up in a cloud. It seemed as if whole generations of them had been waiting our advent.

We heard of several of our friends striking it rich. One young com-panion of mine was out prospecting with two others, and tracing up a small creek came across a waterfall. As they looked, they noticed some-thing glittering under the water and found the rock underneath was a reef showing gold freely in the face. They called it The Waterfall Claim. But though we found plenty of leaders, none of them led to gold; some of the stone showed metal which we in our ignorance mistook for gold. Soon we had a heap of specimens.

We went to no end of trouble getting our stuff ready. A kiln was carved out of the hillside. Some days were spent in collecting a pile of dry puriri and then we made a sleigh and dragged the roasted quartz down to the mill. I remember how we used to sit out on the ridge at night listening to the thud, thud, of the machine, speculating on what each one's share would amount to. After several breakdowns and delay our stuff was crushed, our amalgam put in the retort, and lo! the result — three pennyweight of gold and a tin tack!

The disappointment sat very lightly on the minds of two of us, but with the young Welshman it was a serious matter, and sadly tragical in its consequences. He was a blockmaker, and one of the few who were doing well in Auckland. He had given up everything to join us. When things went wrong he took it so to heart that he went insane, and died some months afterwards in the asylum.

Life at Thames centred round Butt's corner, where the hotel and landing place were. On Sunday mornings the Wesleyans held a service there. A gin case was borrowed, and the preacher, generally a layman from town, addressed a very fair congregation. The late Mr. James Renshaw frequently filled the post with considerable ability.

Our failure at the Hape Creek sent us prospecting once more. Not long after came the rumour of the finding of alluvial gold at Tapu Creek. Quite a rush set in, and we were among the first to venture. Leaving one of the party to bring the gear by boat, two of us walked there. While waiting for the baggage, we strolled up the creek. About half a mile up we came across two diggers working an old-fashioned cradle. One rocked the cradle and bailed in water, and the other shovel-led in the wash dirt and stirred it about with a forked stick. Every now and then one of them would snatch something out of the dirt and pop it into his mouth. Presently he allowed us to see what he had. They were little nuggets of gold of a dark rich colour. We thought this all right, and pegged out a claim just above them. We took out a little coarse gold, and some very pretty nuggets, one of which, weighing eight pennyweights, I have still in my possession. This was the only spot on the Thames Peninsula where alluvial gold was found. An old Californian digger named McIsaacs discovered it, and fossicked out all the likely places in the creek, taking out over one hundred ounces before the news leaked out. Those who came after him had his leavings.

We enjoyed a very welcome change in the bill of fare at Tapu. The rocks on the coast were crowded with fine oysters, and I used to knock off work a couple of hours before the others, go down to the beach, and fill a billy. When the others came home we feasted on stewed oysters and potatoes. Then the peaches! My mouth waters at the thought of them still. On the river flats of the next creek, a mile or so along the beach, were some fine peach groves, all laden with the ripest fruit. It was no unusual thing to see a procession of diggers on a Saturday afternoon returning laden — kits, flourbags, sacks, etcetera, full of ripe peaches, the juice running down their backs.

When we had worked out our claim, then came the question of disposing of the spoil. I, being the only one with an anxious mother in town, was deputed to go to Auckland and sell the gold. When we squared up we found we had made twenty-five shillings a week each for three weeks' work. That was all we got out of our gold mining venture.

However, although he did not find gold in the literal sense, Charles struck a vein which yielded him rich rewards in the development of his artistic powers. While camping in the bush during this period, he was so struck with its surpassing beauty that he determined to transfer its charms on to canvas. Having no teacher and no facilities for learning the practical details of his art, he persevered with his efforts until he had mastered the technique. He recalled all he had been taught while house decorating, in the way of mixing colours, and the different methods of using the brush to obtain different effects.

He finally called on a family friend, William Moore, who was getting some returns for his mining work at a claim called "Rainbow End".

"I'm giving up looking for gold, Willie," he said. "I think I'll do better by painting."

"Good! You can start by painting my hut," replied Willie. But much to his surprise, Charles sat down on his three legged stool, and painted not only the mining hut, but the trees in the distance, and finished off with Willie washing the dishes in the little creek in the foreground. Not quite what Willie had in mind, but on Boxing Day 1871, when Willie married Charles's sister, Frances Blomfield, he was thrilled to receive the picture as a wedding present.

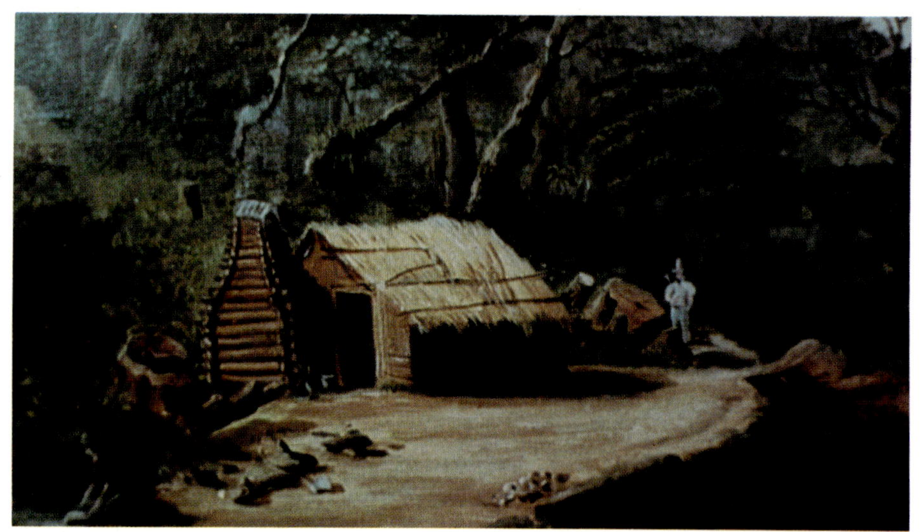

Willie Moore's goldmining hut, "Rainbow End", 1870. Oil on card, 17 × 11 in.

Auckland Harbour, undated. Oil on card, 13 × 7 in.

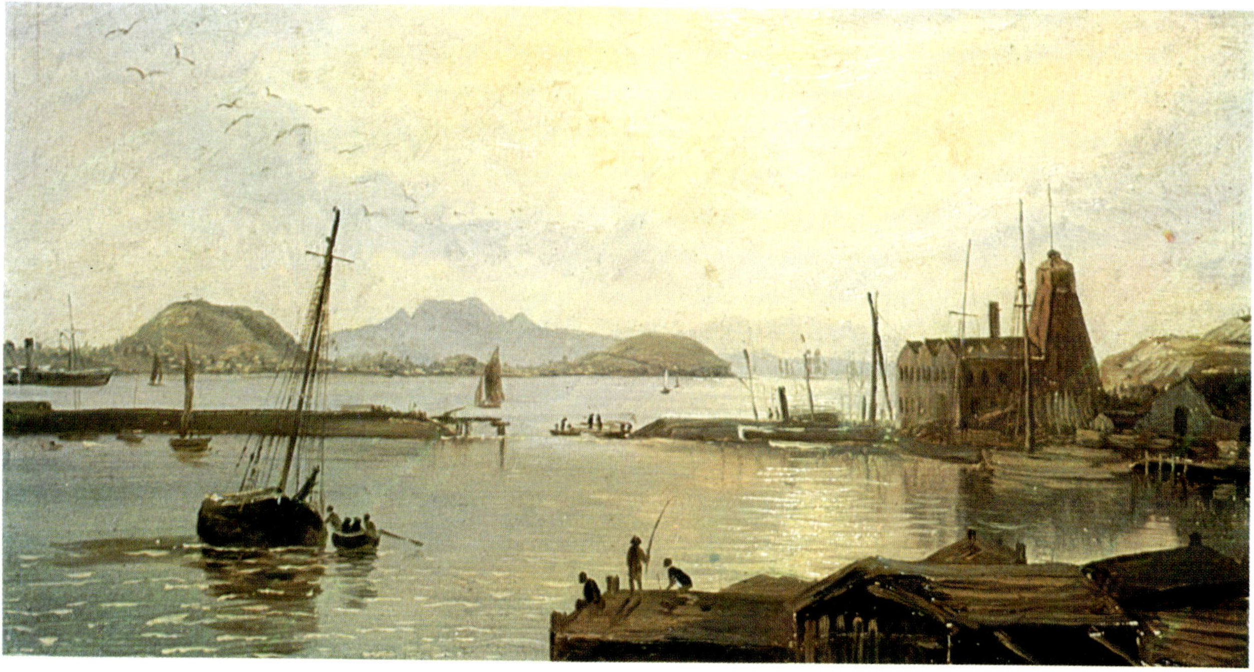

5. A Letter from Thames

Back in Auckland, Charles continued to paint pictures of the scenery, but also found work painting and decorating houses.

After a while he found he needed several pairs of new boots, to say nothing of having his old ones repaired, and became a regular visitor to Mr Wild's shop in Franklin Road. It was not until February 14th, 1871, however, that Ellen realised the true reason for his visits. On that day she received a hand-painted St. Valentine's card addressed to "Ellen Wild, from a loving friend, Charles Blomfield."

Ellen was thrilled! She had always liked this pleasant young man, and now that his beard had grown properly, she thought him quite handsome. He was just over six feet tall, slim, with dark hair, a high brow and dark flashing eyes. Quite a contrast to the petite Ellen with her dainty hands and feet, lily white skin, glossy brown hair and blue eyes. Ellen had come from good pioneering stock, and after helping her father look after her young brother and sisters following her mother's death, she had learned to accept whatever happened, being intensely honest, but keeping a good sense of fun and humour. She had become an active member in the Baptist church and had complete faith in Charles's religion, believing in God as her personal friend.

Their friendship quickly matured into a deep and lasting love, and they were married on January 14th, 1874.

After some months, Charles was asked to go to Thames to do some decorating work. Ellen was carrying her first child, and although she would have loved to have gone with him, travelling conditions were very poor, and she remembered what had happened to her mother when she travelled while pregnant, so decided to stay at home. Charles promised to write, and after a few days his first letter arrived:

According to promise I write this letter tonight. I got down here Monday after about four o'clock. We had a very windy passage, not very rough. The *Crown* rolled about rather considerably, but I was not sick. I spent most of the time down in the cabin beguiling the weary hours with one of Walter Scott's works, *The St. Rowan's Well*, which I bought for the purpose, for the magnificent sum of ninepence, and out of which I read three chapters and have not looked at it since. It will amuse me coming back.

But I have not told you all about the voyage yet. The passengers were quite a study. On the bridge shaded by the paddle cope, sat a whole colony of Irish — men, women and children. As they had all the appearance of either fishmongers (the women) or dustmen (the men), I wondered how they could pay cabin fare, and sure enough when we were about halfway here they were all bundled down to the steerage part and for the remainder of the time they were like Noah's dove, could not find rest for the soles of their feet anywhere.

I of course could do nothing the first day I arrived. The quarters I have are most comfortable, there is a little kitchen behind the shop and a littler bedroom, two bunks, one on the top of the other. I take the top one, a very comfortable one indeed, and the chap who stays here, by name Nat Paine, sleeps in the lower one. I have the advantage of him, as he has to turn out first. If he gets not up by seven o'clock, a carpenter next door opens the little window, pokes his hand through and by means of a stick just reaching to Paine's legs, belabours Paine till pain makes him get up, when I quickly follow.

He treats me as a lodger, finds everything for me, and I pay him again, so I have no bother about anything, and live far better than if I went to Allaway and got shadowy soup, or their watery beef — better even than if I bought my own, although I think Mr Paine is buying more for me than he would for himself, as for lunch for instance, instead of a bit of bread and butter, we have cheese and pickles, sardines and jam.

The work I have to do will take me all my time till next Monday to finish, even if the weather is fine, which is very doubtful, but I shall try to get up by Tuesday night. Tuesday was very fine, but today has been wet. I can do with one more wet day as I have inside work, then it will bother me.

Bob Scott, a chap who used to work at the shop is working down here. He boned me up the first day to do some graining for him at night time. So last night I was working till ten o'clock. Tonight I would not go as I had to write to you, which I liked better, but it will be better still to get a letter from you. Tomorrow night I shall anxiously watch the postman when he passes, and I shall be disappointed if he does not bring one. If you post the letter in town in time for the *Crown*, that is before eight at Newton or ten in town, I should get it the same evening. If posted before five o'clock, I get it the next morning. Samuel's baby is quite well. It is called by the euphonious name of Eva Ellen. I don't see anything remarkable about the youngster, it has two large eyes, some hair, and a mouth for sucking, most little youngsters have.

I have just read a story about a wonderful cave visited by *H.M.S. Dido* a short while ago. The entrance is under water. Anyone visiting it must dive down six feet and then straight along twenty feet, then come up inside it. There is a very deep lake in the middle, the roof is hung with beautiful crystals, and the walls are shaped just like seats, the only light coming through the water, so it is blue and subdued. Many years ago some natives had a quarrel with their chief. A whole family were condemned to die, among them a beautiful girl. A young chief was in love with this girl. One day when pursuing a turtle, he discovered this cave. He kept it a great secret. When this young lady was going to be killed, he determined to save her, so he managed to effect her escape and take her in a canoe to this cave. Diving down, he told her to follow and they both came up inside the cave. For a whole

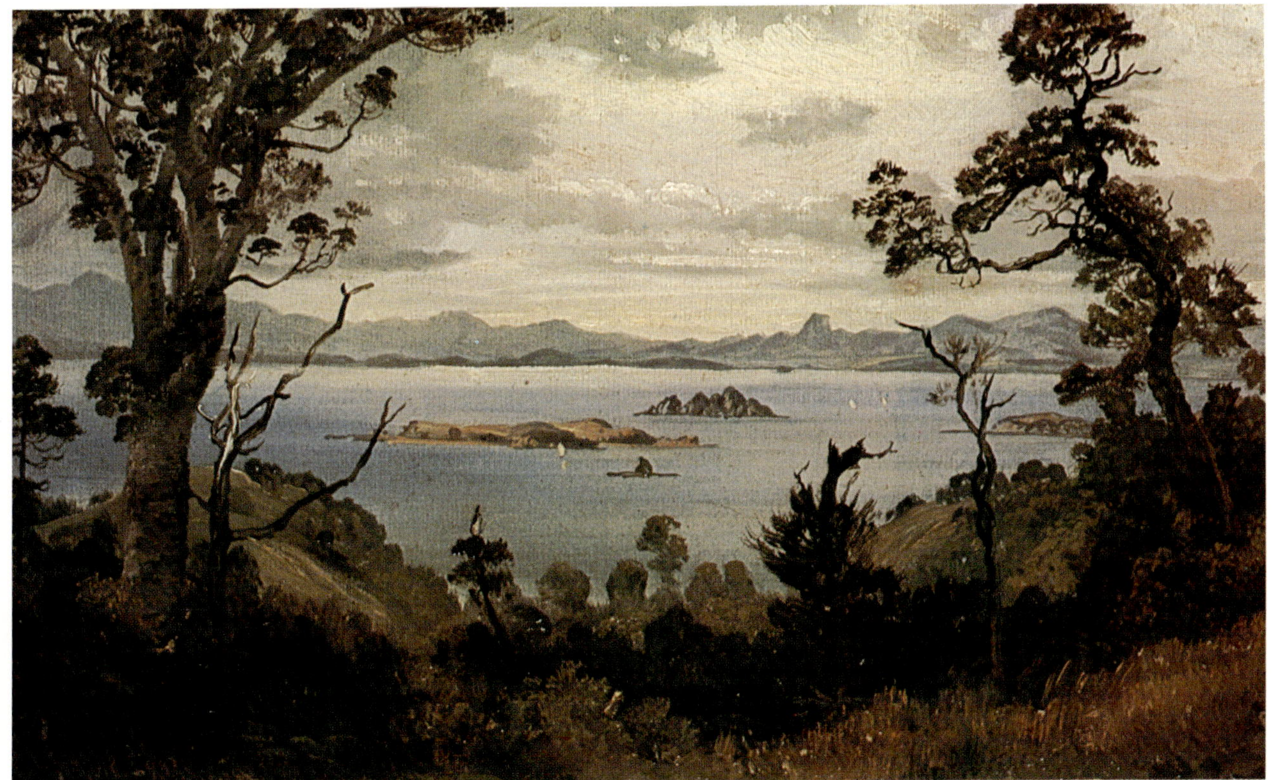

*Coromandel, 1898. Oil on
canvas, 17 × 11 in.*

year he kept her here, bringing her food and every necessary. He then
persuaded a party of natives to embark for Fiji. They asked him why
he did not take a wife with him. He told them he was going to fetch one
up out of the water and when they got to the cave he sprang overboard
and disappeared. They thought he was lost, but he soon reappeared,
bringing this girl whom they had long thought dead. How would you
like that for a year?

There was a very high tide here last Sunday and Monday night, the
sea rising and filling up the gutter on each side of the road in Grahams-
town, so that the space between the footpaths was divided into three
parts, just a narrow strip of road in the middle, the other two parts water.

The other painters here are very curious to know how it is I have
come down to do this place. I shall have plenty of judges to see how I
do the graining.

And now Dearest Ellen, Goodbye and may God bless you and watch
over you. . . .

Charles Blomfield.

2

Exploration
1875 - 1885

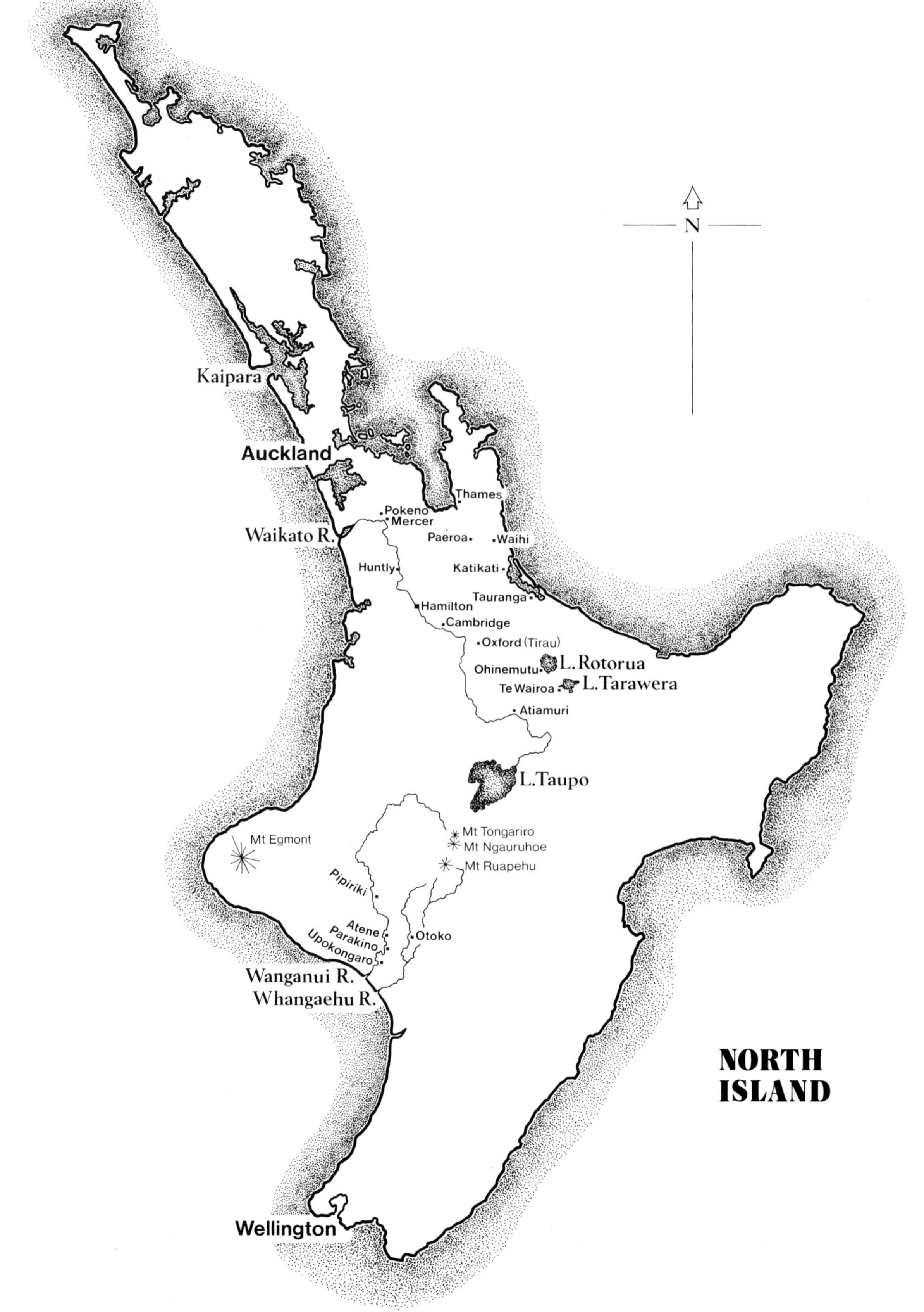

N
Kaipara
Auckland
Thames
Pokeno
Mercer
Waikato R.
Paeroa
Waihi
Huntly
Katikati
Tauranga
Hamilton
Cambridge
Oxford (Tirau)
Ohinemutu
L. Rotorua
Te Wairoa
L. Tarawera
Atiamuri
L. Taupo
Mt Egmont
Mt Tongariro
Mt Ngauruhoe
Mt Ruapehu
Pipiriki
Atene
Parakino
Otoko
Upokongaro
Wanganui R.
Whangaehu R.
Wellington
NORTH ISLAND

6. Hot Lakes and Landscapes

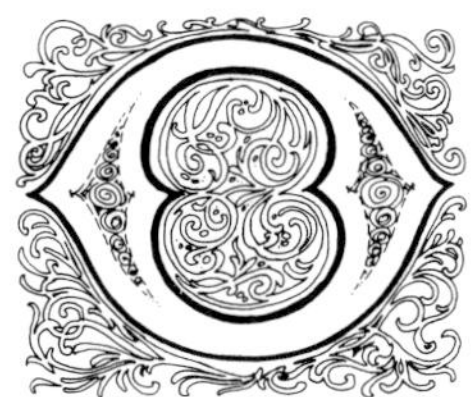

NE DAY CHARLES came home with a stranger.

"Ellen," he called. "I want you to meet my friend, Thomas Spurgeon. You remember how I told you about his father, Rev. C. H. Spurgeon, the Evangelist, preaching in England. Well, Tom has come out to New Zealand to live, and help with the work here."

Tom was soon a constant visitor to their home, and when he had holidays at Christmas time in 1875, Charles invited him to go camping with him to see the beauties of the countryside for himself. He readily agreed, as he wished to make a collection of the various types of fern growing in the bush.

They left Auckland on Tuesday, December 14th, 1875, arriving in Pokeno without mishap, and from there on Charles kept a diary of their trip:

Tuesday, December 14th, 1875. We arrived at Pokeno all right. There we found the river had risen a foot since yesterday. The railway line was flooded, Mangatawhiri bridge quite submerged, and the train could not cross to Mercer. So we had to get out and shoulder our swags across a fern hill about a mile, where the steamer *Bluenose* came and took us off to Mercer. Then on board *The Alert* and off on the waters of the Waikato. In its flooded state it presented a most beautiful appearance. On either side, the tops of cabbage trees, flax, and fern just showed above the water, with here and there the roof of a Maori's whare.

Behind this, bush and trees of all kinds, through the branches of which you might row a boat, in many instances for three or four miles. In some places the river appeared ten miles wide. This sort of scenery with a pleasing variety continued for many miles. In some places very beautiful forms were produced by the reflections as when the under leaves of a head of cabbage tree just touched the water.

At one point we passed a village and flax mill, the mill was seven feet under water and the store containing the dried and prepared flax. I felt it must be a great loss to the owner, Mr Bell. The white house just half above the water looked very pretty with its reflection. Near this there was a small island about a quarter of an acre left dry by the flood. Upon this some twenty cows and a lot of fowls and turkeys had taken refuge. You may well suppose they had pretty well cleared the grass off. They say the oldest native has never seen anything like this before. As we proceeded it could easily be seen the tide had turned as we could see portions of the bank here and there.

Wednesday, December 15th. Started from Hamilton at 10 a.m., the road running for a mile or two through a peculiar gorge, the top being a flat plain through which a gully had been carved by the water leaving steep irregular banks about thirty feet high. After this the road is dead level and very straight. The Waikato here seems to run through a flat delta of large extent bordered on all sides by ranges and hills, the highest in sight being Pirongia and Maungatautari.

Thursday, December 16th. Left Cambridge at 7 a.m. Morning sultry and dull, hills shrouded in mist. Level road first few miles. Crossed two creeks one of which we had to swim, then up a range from the slope of which we had a fine view of the Waikato Valley. It runs through a flat alluvial plain within which a wide rent or chasm has been cut by some power, forming another valley fifty to one hundred feet below the first, through which the river runs, forming a cutting with cliffs one hundred feet high. On the top of the range we passed through some bush and came out on the other side. The character of the country changed — a hilly country broken up every way by chasms and rents showing bare faces of stone — in one place a long valley was bordered by these abrupt rocky walls presenting the appearance of a large quarry. The next thing of note is a large creek running round the Buckland Run, which has carved for itself a wide and irregular passage through the alluvial terrace some one hundred feet deep with banks very steep in places.

Tea at Bucklands and then travelled about four miles on the Te Whetu Road and pitched our tent for the first time on a rising knoll of a fern hill. The weather has cleared up beautifully with a fresh south breeze. From the range we saw a high mountain due south like a volcano peak. We suppose it to be Tongariro. Probable distance travelled from Cambridge, twenty-two miles.

Friday, December 17th. Our journey today has been an uninteresting one. Low fern hills and then a stretch of pumice covered with moss and scattered fern, hour after hour the same country and nearly the same view. Tirau Pah is the summit of one of these fern hills; it is very steep, terraced at the top, and the trees and Maoris' whares looking very picturesque. We missed the track about sundown, and after getting very tired, found ourselves at a native settlement called Korako, where the Maoris were very friendly and intelligent, gave us some splendid potatoes and cabbage, boiled our billy and gave us the best whare to sleep in. In the evening we should have made a fine picture, the chief men and women sitting with us round the candle and singing songs. One of them, George, could talk and read English very well. He had been to school in Auckland. When we sang them the National Anthem, he was delighted and made us sing it again and again till he knew it. Finding he knew the notes of the scales, we gave him the solfa of it, and the words written down. The Elder Native then sang a song in Maori to the tune of Auld Lang Syne which was interpreted to us by George.

Saturday, December 18th. Retracing our steps a short distance we made again towards Te Whetu. For many a weary mile over the same kind of country, once we lost the track altogether and presently picked up another, which has taken us south all day, we went on and on in the hopes of reaching Te Whetu, or possibly Niho o te Kiore by night, but darkness coming on, we were forced to stay and pitch our tent, having to get our tea as we could in the dark with only about an inch of candle to burn, the rest being burnt last night at Korako. We have wood and water here, but no view and there is every prospect of a wet day tomorrow. We don't know where we are or how far we may have to go to the next store, our food is all eaten except the flour. We have crossed four large creeks today, three we had to swim.

Sunday, December 19th. Morning wet and miserable. Breakfasted off flour dumplings. Rain held up a little after breakfast when we managed to bake a little of the flour and take our bearings when we found ourselves too far west. Afternoon very wet and most miserable Sunday.

Monday, December 20th. After some four miles hard travelling through fern and teatree over hill and dale, we managed at last to strike across a track which we followed and found it led the way to Niho o te Kiore over the spur of a high range where we had a fine view of the country towards the Lakes, the Horohoro Mountain, etc., then we went down again through a very broken country for some miles, the scenery getting more wild and rugged till we came to a creek which we had to swim, and here we got our swags wet. Half a mile from this creek we struck the coach road and were very soon on the banks of the Waikato again at Niho o te Kiore. We got a whare to sleep in and some pork and potatoes and made ourselves comfortable for the night. The bridge crosses the river just over some grand rapids, the rush and roar of the water as you look over the bridge making one feel dizzy.

Tuesday, December 21st. We left the river about six o'clock. The scenery at this place is by far the best we have seen yet, the bold and rugged forms of the rocks, especially the Rat's Tooth, the mountains in the distance and the dark turbid waters of the river with the foam of the rapids under the bridge made a good picture. The road over this tableland rises gradually curving round the sides of the mountain until after passing a track of plain, it descends the same way to Taupuaeharuru. We reached this place about half past seven wet through and very tired. Had a good dinner and bed at the hotel.

Wednesday, December 22nd. This morning about six we had a splendid view of Tongariro across the lake backed by Ruapehu covered with snow. After a swim in the lake and breakfast, took a picture of the land from just above the fort. The river runs through a very narrow passage from the lake and after a little smooth water, it commences its rapid course under the bridge. In colour it is a dark cold green, very clear.

Friday, December 24th. With a good stock of provisions we had not gone two miles when down came the rain, so we had to pitch our tent as well as we could, getting wet through in doing it. So we had some tea and went to bed, our blankets keeping nice and dry. Not a very pleasant Christmas Eve

Saturday, December 25th. Passed a very fair night, the morning fine. Started at daylight for the falls. The natives have named this fall rightly when they call it the Snow Fall. With the exception of a very delicate green tinge the whole mass of water is dazzling white. Intending to go round by the river bank instead of the road, we took a track from the falls leading in that direction. We had to climb the high bank of the river now and then, and then a stretch along its margin. It is a beautiful stream running dark and slow in one place and in the next, roaring over rocks and rapids. About two o'clock we came to a Maori settlement where they cooked us some very fine potatoes and showed us the road. We went along a level plain for about three miles after this, when we came to a splendid camping ground, plenty of wood, and the Waikato at our feet, so we decided to stay here over Sunday. The weather has been beautiful today, and in consequence the travelling very pleasant. We made our bed of native grass. It is very soft and even. Altogether this is the most comfortable place we have come to yet. A very pleasant Christmas Day.

Sunday, December 26th. A nice morning, fine and pleasant. Had a swim in the Waikato, in the afternoon took a walk along the banks. The river is very beautiful rushing past here and there in rapids, past little wooded islands looking very picturesque. Came on to rain in the afternoon, glad to turn in early.

Monday, December 27th. Morning wet, tent wet, everything wet. Stayed a while in hopes of it clearing. No signs of change, so we got up, put on our wet things and started. The native grass holds the water like a sponge. We were soon as wet about the legs as if we had waded through a creek. Sometimes the path struck through clumps of tall teatrees, then we got a shower bath all over. However, the worst time must have an end, and about noon it cleared up a little. We came to Orakei Korako and found hot springs and a large pool of boiling water. The natives gave us some potatoes and we slept in the porch of the chief's whare.

Tuesday, December 28th. Rising at day break, I had my first bath in the hot bath. A large cistern of boiling water flows over into another just cool enough to be comfortable. Here is the natural sitz-bath the Hon. Fox speaks of. The feeling of polish is a most delightful one. Altogether the bath leaves a most pleasurable sensation. This is a wonderful place, steam jets and boiling holes without number, the whole earth below you seems boiling, sending up either water or steam through every crevice. After breakfast, and such a breakfast as I never had, the bacon boiled in one of the *puias* (hot springs), the potatoes steamed over another, and such potatoes as I have never seen in Auckland or any where else, so large and mealy. After breakfast, Tom decided to go on while I went to see the cave. I had to cross the river again. It requires a clever hand at the paddle to cross here. They steer up the stream for a good way, taking it easy, then all at once shoot across the current. The rapid stream turns the canoe completely round. The native is all fire and animation in the swift part, and then brings the canoes in the other side as coolly as possible.

The entrance to the cave is nearly at the top of a high hill surrounded on all sides by steam jets and puias. You get one glimpse of the bottom through a dense mass of ferns and trees and then descend, I should think over one hundred feet over boulders and rocks. The rocks get whiter as you descend till at the bottom they are covered with a white crystallized substance like alum. The bottom is filled with hot water of a most remarkable green colour. You can see the bottom masses of rock, clearly twenty feet or so down, yet everything is of a vivid emerald or copper green. The rocks in places are coated with this green which rubs off dry on your hands like colour. Looking from the bottom to the entrance is almost equal to the view downwards, a soft light streaming through the fern leaves at the mouth, a little bit of sky and then the fringe of lichens round the top, the black rocks towering one hundred feet above your head, rugged and threatening, gradually changing through every variety of tint and shade to dazzling whiteness at your feet. There are no stalactites, the size and colour with the hot water at the bottom form the chief attractions. After looking at some of the other puias and terraces I left for the Rainbow Fall. The river just below Korako is so beautiful. I took a picture. Little islands, high wooded banks and a succession of rapids made a pretty picture. I was disappointed in the Rainbow Fall. It can scarcely be called a fall, more of a rapid or cascade — no good surroundings. Close by the fall is the Constabulary Fort, now deserted. I am camped here all alone, having the advantage of a good whare, a good fire, and a good bed.

Wednesday, December 29th. Wishing to paint Atiamuri this morning, I had to wait two hours for the heavy mist to clear off. Afterwards the sun came out very hot. Finished my picture about noon. After dinner started on the road. We had not gone two miles when down came a heavy thunderstorm, wind and rain. We are on one of the pumice flats, not a tree or house for shelter, so we just had to go through it for about six miles when we came to a high overhanging rock under which someone had slept before. We stayed here about an hour, when the rain moderating, we thought we might reach a deserted whare about four miles further on. We went on and on till it became quite dark, when we came across a packman who directed us to the whare where we were very glad to turn in. We lit a fire and made ourselves as comfortable as possible under the circumstances.

Thursday, December 30th. We were soon on the road. We were directed a nearer way to Rotomahana than by the Coach Road, turning off by a Maori pah. We came to this pah about dinner time. We got a few potatoes from them for which we paid a shilling, and had our dinner. We were soon surrounded by a crowd of children with cherries, eggs, etc., for sale. We invested ninepence in cherries. They were quite a treat. We left this place about two o'clock, and after going up and down a great deal, we came to the first lake, Roto Kakahi, about a mile and a half long with two small islands. The water is of a dull green colour, the hills around high, but very little bush. We took the wrong track here, and after climbing up a high hill we had to retrace our steps to the margin of the lake. Here it commenced raining, so we pitched our tent

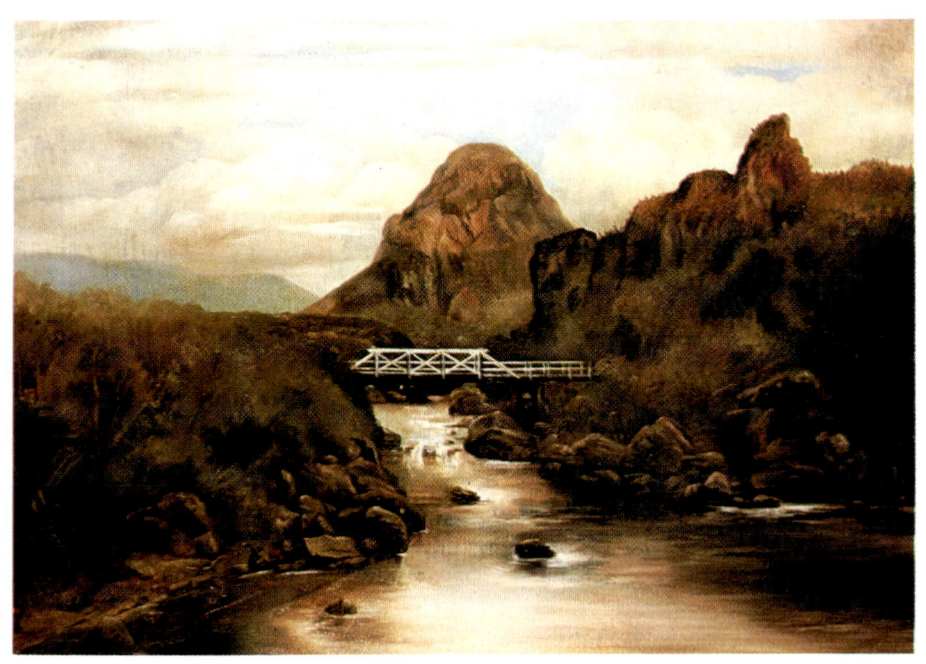

Atiamuri, 1875. Oil on canvas, 18×12 in.

Mud Valley, Rotomahana, 1912. Oil on canvas, 27×12 in.

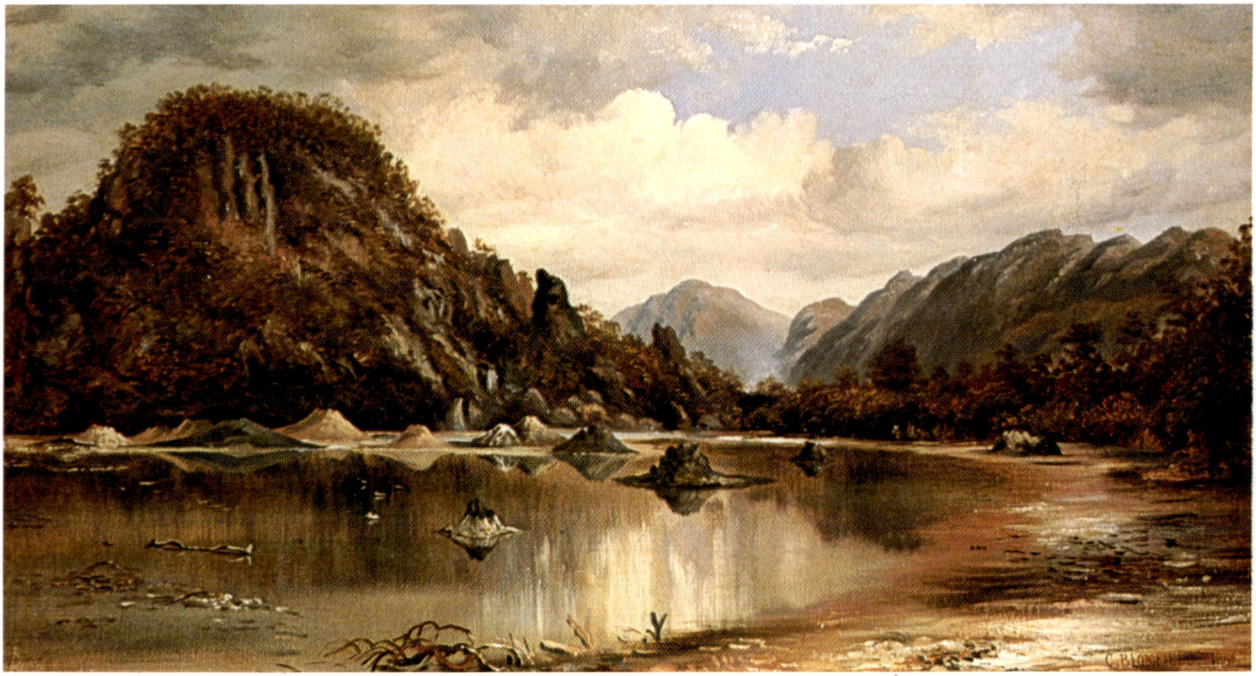

50

and camped for the night. The banks of the lake here are low and covered with the softest moss and ferns.

Friday, December 31st. We left our camping place soon after sunrise. The fern was very wet. We went round the lake to the settlement on the other side and were directed the right path to Wairoa, a station on the north end of Tarawera. A creek connects the lakes Kakahi and Tarawera. It is shaded with bush and very pretty. Wairoa is a large settlement. The natives get their living by paddling people over to Rotomahana in canoes. They are very jealous of anyone finding the way by themselves. We had our dinner at the Frenchman's who keeps a lodging house here in a whare. He has every convenience, good beds and is a good cook. He showed us the track, but warned us the Maoris would not let us go without some bother. However, we made the attempt and succeeded without any difficulties, and after losing ourselves once or twice, we are camped on the bank of the far-famed Rotomahana opposite the Great Terata, with a spring of cold good water not far from us, a desideratum in these parts.

Saturday, January 1st, 1876. A glorious day and a glorious place for New Year's Day, all by ourselves on the spot so many have come thousands of miles to see. We made for the pink terrace first. The colour is the chief attraction. With the morning sun shining brightly on it, it is almost white, but when the sun gets round and you get more shadow, the lovely salmon colour is very marked, varied with grey and white.

White Terrace, undated. Oil on canvas, 27 × 17 in.

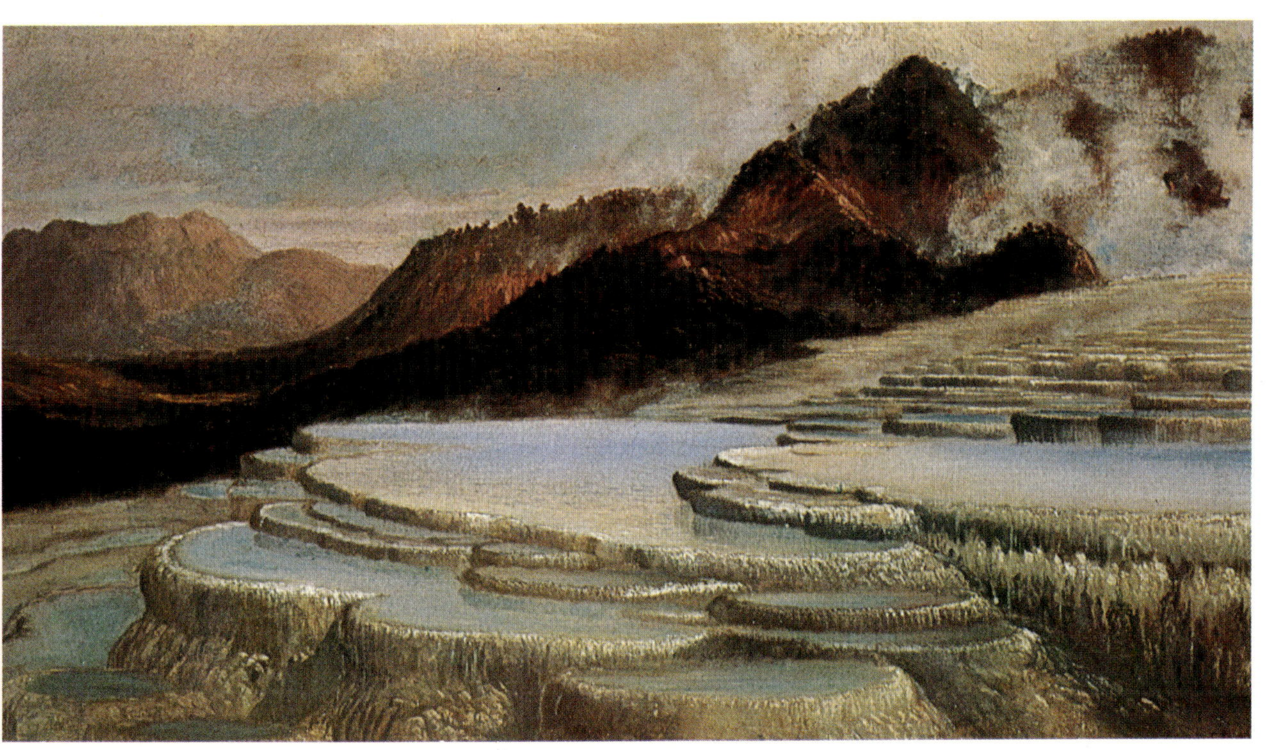

The overhanging lips of the basins are exceedingly beautiful and graceful. The pools are all near the top, so that it is impossible to see the carved lips and the pools of water at the same time. You get a good view of the lake and the white terrace in the distance from just above the pink terrace. At early morning the whole lake steams. As the sun rises and the air gets hot, the only steam you see is from the puias and steam vents. After taking two pictures here, I went over to the white terrace. Although we were camped between the two, we have to cross a swamp to get to the pink, and a creek to get to the white terrace. The colour of this terrace is of a greyish white, but on a far grander scale than the pink terrace. Several large pools of water lie near the bottom, nearly cold, but the same lovely blue as the others. You ascend the marble steps here only three and four inches high — there as many feet. After passing some fine specimens of the chiselled steps for which the terrace is so famous, you stand before what really seems to be the work of some cunning artist. A round basin of water about five yards across is surrounded by a marble rim overhanging in beautiful fringe work, with a mouth cut out of the lip about a foot for the water to run out, the fringe work finishing off on either side of the mouth with the utmost symmetry. Beneath the mouth a spout of rock conducts the water into the cistern below. After several more pools, each hotter than the last, you reach the highest just below the great geyser. Behind this you see nothing but a great crater as it were in the rocky mountain, and a glimpse now and then of the blue depth of boiling water through the clouds of steam. A little further on are three geysers and a blow hole. Two of these boil up six or eight feet every few minutes. The other is continually splashing up boiling spray from under a high rock. The whole place is enveloped in steam and the air is rank with sulphur. Tonight we had a beautiful sunset again. The light as it leaves the high mountain tops tints them a beautiful violet hue.

Sunday, January 2nd, 1876. Another fine day, though cloudy before breakfast. Went and got a bath in the pink terrace. Did not enjoy it as much as the bath at Orakei Korako. It had not that feeling of smoothness, and felt as if it wanted stirring up. The warmest water is at the top, running off before the bottom, leaving the cold at the bottom. After breakfast went again to the Great Terata. It was very active, the upper pools far too hot for bathing. Got nearly scalded in the steam trying to get a view of the water boiling up in the upper puia. The wonderful tattooed work seems more wonderful the more you look at it. The afternoon was fine and peaceful. We have had a most enjoyable Sunday.

Monday, January 3rd. Left the lake at dawn and arrived without mishap at Wairoa about nine o'clock. We were congratulating ourselves upon seeing the lake and the terraces so easily, but when we got to the Frenchman's, the natives laid a complaint against us for trespassing on forbidden ground without leave, and for smashing the terraces with the hatchet. To the first charge we pleaded guilty, but said we did not see any notice that people were not allowed on the lake. To the second we gave the lie direct. One old woman took up our little axe and refused to believe but that it had been used to break pieces off the terraces. We declared we had not taken it away from the tent where we camped and that it had only been used to cut firewood. It was no use. This woman, who we heard owned the white terrace, and her brother who also owned land there, wanted utu or money for the trespass. We went with them to an Englishman who heard the case stated on both sides, and acted as interpreter. He said they had no legal claim upon us, and advised us to take our swags and march off, and if anyone interfered with us to knock them on the head.

After we had had a meal at the Frenchman's we acted on the first part of his advice. Fortunately a great row was taking place not far off, which drew off the attention of the natives from us. As it was the man watched for us to go, and then stopped us and demanded £1.0.0. We refused, and walked away, and felt greatly relieved to put three or four miles between us.

The road to Ohinemutu passes through bush part of the way. It is very pretty. Lake Rotorua is large, but the banks are low and uninteresting. A most intolerable smell pervades the air round about.

Finding the steamer leaves [Tauranga] for Auckland tomorrow night, we determined to start away at once and walk as far as we could through the bush. When we started, the morning had been very hot and some threatening clouds were hovering about. We had proceeded about five miles on our journey, and were in the plain, no shelter, nothing but fern, when a very heavy thunder shower passed over us in half an hour. We were drenched to the skin, and the roads were running with water like a creek, making walking very heavy, but there was nothing for it but to push on. At last we came to two weatherboard houses. We tried the doors and windows, but they were both locked up, so we started again in hopes of gaining the bush before dark, as there, probably, we might light a fire and warm ourselves. The bush was still some three or four miles distant, and when we got there we might be no better off, as there would be no place to lie down even if we got a fire. Just as darkness was gathering in, we espied two houses, both unoccupied. We got into one of them, and finding plenty of dry wood about, were not long in getting a good fire and making some tea. We took our wet clothes off, and wrapping ourselves in our dry blankets like Maoris, we felt devoutly thankful for finding such a nice place in our necessity. We never enjoyed a meal better, by a warm fire which warmed us while it dried our clothes. We drank our tea and ate minced mutton hot, with bread, and felt it almost too good to be true.

Tuesday, January 4th. After having our breakfast with cherries, which grow wild just here, we started off again through the bush. It was a pretty walk, a good road, and very interesting. The bush is pretty but scraggy here, no large trees, a few rimu, and one moderately sized rata, but very small after the Thames bush. About midday we came to the place where the coach changes horses. We here found an empty dray going to Tauranga, so we took advantage of it to get a lift, and arrived in Tauranga about six o'clock. After leaving the bush, you have a fine view of the Tauranga harbour stretching away to the right, and left land-locked and guarded by islands. Just here is the settlement of Uropi and the Constabulary camp. As we neared Tauranga, marks of cultivation became more apparent till within about five miles of the town the country presented a lovely appearance, dotted over with country homesteads and small farms, fields of wheat and grass. The town itself is very picturesque, clumps of trees surrounding the neat little houses and a row of shops facing the water, a wharf and jetty with a vessel or two lying alongside.

When we arrived we found the steamer had left on Monday morning, so after all our hurry we were too late. We put up at a very decent boarding house and waited to see what the morrow would bring forth. *Wednesday January 5th.* Finding that if we could get a boat to Katikati we could then walk to Ohinemuri in a day, we hunted up the watermen to try and get a boat. We found them nearly all engaged. They seem to occupy the place of the cabs and buses in Auckland. At last we persuaded an old man named Jones to take us across in a very old and rickety boat. It was a pleasant trip with a fair wind. We crossed in about five hours. The scenery is pretty wooded headlands and long sandy spits. One place can only be crossed at high tide. We got there only just in time, as at one stage we were sailing right through the tops of mangroves. However, we got across and landed at Katikati and walked a distance of five miles close by the sea beach to a Maori settlement called Waihi, where we stayed for the night. Pipis and potatoes and Maori bread for tea.

Thursday, January 6th. The sound of the wind in the trees and the waves breaking on the beach made pleasant music last night. We were very comfortable in the whare, barring the mosquitoes. We were up at daybreak, and were just starting when our host asked if we wanted any breakfast. He offered us some stewed goose. They had evidently killed the goose on purpose for us. If we could have stayed we should have had a fine breakfast, but we wanted to get to Mackaytown by dinner time, so we had to be satisfied with cold goose and bread. We started just as the sun rose out of the sea, gilding the tops of the breakers. Our road lay first over a few fern hills then across a flat for eight or nine miles, then over more ranges till we came to the bush on the Thames side. We went for some distance along the banks of the Ohinemuri river, then crossed it at the ford and were soon at Mackaytown. Here all was bustle and stir with the elections, Maoris and white men making a great noise. The scenery round Ohinemuri is very good, bush and river.

Friday, January 7th. The steamer did not go to Shortland till night. We walked leisurely down to Paeroa where everything was quiet, everybody being at the Poll. The Ohinemuri river here runs through the flat, a good sized stream, the tide affecting it as far as Mackaytown. The steamer comes up as far as Paeroa.

And so, after an energetic three weeks, Charles returned to his wife in Auckland.

7. Wanganui Waters

Tragedy struck Ellen and Charles when their first born child, Fanny, died in infancy. But on April 30th, 1876, another daughter, Mary, was born, and she was a bonny child, bringing joy to her parents. Two years later, they were blessed with another daughter, Nellie, a pretty little thing.

By now Charles had opened his own shop in Wakefield Street, advertising in Brett's Auckland Almanac, and in July 1879 he was able to buy a section in order to build their own home. It was a lovely thirty perch section on the corner of Wood and Ryle Streets in Ponsonby, with a gentle slope to the north, and a beautiful view over green fields and trees to the beach at Freemans Bay and across the harbour to North Head and Rangitoto, with Coromandel in the distance, and it cost the princely sum of £169.0.0.

Sam returned from Thames, setting up his home in Upper Queen Street, and by this time his family had grown considerably. He and Charles went into the bush and chose a good straight kauri tree, which was felled when the sap was down, lifted off the ground, and left to dry for about six months, after which it was dragged to the sawmill and cut into timber to build his big two-storeyed house on the section.

Charles and Ellen spent long hours in designing their home, and when it was finished it was a lovely home. Upstairs there were three large bedrooms, with an open fireplace in the main bedroom and a connecting door between the two larger rooms. Halfway down the stairs was the bathroom, which held not only a bath, but a steam bath similar to a modern sauna. The ground floor had the parlour in the front, a large dining room, a big kitchen with a walk-in pantry under the stairs, and a back room which Charles was able to use for his studio. There was a verandah top and bottom, on two sides of the house, facing the sun and the view.

Sam built the whole house of the solid kauri, and made a real feature of the banister of polished kauri, which came down to the landing, then curved right round and descended to the foot of the stairs opposite the front door. At the bottom he put a curl like a snail's back, instead of the usual knob. He loved making these banisters, and made several for the larger buildings around the town, including Victoria Arcade.

When he had finished the house, he made built-in cupboards in the dining room, with glass doors at the top for Ellen's best china on the left hand side, and bookshelves on the right. He also constructed the bedroom furniture, including a large chest of drawers, and half-round tables for the washbasin and the dressing table.

While Sam was finishing off the house, Charles began to decorate it. All the skirting boards, doors and architraves were wood grained, and in the main bedroom, he achieved a bird's eye maple effect. The cornices in

the hall and two main rooms downstairs, and the large ornate ventilator
in the centre of the room were tinted in pastel shades of pink, blue, and
gold. Then he wallpapered the rooms, and finished by painting murals
around the tops of each in the form of a frieze, and painting the mantel-
piece in the dining room to look exactly like marble.

At last it was finished, and Charles and Ellen moved in with their two
little girls, and a short time later their third child, Bessie, was born in their
new home. They prayed that it would always be a happy family home.

About this time, Sam's eldest son, William (later known as 'Blo') aged
about fourteen, became well known for his artistic efforts, and tells his
own story:

> I wagged it from school time and again and at last applied and got a
> job as office boy to a stockbroker in the N.Z. Insurance buildings in
> Queen Street, where the sharebrokers were nested up in an arcade with
> the offices around. As I was understood by my parents to be still
> attending school, I had to carry my school bag, etc. to work. Five
> shillings a week wages to spend all on my own but that nearly all went
> in 'hush money'.
>
> However, my guilt was discovered through my artistic efforts. There
> were some real gems for caricature amongst the mining touts and brokers
> and these characters I practised on and pasted my efforts on the public
> noticeboard in the arcade. These efforts caused much amusement and
> not a little trouble. My bit of notoriety reached the ears of my Uncle
> Charles Blomfield, who was a leading man in the New Zealand artistic
> world then. I was discovered, and put to work, but sacked myself from
> the broker.
>
> My Uncle Charles placed me in Phillips and Sons paint shop, on the
> 'picture side' in Queen Street. I revelled in the engravings, chromos and
> many illustrations that I had to keep clean, between my duties of putting
> into racks many rolls of wall-papers and running messages.

During these early years of his marriage, Charles stayed at home most
of the time, looking after his business, his home, and his family. He was
already a member of the Society of Artists, exhibiting regularly with them,
and in 1880 he was elected to the committee of the new Auckland Society
of Arts, a position he held for seventeen years.

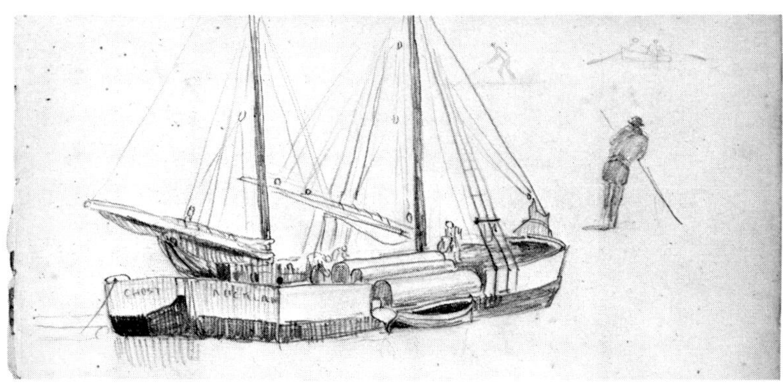

Logging kauri, 1879.

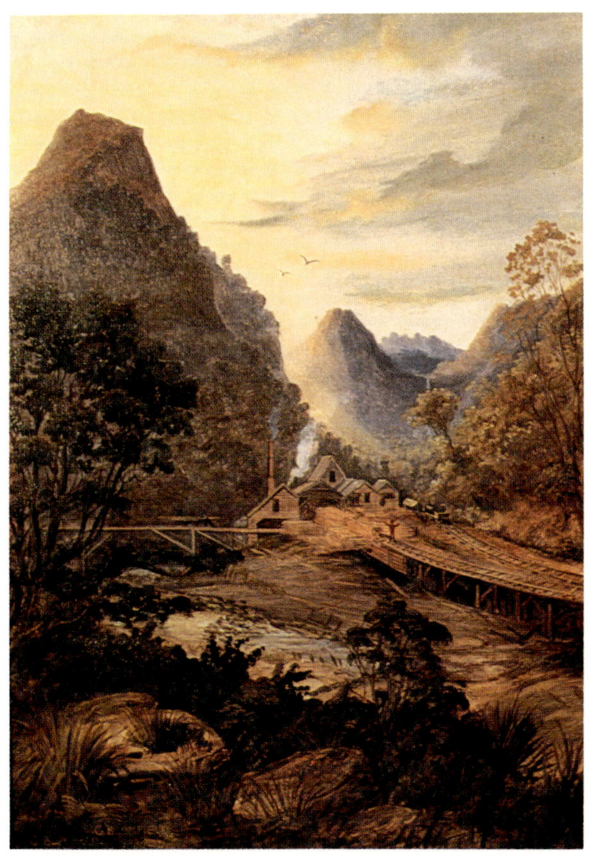

Pararahi Logging Mill, undated. Oil on card, 15 × 10 in.

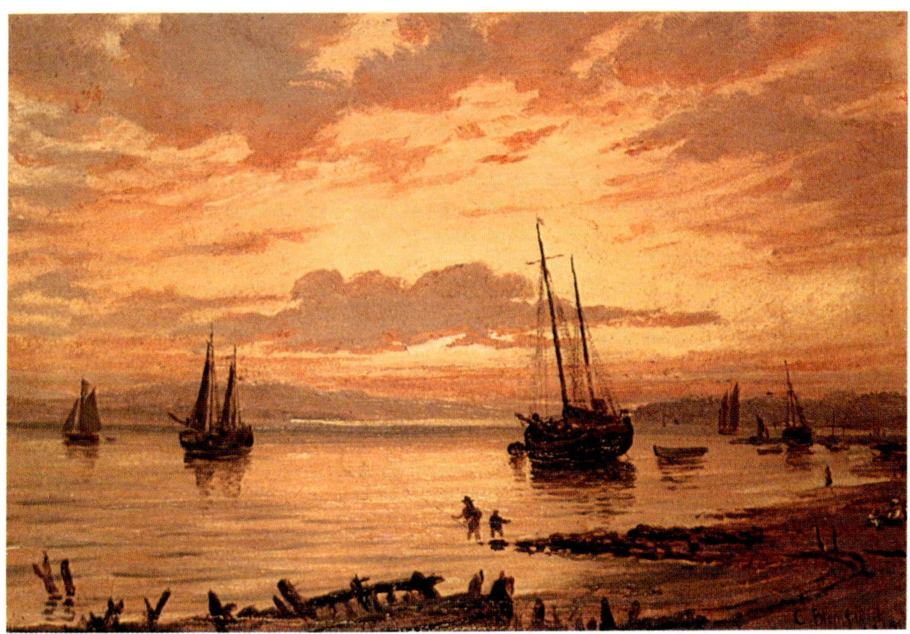

The Waitakeres from Devonport, 1914. Oil on card, 16 × 11 in.

However, he made a few short trips away from home, bringing back paintings from the north and the Wanganui River. Of his Wanganui exhibition, the local newspaper reported:

During his late trip up the Wanganui River, Mr Blomfield, the artist, executed several paintings of some of the more striking pieces of the beautiful scenery which he came across. They are at present on view in Mr A. D. Willis's window, where they are attracting much attention.

They are evidently appreciated for the majority of them have already been sold, and as they are of great local interest, as showing some of the most beautiful and almost unknown scenery of our noble river, we venture to give a description of the several paintings.

There are five large sketches and seven small ones, all in oil, and all unfinished — in fact, just as Mr Blomfield brought them back with him — but unfinished as they are, they give a vivid idea of the varied and romantic beauty of the upper part of our noble river.

One that will perhaps command the most attention is a view of the entrance to the limestone caves only just discovered; the mouth of the cave is hung and festooned with creepers and hanging plants — one like a great living chandelier. Just discernible, amid the gloom of the interior, is a fine waterfall — the outlet of an underground river — and the foreground is a rich border of ferns and lichens, making a strange but beautiful picture.

Another one, very different in character — but very striking — shows the entrance of the Manganui-o-te-Ao, which river is enclosed on all sides by high walls of rock, which rise boldly from the water's edge to the height of many feet. The foreground cliffs are in deep shadow, bringing out by contrast the sunlit masses of rock in the middle distance.

The view from the mouth of the Omorehu creek is also a very fine one, showing a fine perspective of cliff and mountain reflected in the placid waters of the river. An upright sketch of the river at the Arawata — about twelve miles above Pipiriki — is remarkable for the rich colouring of the distant hills and sky. Perhaps one of the best is a view of the valley of the Wanganui, from the height above Parakino, where the river is seen winding about among the Maori settlements, enclosed by its lofty mountains; while, beyond them all, rises Ruapehu, the mountain King.

There are some lovely views among the smaller sketches, and no doubt Mr Blomfield will work up several good paintings from some of these. The Ngaporo rapid and the view at Otuku are perhaps the best.

There are two finished paintings framed in upright oval mats — forming a very pretty pair — both representing waterfalls to be seen in the Wanganui. One is a short distance up the Omorehu creek which falls into the Wanganui a mile or two below Pipiriki: the water falls over a peculiar shelf of rock, while just underneath, to the right is another fall. The other one is a very fine fall, situated about two miles above the caves, where a large body of water comes over the cliff, and falls some distance intact: it then strikes the projecting rocks, and makes a handsome cascade till it disappears out of sight behind the fern and trees in the foreground. Either of these falls would alone be worth seeing, but we understand Mr Blomfield obtained pencil sketches of several others, equally good. There is also on view a painting of the river, which will be recognised by everybody — an evening view taken from the river bank, showing Mr Nixon's house on the opposite side, and Ruapehu in the distance.

Charles, himself, also wrote about his experiences on the Wanganui River:

When I came to Wanganui a few weeks ago everybody said, "You must go up the river." But I had no intention of going up the river; I thought it was the wrong time of the year. Eighteen months ago I stood at the source of the Wanganui, I crossed it on foot, I travelled down it, from the slopes of Tongariro past the Pourere Pah where Captain St. George was killed in the last fight with Te Kooti, and on for ten miles until it enters a romantic bush country, and I made up my mind that some day I would follow it down to do it properly, ending where I have now begun.

But being here, and also being favoured in my trip up the Mangawhero with charming weather, I thought, "Well, I will get a boat and go up as far as I can by myself." But that was voted impossible.

"You will never get up the rapids," people said, "You must go up with some of the Maoris when they return in their canoes."

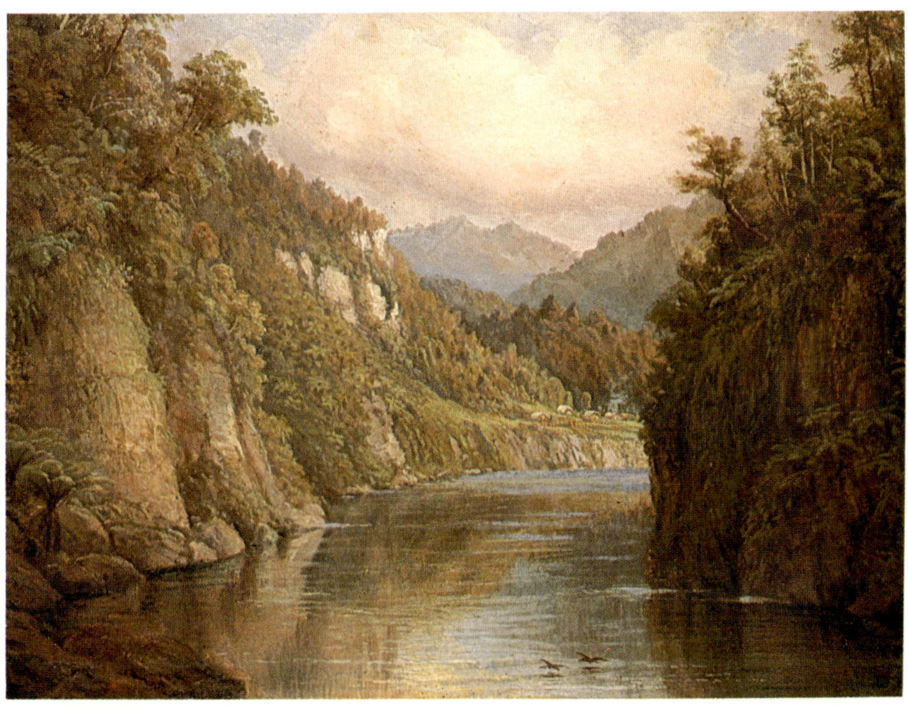

Wanganui River, undated.
Oil on canvas, 26 × 20 in.

But that did not suit my fancy, for they would most likely want to go on just when I wanted to stop, and to stop just when I wanted to go on.

At last I heard of a person who happened to be just the man for me — Andrew Anderson, the mailman. I found him out at last, and fortune favoured me, for I could not wish for a better fellow: steady, obliging, courageous, a splendid hand with the canoe — either pulling, poling, or paddling — and just as good a bushman when camping time comes. He was a man who can make you comfortable under any circumstances, as I have had good evidence of more than once. Fancy, for instance, being benighted on the river, no houses near, rain pouring in torrents, everything wet, not an inch of level ground to plant the tent on, nothing to burn but half-rotten wood sodden with moisture, and it does not look much like comfort for the night, does it? Yet Anderson went patiently to work, and before long there was the tent pitched, the billy boiled, and a dry comfortable bed to lie on, and I slept as soundly as if I had been in my own bedroom.

Now a man who could do this under the circumstances is worth something. Wishing to visit some plains on the way, I arranged with Anderson to pick me up at Kennedy's, and when there I heard that there was a short cut over the hills to Parakino, saving seventeen miles of canoeing, so I determined to walk on, and was well repaid for my trouble by the magnificent prospect from the top of the hill. After going a mile or so through bush, I suddenly came to the top of a rocky bastion, overlooking — well, when I got up there, it overlooked nothing: it seemed all sky, a dense mist filled the valley and blotted out every vestige of the landscape. The sun was shining gloriously overhead, and by-and-by I caught a glimmer of water far below, and in half an hour the scene slowly unfolded itself.

As this spot is only eleven miles from Wanganui by road, it ought to become a favourite spot for a day's excursion. After taking in the scene, literally as well as mentally, and waiting half an hour, up came Anderson and the canoe, with Her Majesty's mails aboard. So now I was fairly on my voyage.

As the mail was due at Pipiriki on a certain day, we had to push ahead, and there was no time for anything more than a passing glance at the exchanging panorama, which, from Ruakino to Pipiriki forms an endless series of pictures, some of them grand and beautiful in the extreme. But having arrived at Pipiriki, the canoe was at my command: I could go or stay as I pleased; and from there onward I found so much to occupy my time and my pencil, that it took the best part of a week to go twenty miles. We got as far as the caves on Saturday, four miles above Pipiriki.

The next day being Sunday, a day on which I never work or travel, here we pitched the tent, and I dismissed my boatman, who was glad to spend the Sunday with his family at Pipiriki, and remained in solitary confinement, like Crusoe, 'Lord of all I surveyed' till Monday morning. But what a lovely spot for a Sunday's rest! Just in front of the tent a little plot of the softest grass, a tall fern on one hand and a cabbage on the other, both magnificent specimens of their kind, high cliffs behind, a waterfall on either hand, flowing out of dark mysterious looking caves. In front, a few feet below me, the river deep and still, reflecting its rocky banks. And when:

<blockquote>
At eve
The moonbeams softly gliding in between
The sleeping leaves
</blockquote>

added their soft witchery to the scene, and any sound but the slow murmur of the waterfalls would have been an intrusion, the time and scene formed one of those sweet images that linger for ever in the memory.

The caves are said to be very extensive and rich in stalactites, but the entrance is guarded by a large pool of water and a waterfall of considerable volume, so it is almost inaccessible in winter. The view of the entrance is like a fairy scene; the ferns and lichens hanging round form a fitting frame, and from the ceiling hangs by a slender cord a mass of living creepers like a great chandelier.

From here to Teheke I consider the best part of the river for scenery; certainly there are some very fine views about Atene and just above, and a mile or two below Pipiriki the banks are very high and imposing; but from the caves for some ten or twelve miles the river rises between perpendicular walls of rock all festooned with a hanging drapery of ferns and lichens, while above higher still rise lofty hills covered with luxuriant bush. Over these cliffs fall numerous streams making a succession of fine waterfalls, all different and all beautiful, now a thin gauge like a sheet of water falling from a projecting cliff high above our heads, then a roaring cascade of sparkling water, then again one away back of a deep dark ravine almost hidden by ferns and creepers; in several places two or three are visible at the same time, and some of these are double ones.

Thus the visitor is led on from one fine sight to another, his admiration growing at every turn, again and again he is ready to declare the view inimitable until the next turn of the river reveals new beauties and calls forth new praises, until at last the interest culminates at the Manganui-o-te-Ao where an immense cliff rises like a mighty pillar on the right and the two rivers meet like two lanes in a great city walled in by many massive piles of masonry.

I had always been led to expect something very fine up the Wanganui, but it certainly far surpassed my expectations; the broad river, always interesting and beautiful both in the rapids and in the long reaches of still water, the steep rocky banks, the lofty trees, with white cliff faces peeping out, tier above tier, from the varied foliage, the beautiful ferns rising as thick as they can stand, acres of them, from the water's edge right up to the top of some of the mountains, the natives in their long canoes and picturesque costumes all combine to make up a series of pictures which I think would be hard to equal anywhere.

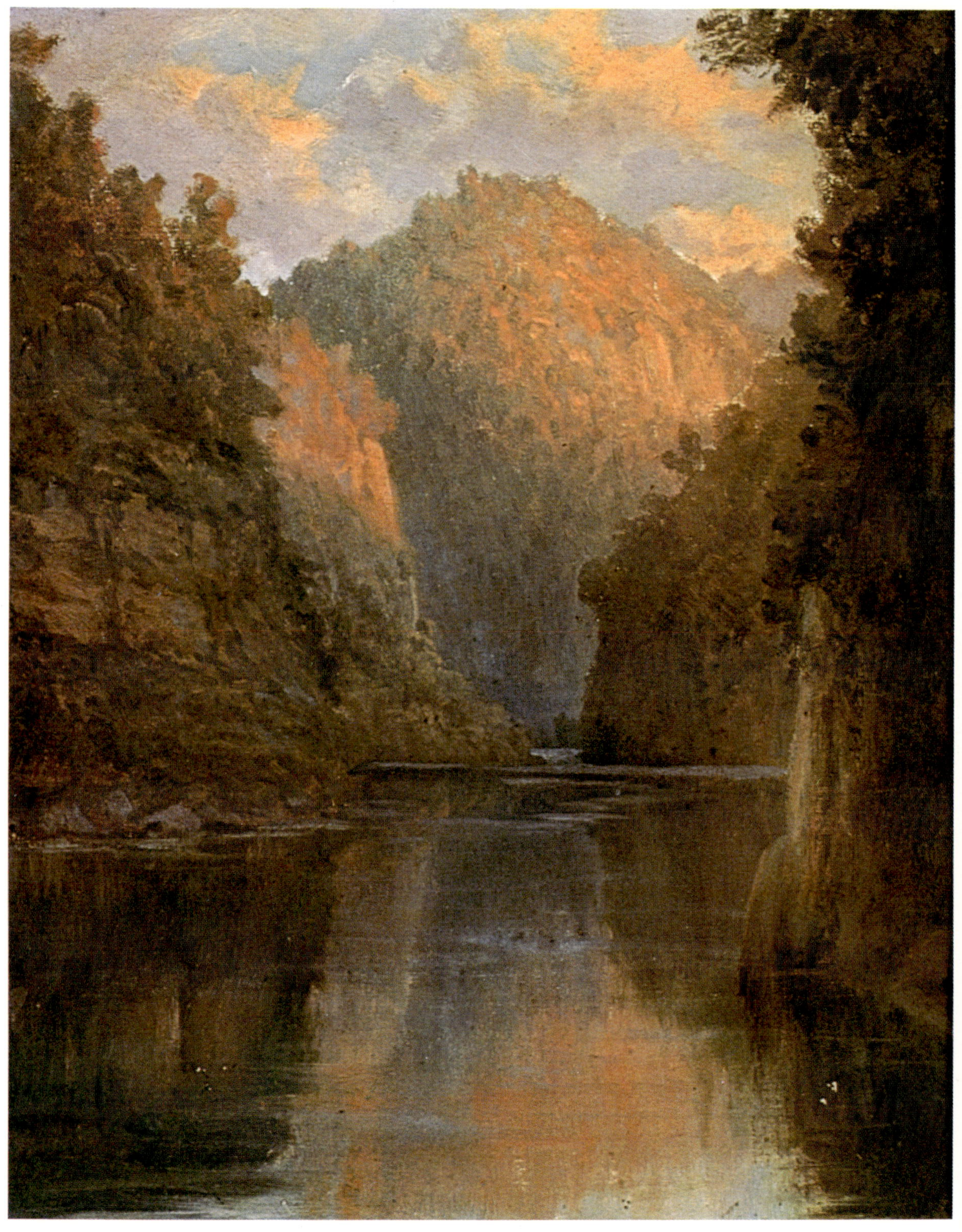

Not content with travelling up the Wanganui River, Charles decided to journey up the Mangawhero River also, in search of an almost unknown waterfall. Once again, he records his experiences:

A waterfall on the Mangawhero, unvisited and almost unknown, virgin ground to the artist and photographer! This was quite enough to induce me to start on a sketching tour up the Mangawhero.

It is true this time of year was very unsuitable, the nights were cold and the roads bad — but after the wind, rain, and frost of Taranaki, where I only had six fine days in seven weeks, the beautiful weather I have been favoured with in Wanganui seems like a young summer. So, after getting reliable information about Field's track from Mr Field himself, I left early one morning in the last week in July in search of the falls.

The road leads along the river bank to Upokongaro and through the valley of that stream. There is nothing worthy of remark until, ascending by an easy gradient, the top of the dividing range is reached, where a grand view is obtained of the valley of the Mangawhero. After the rough country traversed, the verdant fields and rolling downs that form part of the runs belonging to Mr Mason and Mr Fernie are very refreshing.

Descending rapidly, I reached the crossing. My instructions were to cross in an iron cage, which runs on a wire rope, but unfortunately I found the rope broken and the cage useless, so I had to ford it.

After leaving Mason's the road goes through open grassy plains and gentle slopes, and then commences to ascend the valley, and the river, which meanders through this open country with many a bend, is kept on the right. The scenery improves as you get on. The track — for after leaving Mason's it is little better than a horse track — ascends very gradually, now making a wide detour to get a good crossing over some tributary, and now cut out of the steep hillside, sometimes shut in by a lofty avenue of tall pines and ferns, and sometimes coming out on the top of a steep incline, with the river full below, shut in by its precipitous banks.

Mr Roger Montgomerie's place is the next and last station. The house, hidden from the road, nestles prettily amid the surrounding hills. On the opposite side of the river there is a high bush-covered ridge, where in fine weather a splendid view of Ruapehu can be obtained; you look right up the valley of the Mangawhero, range beyond range, leading right away to the dim blue distance, while beyond them, in silent majesty, the noble form of Ruapehu is seen, a giant mass of glittering ice. It is now all Maori land, and the traveller must put up with such accommodation as they are able or willing to supply.

I found the settlers kind and hospitable to a degree, but the Maoris — well, anyone who has met with the natives knows what to expect. The Maori seems to judge of a visitor by his equipment. A good horse, flash saddle and rugs, and you are a person of some importance — but on foot, as I was — carrying all your belongings on your back — then you are a nobody and anything is good enough for you. So when I reached Parapara, on the evening of the second day, tired and hungry, I met with but scant courtesy.

"You got no blankets?"

"No."

"Well, we got none."

"Oh!" I said. "You must find me something to keep me warm."

"Well how much you pay?"

"Oh! how much you like?"

"Oh, one blanket, one shilling; two blankets, two shillings; three blankets, three shillings," etc.

So I had to pay them two shillings for the privilege of sleeping in a crowded hut, wrapped up in a villainous bit of dirty blanket and the fly of an old tent.

Some very fine views meet the eye between Montgomerie's place and the first Maori at Otuku — one especially fine, where the road passes round a steep spur and the river makes a sharp bend round the base of rocky cliffs. Otuku consists of a few scattered whares on an open plateau, some distance from the river, but passing this, the road comes out again above the riverbed, and here a most spectacular sight presents itself, coming upon the traveller quite as a surprise. A cluster of little gem-like lakes lie nestling among the tall pines and rimus. Being so far below the spectator, the water takes a dark indigo colour here, contrasting strongly with the light buff of the dead raupo fringe around them. I passed on regretting I had not time for a nearer inspection.

Some four or five miles further on, the valley narrows and the road leads close down to the bed of the stream. This, to my mind, is the finest part: the scenery is truly magnificent. The precipitous banks, rising hundreds of feet on either side; the rapid river, sometimes rushing over rocks and boulders white with foam; and sometimes pausing in dark still pools, mirroring back its shaggy bank — these alone would make up a fine picture, but when we add the varied and enchanting beauty of the native bush, when from base to summit the steep mountains are clothed with dense vegetation, when even the precipices are festooned with ferns and lichens, when tall shaggy pines rise from the river bank and the giant fronds of the graceful tree ferns peer out among the darker growth — the picture is so varied in colour, so full of grace and beauty, that the mind revels in it, and all the trials of the way are forgotten.

A little further on Maroetawa is reached, situated on an open part amid very picturesque surroundings. What splendid runs some of this country would make. The land is very good, the bush light, and there are some nice flats here and there. It is only a question of time, no doubt, and this fine country will be in the hands of Europeans, and then, alas, the most charming feature, the native bush, will soon be a thing of the past.

The road, which was bad enough before, gets worse after leaving this place, and in the shady places is just a sea of mud, worked by the pack horses treading in one another's footsteps, into a series of corrugated humps, on which the feet slip and slide, and hollows where you reach bottom somewhere about knee deep. But the longest and worst road has an end, and by the by the Parapara is reached, just at the point where Field's stand turns off the Mangawhero Valley — a cold, bleak spot.

On the morning of the third day I started, after an early breakfast, in search of the falls. The only information I could get from the Maoris was that they were about five miles up the valley, and I must go up the riverbed. So finding a track that led down to the river, I got into the water and tried to make my way up, but I soon found out that the middle of winter was the wrong time to wade waist-deep for five miles up a rapid ice-cold river. I tried both sides of the river bank for a way through the bush, but there were no signs of a track, and to push through scrub and supplejacks, and over hills and gullies for five miles would have meant a night or two in the bush without blankets or food, so I was reluctantly compelled to give it up, and leave the search for the waterfall to a more favourable opportunity. Although distant five miles, the roar of the falls was distinctly audible, and no doubt "Raukawa" as the natives call it, is a grand sight.

I could not help wishing this road were better known, as it would, I am sure, prove a favourite route for tourists coming overland from Taupo to Wellington. The road would be an excellent one in summer, and the scenery abounds with game, and if the Maoris at Parapara would only wake up to their own interests and cut a good track to the falls it would prove an extra attraction.

In conclusion, I commend a trip to the Mangawhero to anyone wishing to spend a pleasant holiday; but take my advice — go in summer, and take your own blankets!

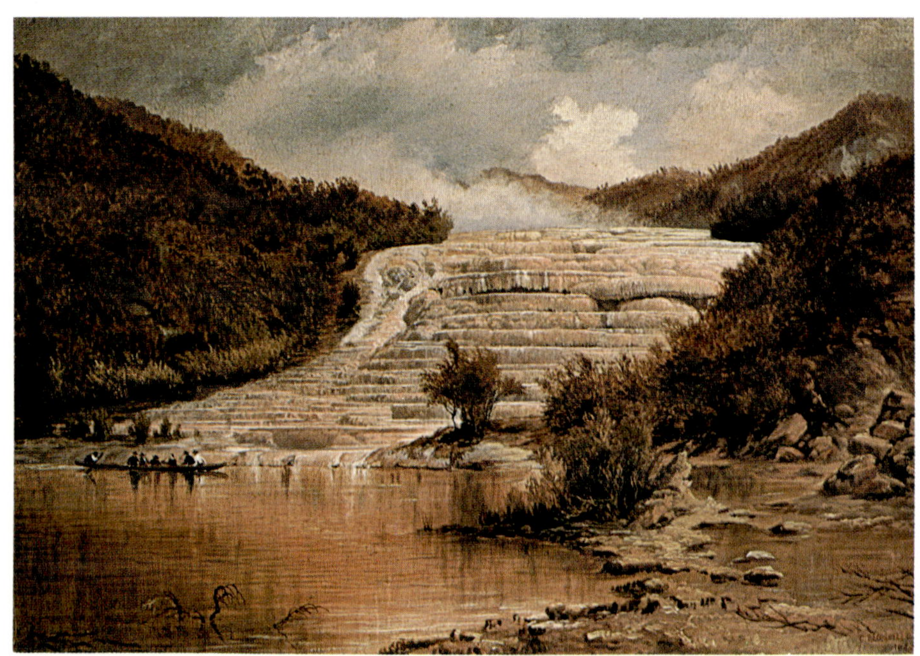

Pink Terrace, 1885. Oil on canvas, 27 × 21 in.

White Terrace, 1908. Oil on canvas, 30½ × 22½ in.

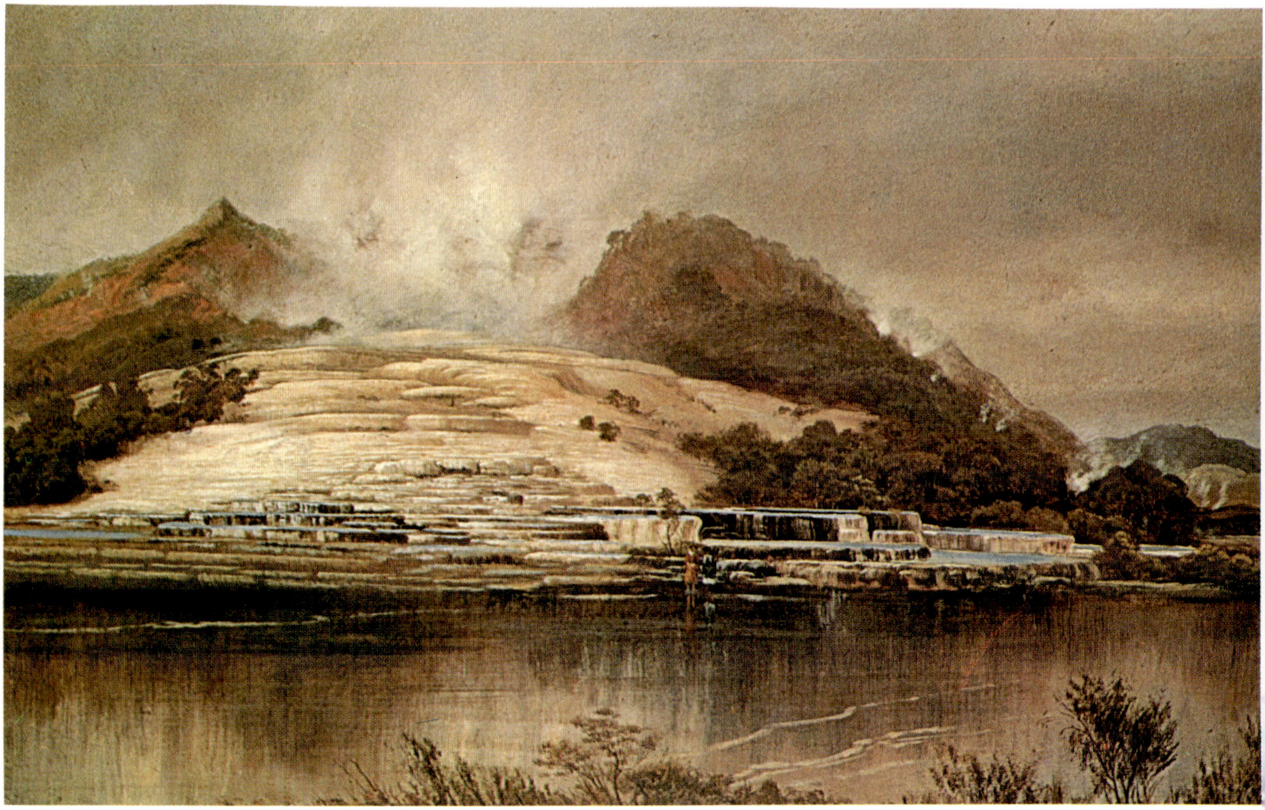

8. Painting the Terraces

Tom Spurgeon was quite excited when he called on the Blomfields.

"Charlie," he said. "They've asked me to replace Allan Webb as pastor of the Baptist Church."

"Yes," replied Charles. "We were at the meeting when they decided to send you the call. We're very pleased, and know that you will make a good pastor."

"Now I'll tell you of my vision for the work here," said Tom. "I can envisage a really big church on the lines of my father's Tabernacle in London. The Metropolitan Tabernacle holds nearly six thousand people, but our church will only need to seat about one thousand five hundred."

"What a wonderful idea," said Ellen. "Do you think you will be able to get it built?"

"Oh, yes," replied Tom. "We will take up collections here to buy some land, and then I'll go home to England with an appeal for help from my father's congregation."

True to his word, Pastor Spurgeon inspired his congregation to raise enough money to pay for a large section on the corner of Queen Street and Karangahape Road. This was a good residential area at this time, and several churches were built nearby — Pitt Street Methodist, Beresford Congregational, St. James Presbyterian, and St. Benedict's Catholic. At the same time, Tom carried on with his design for the church to be built on the site.

Finally, in 1884, they were ready to commence the building, and Ellen was asked to turn the first sod for the foundation to be laid. Then in 1885, when it was almost finished, Ellen climbed up the ladder and laid the last tile on the roof, and it was ready for occupation in May of that year. Meanwhile Charles was commissioned to decorate the inside, and he made a marvellous job of it. The beams in the high ceiling were all hand printed with intricate designs, and the cornices were shaded in pinks, reds and blues, edged here and there with gold. He must have felt like Michelangelo while he was painting forty or fifty feet above the ground, high up on a scaffolding!

He also offered to write a text in the white alcove behind the pulpit. The text chosen was "Praise Ye The Lord" and he finished it in beautiful gold lettering.

A few years later the church bought a pipe organ, and this was built in the alcove, hiding the text, but as the organ led the members in worship and praise of God, it was accepted as complementing the text.

In September 1884, Charles was also appointed as a singing inspector for the schools in the Thames area, receiving £2.2.0 a day while examining country schools, and £1.11.6. a day for town schools.

Then during the Christmas holidays of that year, Charles decided to return to Rotorua and paint the Pink and White Terraces, taking his eldest daughter, Mary, now eight years old, with him. While away, he wrote home to Ellen:

It is just about five days since I left home, yet it seems a fortnight at least, so much has happened and so much change and excitement that it makes the time seem very long. We are both very well.

I left town, and Mary is happy as the day is long, and seems to like this kind of life almost as much as her dad. The tent is nice and large and comfortable and perfectly watertight, and the weather is very warm so that although the weather is still unsettled, it is no hardship to stay in the tent when it rains, and when it is fine she seems never tired of sitting reading by me, or drawing or paddling up and down the steps of the Pink Terrace. She has had some hot baths, but in the morning she has a cold or tepid bath in a little basin about half way up the terrace — I think this is better for us than hot baths every day. She sleeps at night like a top.

I must now tell you of the adventures we have had since we came down. The first was in the coach which was too crowded — eleven passengers and such a large mail and a lot of luggage. We left at half past nine and did not get to Ohinemutu till nine o'clock at night. They go now all round by Rotoiti and Te Nga, about sixteen miles further than the way we went. The gentlemen had to walk a good bit of the way, the roads were so bad, or I don't think we should have got here yet. We stayed at Lake House and the next day was wet. We did not get away till three in the afternoon, and then had to hire a buggy for myself and my things. I forgot to tell you I had to leave two of my boxes at Tauranga, as there was not room for them in the coach. The coach-man promised me faithfully he would send them on Christmas Day and would forward them to Wairoa yesterday or today.

I hope he has kept his promise, for one of them is the box with all the food in and we have been living on bread and meat. Well, Tuesday was wet and just after we started from Ohinemutu the rain came down in torrents. We had our overcoats on and a lot of dry sacks, but the rain soon found its way down my back and soaked me through about the seat, and got into our carpet bag and spoiled the look of some of the nice clean things you put up for Mary. Just as we passed the green lake, it seemed just as if someone was pouring water out of a bucket. However, we got to Wairoa and found our way to Haszards', where Clara gave us a cordial welcome. Mr Fairbrother, I must tell you, we met at Ohinemutu, and he rode to Wairoa before we did, and met us there. We were very wet, but a change of things and tea soon put us to rights.

At Lake House I saw Mr Robert Graham, the proprietor, and the owner of Wairakei. He said he had been looking out for me to go to Wairakei and paint the Huka Falls and geysers there, and gave me an invitation to go there and stay there as long as I like. He said Mary and I could go, and live at his place for three or four weeks and it should cost me nothing. I told him I would see about it after I came from Rotomahana. I think I shall go, if there is nothing to hasten me back to town.

Well, we got the loan of a boat and put our things on board and started off on Christmas morning about half past nine, for Rotomahana. It was such a fine morning and it was calm, and we got on very well and crossed the lake in about two hours. Mary pulled some time. We got to the creek all right, but here our troubles began.

I have written an account of the bother we had with Thompson at Rotomahana separate, as you may have to show it to someone. If Mr Haszard comes to see you, let him read it. Also brothers and sisters. I shan't have time to write it all over again for them. I should like also for Mr Maine to have it. If he asks you anything about it, let him have it, for it will do me good to have the affair published. As it is I am quite a centre of interest here, and the last party wanted to see this formidable Thompson and asked me to point him out. Mr Alexander, the lawyer, was among them. Another gentleman of the party from Christchurch gave me an order for two pictures of the Terraces for £15.0.0. so you see how God can bring good out of evil. Dr. Campbell is also here from Auckland, staying at McRaes.

We had a long wet walk in on Saturday night, but are none the worse for it. Mary tripped along splendidly and yesterday she was as lively as ever, in fact too lively for Sunday. She and Adolphus, the boy, are inseparable. I think this will do her good, she has such an appetite.

I expect to go back this morning in the native boat if they will take the things. If not, we must walk back and carry enough *kiki* to last a week. Yesterday was wet and this morning is not very bright, but it may clear up. Hope springs eternal in the human breast. How are you getting on, dear? I hope you are well and the dear children. Give my love to Bess and Nell, and the largest share for yourself . . .

The food was rather monotonous last week. We had two loaves of bread, beef steak and suet. We had the steak in small portions boiled, fried and stewed, and when that was gone, melted some of the suet and had bread and dripping, and for a change boiled bread and sugar for breakfast. There is a little boiling hole close to the water in front of our tent, and there we cooked our food. When we get our oatmeal, I fancy it will be a splendid place to make porridge, as you can leave it as long as you like and no fear of it burning. We call this our gas stove, and it is just as handy and just as clean.

As we had no candles, we lit a nice fire in the evening just in front of the tent to see to read and go to bed by. So you see when we get our flour and wheatmeal and oatmeal and candles and cocoa and eggs, etc., we shall be well off. You need not be the least uneasy on our account. Just as if you would. Now goodbye dearest, and may God bless and shield you as He has been with us, and bless the dear little ones, Amen.

Your loving husband
Charlie.

P.S. Will you send me in the next letter some five or six of my cards. You will find them in one of the drawers in the dining room, and two sticks of charcoal from a green box in one of my drawers, also a piece of transferring paper, black one side and dark green the other, on my shelf near the hole in the chimney.

C.B.

Then a few days later:

I expect we shall go into Wairoa tomorrow when surely there will be letters. I am getting on very well but slowly. I have four finished pictures as well as a number of small sketches. I have not finished with the Pink Terrace yet, but shall do so perhaps by the middle of next week, then I shall move the tent and things over to the White Terrace and camp there. I expect I shall be longer over that side as there are so many fine views to be taken there. I have been sketching on the White Terrace twice. It is very awkward when the hot water is running over. I don't quite know how I shall manage. Some of the pictures I shall have to take standing in the hot water. Perhaps the South Wind may blow, and then it will be dry.

Now goodnight, I am getting sleepy. Mary is fast asleep long ago. She slept this morning till about half past eight. She is very well and jolly. Nearly all this morning she was paddling about the top of the terrace. God bless you. Good night. Kiss the dear littles ones for me xxxx Bessie from her delicious dada xxxxx. Nellie xxxxx.

Sunday morning. We came into Wairoa last night in the Maori boat and another disappointment awaited us. There were no letters. It is now nearly three weeks and no news of any sort from you or anyone in Auckland. It is really too bad, and I can't understand it. Surely someone must have written before this. I am afraid there has been some mistake in the address. You should always address them, Lake Tarawera. If not they will go all over the country before they come here and perhaps I may never get them. Tell the others, Fred and Will, to address all letters, Charles Blomfield, Artist, Lake Tarawera. This will be sure to come direct.

Mr and Mrs Haszard are expected home about the end of next week. I shall be glad to see Mr Haszard before I leave. Thompson the Thunder Cloud of Rotomahana, as Clare calls him, is very civil to us now and seems to treat me with great respect. He comes over sometimes with the tourists and comes into the tent and chats away and I think I shall have no more trouble with him.

The Maoris seem to think they can charge as long as people will pay. They are charging 2/6 now for people to come back in the canoe down the creek, and yet with all their charging and all the money they get, they are very poor. A little while ago before the potatoes were grown, they were living on fern root and sow thistle. The money goes as fast as it comes.

This morning the sky is cloudy and the air cold, and it looks like rain.

It is much colder here than at Rotomahana where the whole atmosphere is warmed by the large quantities of hot water and steam.

Have you got another letter from Tom yet? I should think it was nearly time there was one. I wonder when he will be back. How is the Tabernacle getting on? Have you seen it lately? How are you dear, and dear little Nellie and Bessie. God bless you all and goodbye. From your loving husband,

Charles Blomfield.

January 13th.

Dear Ellen,

We have almost given up expecting letters from anybody or indeed any news from the outside world. There is one good thing about it, I cannot bother myself about the way things are going at home, as I don't know anything about it, but I should like so to have a letter from you.

Mr Fairbrother said on Sunday he was going to Ohinemutu on Monday and he would see if there were any there, and also send a telegram to you to tell you the right address, as I feel sure you must have written long ere this. I hope and trust you and the dear children are quite well.

This morning was fine but about ten o'clock it came on raining, and has rained more or less ever since. We thought of going over to the White Terrace and pitching the tent there today and this morning before breakfast I went and chose a place and spent a lot of time clearing the fern away and getting the place ready, but when the visitors came, Sophia told us there were three men. Photographers came to stop ten days and they appear to have jumped our claim, and I believe pitched their tent in the very place I cleared for ours. It has been too wet to go and see since, but I shall go in the morning if fine. If they have pitched there I shall stay here a day or two longer as this is much the best place to live, but I have nearly finished the Pink Terrace. My last picture is taken near the top showing the bath and top steps. It is a very good one. This makes five finished ones.

Sophia says that Mrs. Snow's things are all up, so I expect she will be here soon now. The Maoris are all expecting her up here. They think she has stayed too long in Auckland. Clara says she rather dreads her coming, as the Maoris will hold a great tangi over Mr Snow when she comes home. I have got her oars, but Mrs Way's boat. I don't know how I shall manage if she wants the oars, as we use the boat a great deal going about, and also for fetching water to drink. I took Mrs Way's boat in mistake for Snow's, and when I told Mrs Way she said she was glad I had it, as the Maoris were always taking it away for something or other, and now she knows where it is. She is all by herself. Her husband has not been home for a long time except two days at Christmas, and she is expecting her confinement very soon, and is living still in that old ruin, the Manse. Fairbrother has had a nice whare built in

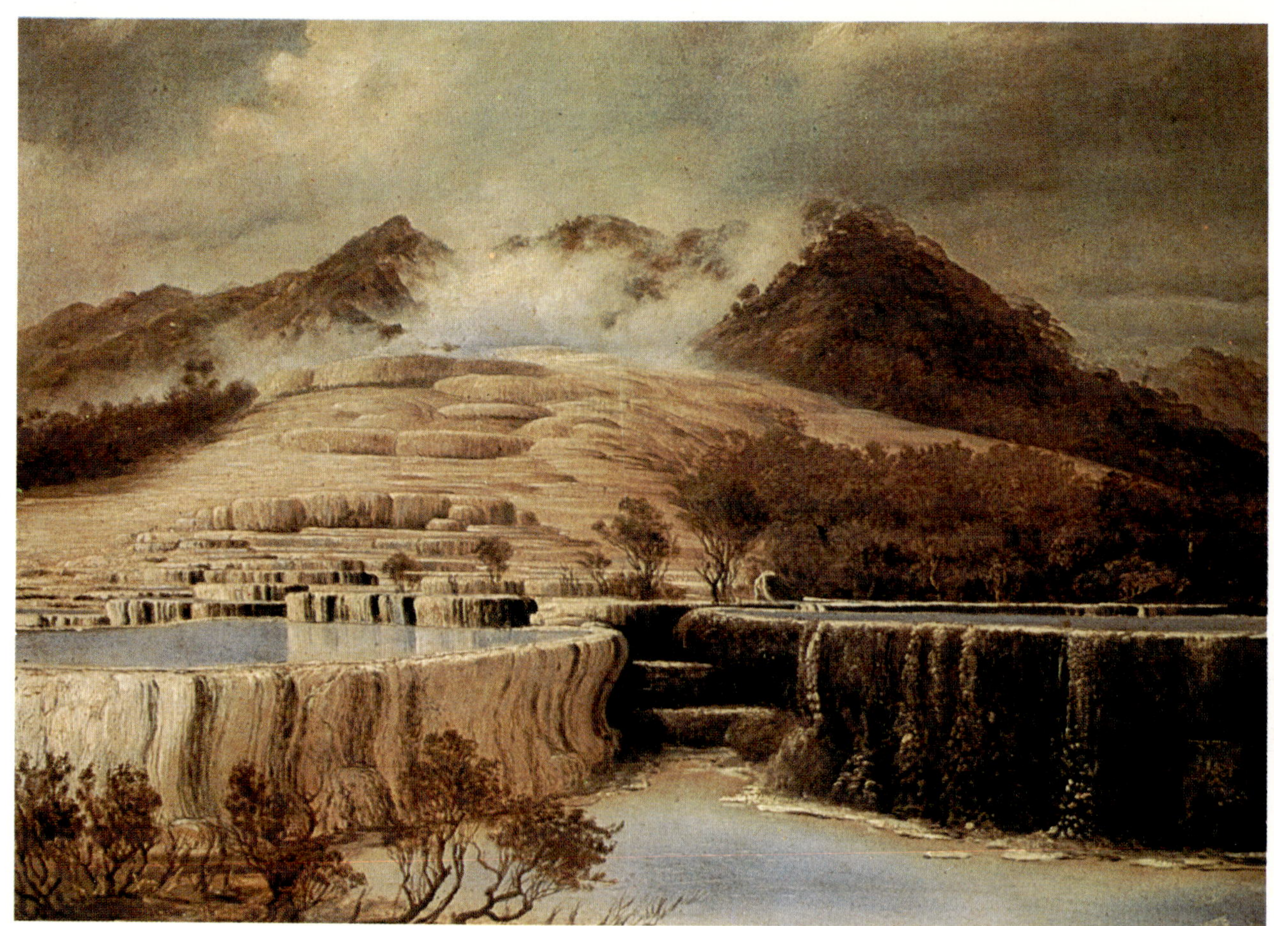

part of her ground, and professes to look after things, but I don't think
he does much of that, and is more often away than there, and I think
he has most of his meals either at Way's or Haszard's, and he is often
at Ohinemutu. He said he was coming to stay a day or two with us,
but he has not done so, and I don't think he will somehow.

8 o'clock. The rain held off for a little about half past six, and we
went in the boat to the White Terrace and saw the new arrivals and
found that they had not got our place, but just close to it, in among
some teatree. One of them is Mr Chapman, of Auckland, bookseller,
and another, Ballantyne, a photographer. Thompson the Dreadful is
with them taking care of them, and so he will be happy. He looked half
frightened when he saw me. Over there they are disappointed about
the weather. They have waited for fine weather, and thought it was
quite settled, and now it seems very unpromising. Mr Ballantyne said
another wet day would be enough for him, and he would clear out. I
asked them if they had any news from Auckland, but they said they had
no papers.

They said they had heard all about me in Auckland and the trouble
I had had with the Maoris. I hope you have saved the account in the

*White Terrace, 1896. Oil
on canvas, 25 × 19 in.*

72

papers of it. I shall be glad to read what their version of it is. These people had a lot of trouble last night with the natives of Wairoa before they got their consent to come.

If it is fine tomorrow I shall shift the tent over, and so shall have company, not that I care for that, as Mary and I are happy enough by ourselves. Coming back in the boat we got caught in a heavy shower, and I got very wet rowing.

I must now turn in. God bless my darlings and good night dear Ellen. Much love and many xxxxx from your affectionate husband,

Charles Blomfield.

On his return to Auckland, Charles held an exhibition of his paintings, and this was reported in the *Herald*:

Mr Charles Blomfield, the well-known painter of New Zealand scenery, has just completed a fine series of oil paintings of the Pink and White Terraces, Rotomahana, and of the most picturesque views in their neighbourhood. Mr Blomfield spent three weeks on each of the Terraces, and painted direct from Nature, with the result that he has produced perhaps the most faithful representations of this locality, together with the varied tints of blue, pink, and yellow, which are so peculiar to these now famous Rotomahana springs. One of the peculiarities of the White Terrace is the intermittent rise and fall of the waters, certain atmospheric changes bringing about an overflow of the terrace. Out of the upper basin a geyser is thrown up twenty or thirty feet occasionally; then again the water recedes into the bowels of the earth, and the upper basin, which is said to be fifty feet deep, becomes perfectly dry, when the vapour only, rising from the hidden waters, is visible to the eye. On such occasions the tourist may walk with safety along the ledges of the various blue pools, and examine for himself the beautiful fretwork-like patterns of the silica formations. One of Mr Blomfield's paintings represents the Terrace when the great cauldron is empty — a sight which many tourists have no opportunity of seeing. There is a constant overflow on the Pink Terrace, and a series of cascades on the various terraces. The upper basin always wears a glassy surface, a large quantity of vapour rising up from the heated water. This pool is remarkable for its great depth and the clearness of its waters. The tourists invariably bathe in the pools of the Pink Terrace, because the formation is more even, and the bottom of the pools is soft and sandy-like. Mr Blomfield has painted twelve pictures in all, and they are worthy of inspection. They are at present on view at his private residence, Wood Street, Ponsonby. We may add that Mr Blomfield is now engaged executing orders for several distinguished tourists.

A few years later, Charles told his own story:

I have often been asked to tell the story of how I obtained my paintings
of the Terraces. It was Mr Thomas Spurgeon who first suggested it.
We were visiting Rotomahana together. He was enraptured with the
wonderful beauty and what he called the "heavenly colour" of the water
in the pools. "Charlie," he said, "you should come here and paint some
real good pictures of these exquisite scenes; you would do very well
with them."

At that time the natives were very chary about allowing anyone to
sketch or take photos at Rotomahana. They demanded £5.0.0 for the
merest drawing or negative, so that no important paintings had been
attempted by any artist. Any sketch had to be taken surreptitiously,
and if the culprit was caught he had either to pay their exorbitant price,
or the sketches would be taken away from him and destroyed. As I was
determined to spend some weeks there, and do the thing properly, it
was necessary to make arrangements with the natives beforehand.
Fortunately, I had a friend at Court in the person of the Maori school-
teacher at Wairoa, Mr Haszard, who lost his life soon after in the
Tarawera eruption. He was in treaty with the different chiefs interested
for some weeks, and at last a big meeting was called to decide the
question. Finally after much talk, an agreement was come to. Upon the
payment down of a lump sum, I was to be allowed to come and camp
on the lake, to bring my own boat, to stay as long as I pleased, and not
be interfered with by anybody.

But my troubles were by no means over, for when I arrived, Thompson, chief of Te Ariki, took charge of me and insisted that I give him
£5.0.0. and ten shillings a day to look after me. As chief of Rotomahana,
he claimed that my payments to the Wairoa people had nothing to do
with him. I was threatened with being thrown into the lake, and as I
obstinately refused to be further bled, things were very unpleasant
until the arrival on Christmas Day of Clara Haszard, Mr Haszard's
eldest daughter, who had ridden over with a party of friends. When I
told her how I had been treated, she was very indignant! She could talk
Maori like a native and gave him an awful ragging, and threatened to
bring Kepa over to him; he would teach him his place. Kepa was the
head chief of the district at that time. His monument may be seen at
Whakarewarewa, just below that singular mound at the top of which
his body lies.

After this Thompson packed up his traps and left us in peace. I had
no more trouble with him. We became good friends. He would often
ask me about the visitors: "You know this man; you think he plenty of
money?" He would often bring his little daughter to play with my
Mary. They did not understand each other, but they were great chums.

The tourists came every weekday, from ten to thirty of them, mostly
moneyed people, from all parts of the world. They would arrive at the
White Terrace about eleven a.m., view the sights there, the mud flat,

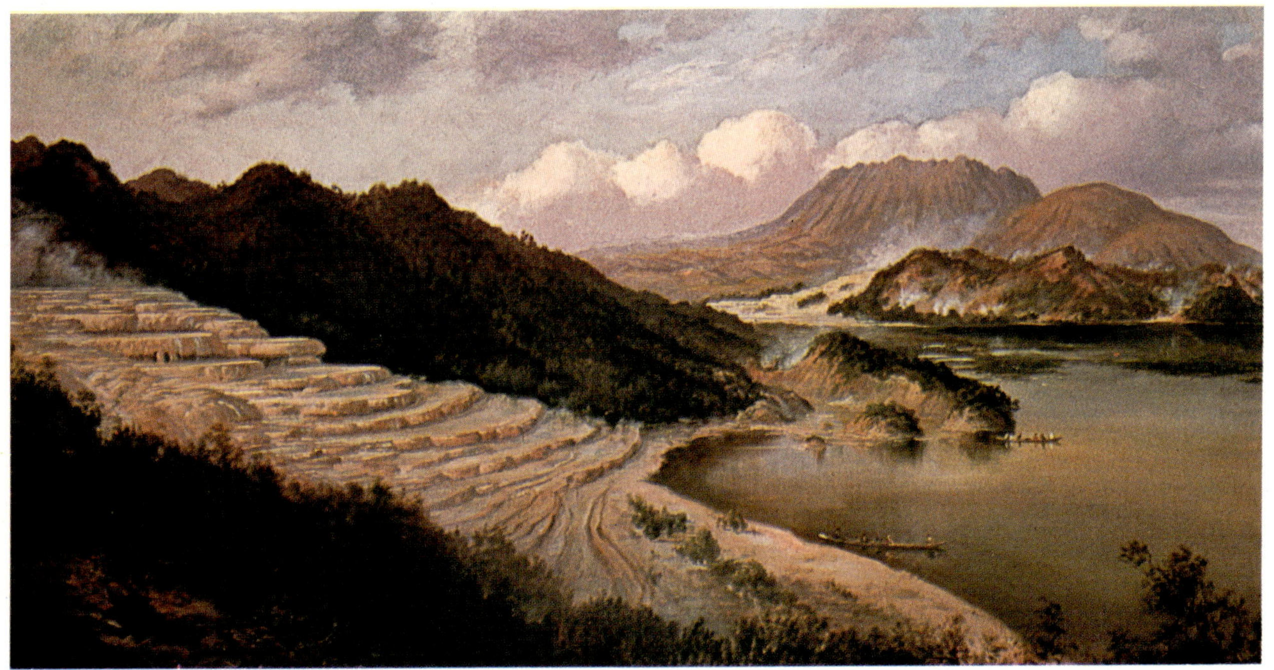

etc., and have lunch at a little boiling spring where they ate potatoes and koura cooked in the boiling water, cross over to the Pink Terrace, bathe there and then go straight back. From the time they left until another party came next day, we had the lake to ourselves. It might have belonged to us. My little girl, far from being lonely, amused herself splendidly, bathing in the hot basins, making mud pies, plastering up the baby mud volcanoes with clay to hear them go off with a pop, hunting for petrified ferns and birds' feathers in the hot water. She got so used to the strange, weird sights that she skipped about fearlessly among the geysers, greatly to the horror of the visitors, who hardly dared venture out of the guide's footsteps. We sometimes lit a fire for our cooking and sometimes cooked in the boiling springs. Our plum puddings we tied to the end of a long string and threw them in the great boiling cauldron at the top of the White Terrace.

I often felt vexed at the careless way the visitors were shown over the sights by the guides. Some of the best things were missed. Camping there for six weeks, and having the place so much to ourselves, we explored every corner of the lake, finding many strange and lovely sights out of the beaten path.

In one spot there was a hollow where the stream was gently rising, keeping up an even temperature. It was filled with a luxuriant growth of tropical ferns and mosses. In another place we found a hot stream flowing into the lake between two high cliffs. Forcing our boat up this, we came to the queerest place imaginable. The ground was hissing and simmering like hot fat in a frying pan. Just beyond, a very hot lake of intense green colour with steam jets all round. On a cool night the whole of the lake was steaming, the great geysers sending up immense

columns far into the sky. Often on a moonlight night I would take the
boat, and leaving my little Mary fast asleep in the tent, pull slowly
around the lake. It was a most uncanny experience, the mysterious
shroud of vapour, the absolute solitude, the strange weird sounds on
every hand, hissing, gurgling, muttering, moaning, sighing, seemed like
some unknown world, while every few yards a wild duck would rise from
the water with a startled cry, and vanish in the gloom.

When we moved our tent from the Pink Terrace, we pitched it in the
fern in full view of the White Terrace — in fact one of my best pictures
was painted from the tent door on a wet day.

I awoke one night with a strange sensation as of something unusual
happening. Then I became conscious of a singular stillness, the usual
sounds of activity had ceased. I had become so accustomed to the
constant seething and boiling that the sudden quiet had wakened me.
When daylight came, the cause was apparent. The great geyser at the
top of the White Terrace had ceased playing, and in a few hours the
immense cauldron at the top was empty. It was a wonderful sight, a
sight seen by very few. I hurried up with my canvas and brushes and

White Terrace geyser, 1904.
Oil on canvas, 29 × 19 in.

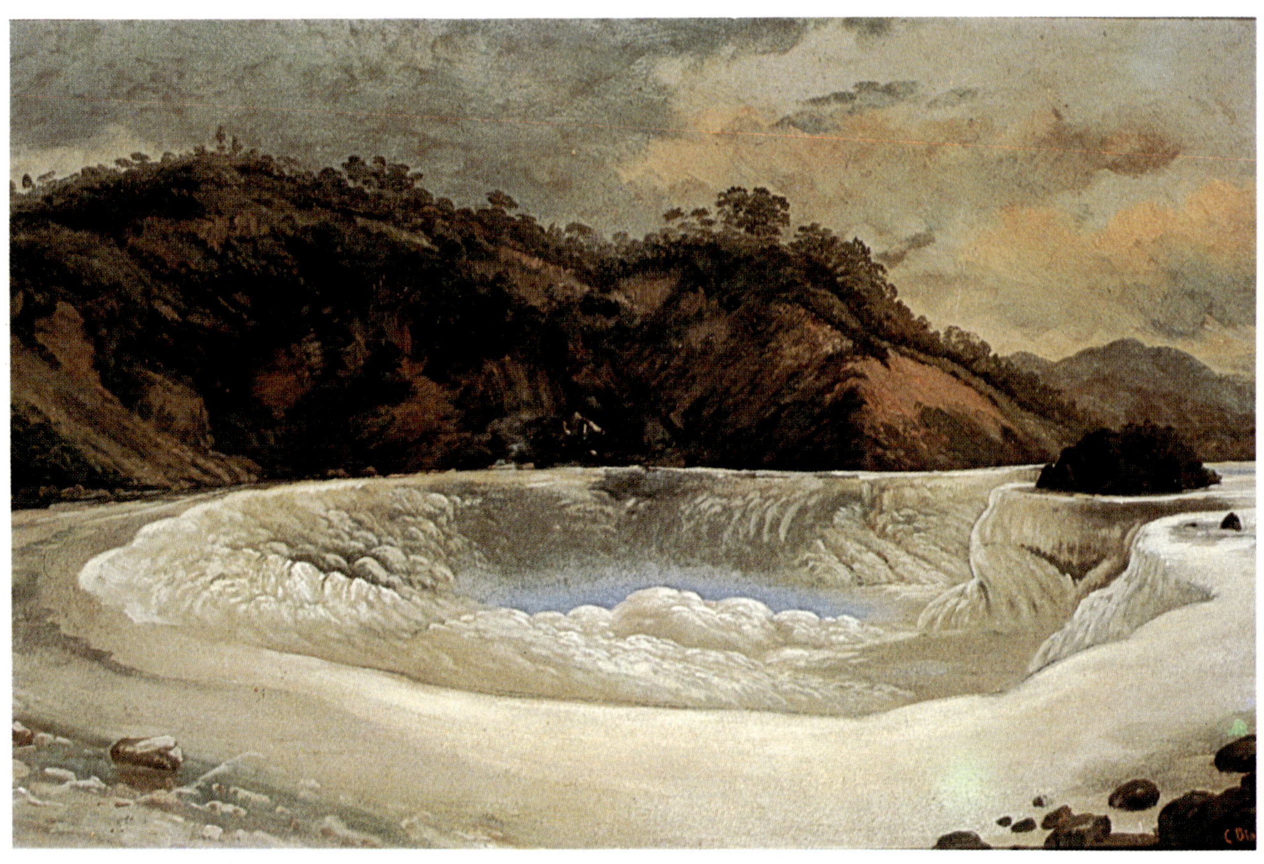

began a picture of it, getting it only half finished when the boiling fountain began to work again, slowly filling the basins, and it was a fortnight before it emptied again and gave me a chance to finish my picture.

In the centre of the lake were two little islands, the larger of the two a very hot spot, steam rising in many places. It was here the Maoris brought the victims of rheumatism as a last resource, and laid them on the hot ground. Thompson's grandfather, Rangihua, an old tattooed warrior of a hundred summers, was lying here when the great eruption occurred. Poor fellow, he must have had a fiery transition. He would come sometimes and sit by my side and watch me paint. As for Thompson and his little daughter, they were buried with all their people eighty feet deep by the rocks and mud of the volcanoes.

Rotomahana was unique. There was never anything like it before and never will be again. It was beginning to be known as one of the sights of the world. The number of tourists visiting it doubled every few months. Soon the Government would have taken control and then all kinds of incongruous "improvements" would have been introduced. The Maoris may have control of a beauty spot for years without altering its natural aspects, but as soon as the European steps in, it soon loses its native purity. They form shell paths and build trim shelters at Whakarewarewa, turn the slopes of Ruapehu into a Scotch Highlands, and make a hideous wilderness of many a fine stretch of bush. One dreads to think of what Rotomahana would have looked like with shelters, tea kiosks, signboards, steam launches and perhaps a big hotel just where I pitched my tent.

It was a very pleasant life. Time passed all too soon. But at length the day came when our stock of provisions ran low and we had to pack up and come away. I was loath to leave the lovely spot. It was like parting with an old friend, and when the boat was gliding down the hot stream towards the Tarawera Lake, I had a feeling I should never see it again. Was it a presentiment, I wonder, of the coming doom?

And later still, Mary adds her version:

Some time during the summer of 1883, Mr Charles Blomfield with his wife and a friend paid a visit to the Terraces. At that time the only way to get there was by boat to Tauranga, by coach to Ohinemutu to put up at Lake House, then on by coach next day to Te Wairoa. From there by pulling boats across Tarawera Lake to a beach beside the stream from Rotomahana, thence to walk a track which followed the stream, to the foot of the White Terrace.

The guides conducted the visitors first over that Terrace, and then after lunch, across the lake in a canoe to visit the Pink Terrace.

This visit so inspired Mr. Blomfield with the unique beauty of the Terraces and with the desire to paint them, that after his return to Auckland he decided that during the following summer he would go again; this time fully equipped with all necessary gear to make a long stay. Knowing Mr Chas. Haszard, the school master at Te Wairoa who was also a Justice of the Peace, he requested him to make all arrangements with the natives, getting permission to camp at the terraces from them.

After some time and the payment of £5.0.0., things were finalised and a few days before Christmas 1884, he left Auckland taking with him his eldest daughter, a child of eight years; boxes containing canvases and all the painting and camping gear and food for a stay of six weeks.

We reached Mr Haszard's home after a trip in the rain from Rotorua and were made welcome. Next day the stuff was packed into a small boat which had been hired for our use, and in that we journeyed across Lake Tarawera. A Maori man, wading breast high in the swift narrow stream, pushed the boat up from one lake to another while we walked.

On reaching Rotomahana my father took charge, and we crossed the lake to the Pink Terrace, where against the teatree our first camp was made. Fresh water had to be obtained from a spring some distance away. The lake was a dirty colour and shallow and warm, with the water from many hot springs running into it.

Our first morning there was Christmas Day and showery. However, father was so eager to start that he soon had his easel set up on a small islet from which a good view of the terrace could be obtained. He made full pictures of every view that he decided upon, painting from one site in the morning and from another in the afternoon. We stayed three weeks at that place, and then shifted camp to the foot of the White Terrace.

Twice a week parties of tourists visited the Terraces, and they were always interested to find us there, often expressing amazement at seeing a little girl, unafraid of all the weird things which abounded. The Pink Terrace was very steep and only one way on the left hand side gave access to the top. The pools were all near the top on the Pink Terrace, and some of them made beautiful bathing places. The boiling spring at the top was wonderful, clear and deep and having beautiful colours in its basin, but the water in the pool was a lovely blue. The surface of the terrace was smooth, unlike the White Terrace, which was rough, like the terrace formations we can see at the present day. From the hill at the back of the Terrace, led a track for eight miles to Wairoa, and the first Saturday we walked that, missing our way towards evening, and not reaching Mr Haszard's house till after dark. After spending Sunday with them, we returned on Monday by the boat, and each weekend we spent in this way. Having our boat, we were able to explore the sides of the lake, and found some queer places.

Near the White Terrace, there was much more thermal activity and many interesting spots within easy walking distance of the foot of the terrace. The Terrace itself was very much larger than the pink one, with many very large and deep pools near the base. Other pools and high buttresses were scattered about the steep slopes. The spring at the top was quite different from that on the Pink Terrace and the blue water filled a very large round basin.

When the East wind blew, the water sank away, leaving the basin empty and a huge pipe from the centre made the resemblance to a wash-hand basin very marked. It was here one day we witnessed a most wonderful geyser. The basin was empty. As the afternoon waned, the water began to rise. All at once geyser activity began in the centre. A dome of water formed which rapidly rose till in a short time there was a column of boiling water which was like a ship's mast, only having the movement of the force which was raising it constantly, lifting it higher and higher. We stood spellbound, yet afraid of what was going to happen. Then suddenly the whole column fell like a tree, keeping its form till it crashed across the basin and the flat rim beyond it. It was an unforgettable sight. By night the basin was again full and overflowing as usual.

It would take too long to describe other sights and experiences we had. At the end of six weeks we returned home, father with a valuable collection of pictures. These he kept and used as models for all his Terrace pictures. He was very particular about reproductions, taking tracings of the original pictures and enlarging or reducing by scale.

It was exactly eighteen months after this memorable visit that the eruption occurred, and Rotomahana blew out also, and the Terraces were lost for ever. At that time the English and Colonial Exhibition was being held in London, and Mr. Blomfield had sent several copies of his Terrace pictures there. These were remarked upon when news of the eruption was published in England, and people who had visited New Zealand and seen the Terraces were especially interested, and all the pictures were sold.

For years copies of Terrace pictures were sent abroad as well as being sold in New Zealand, and helped to make Mr Blomfield's name known as an artist of no mean ability. He was skilled in all branches of landscape painting, but in the painting of the Terraces he was unique.

3

Eruption

1886

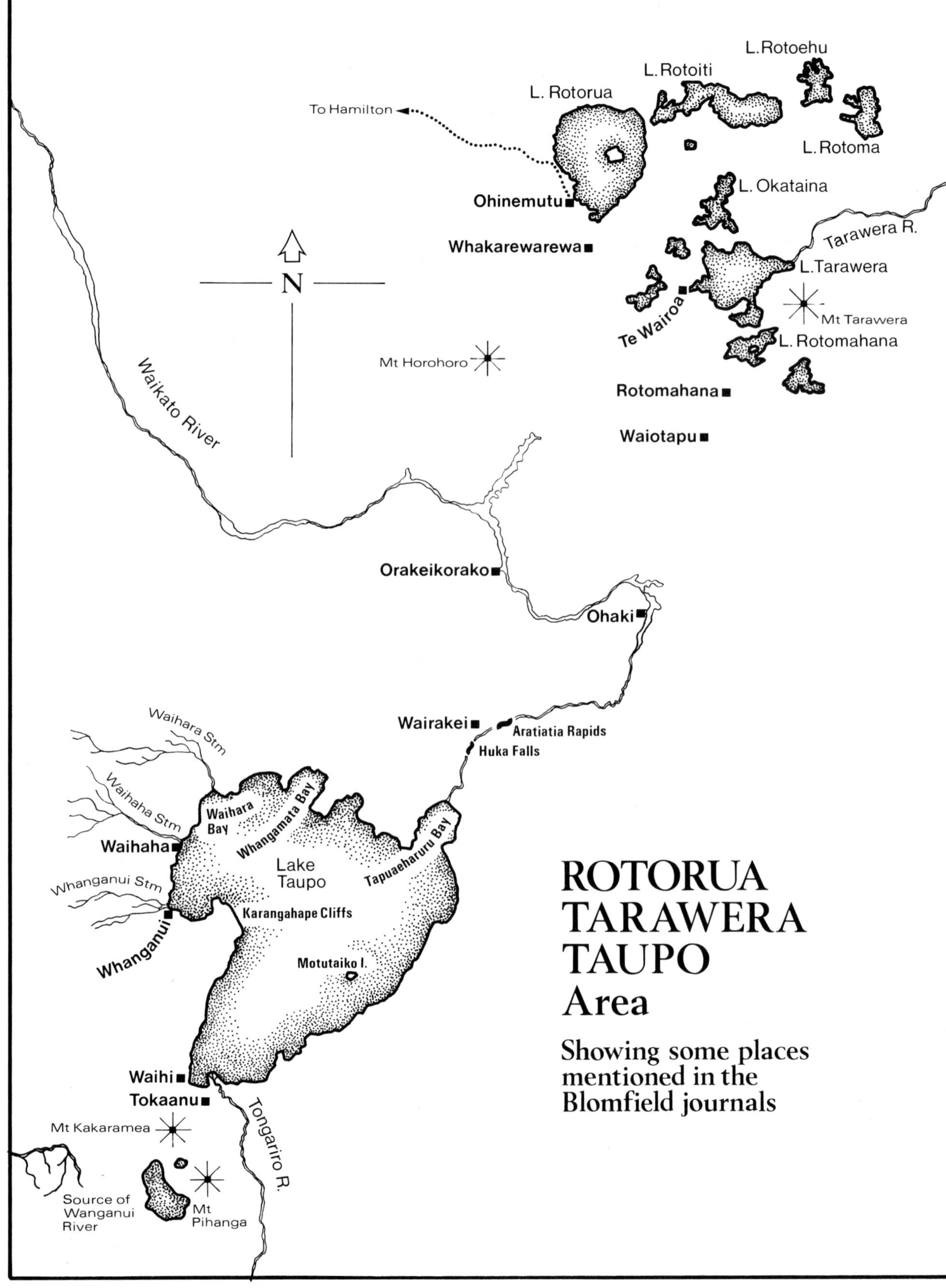

To Hamilton
L. Rotorua
L. Rotoiti
L. Rotoehu
L. Rotoma
Ohinemutu
Whakarewarewa
L. Okataina
Tarawera R.
L. Tarawera
Te Wairoa
Mt Tarawera
L. Rotomahana
Rotomahana
Waiotapu
N
Mt Horohoro
Waikato River
Orakeikorako
Ohaki
Waihara Stm
Waihaha Stm
Whanganui Stm
Waihara Bay
Whangamata Bay
Waihaha
Lake Taupo
Tapuaeharuru Bay
Karangahape Cliffs
Whanganui
Motutaiko I.
Wairakei
Aratiatia Rapids
Huka Falls
Waihi
Tokaanu
Mt Kakaramea
Tongariro R.
Source of Wanganui River
Mt Pihanga

ROTORUA
TARAWERA
TAUPO
Area

Showing some places
mentioned in the
Blomfield journals

9. Volcano

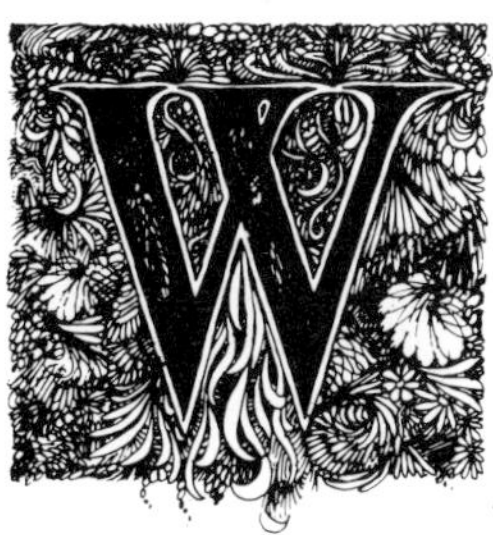

WAKE UP, GIRLS! Mary, Nellie, Bessie, Wake up!" Charles gently shook his daughters. "You've got a little baby brother!"

Bessie rubbed her eyes and sat up sleepily in the stretcher bed by the door. It was half past two in the morning and hard to wake up. But Mary and Nellie jumped out of the big bed and clapped their hands with joy: "A brother! Oh! How lovely!"

But before they could go in to see their mother and the baby they heard a terrible noise: *Boom!! Boom!! Boom!! Bang! Bang!*

"What was that?" they all cried, as they ran out on to the top verandah. Bessie clasped her father's hand, and felt it tremble, as he whispered: "They've come. It's the Russians!" But although they all gazed towards the darkness of the harbour and Rangitoto, there was nothing to see. No ships and no cannon fire; but the noise continued.

After a few minutes they returned inside and remembered about the new baby, and tiptoed into their mother's bedroom, where Grandma was holding the infant in her arms. Bessie took one look, but the baby started to cry, so she crept slowly back to her own room and climbed into bed. She had never been more disappointed in her life. For a whole year she had prayed for a baby brother, and all she got was a wrinkled-up little thing with a yellow face that puckered and cried when she wanted to play with it.

Mary and Nellie soon followed Bessie back to bed, and Charles tucked them all up again and kissed them goodnight. After seeing that his wife, new son, and mother were all right, he soberly left the house and walked down the hill to the *Herald* office to try and find out what had happened. He met several other people who were standing around in the street waiting for news, and there were all sorts of different reports and explanations as to what was causing the noise:

From the continuousness of the firing, the loudness of the reports, and the apparent occasional sound resembling salvoes of artillery, many people both in Auckland and Onehunga were under the impression that a man-of-war, probably the Russian *Vestnik*, had run ashore on the Manukau bar, and that these were her signals of distress. Vivid flashes, as from the firing of guns, were also witnessed both at Onehunga and also from the cupola of the *Herald* office, which served to almost confirm the impression that there had been a marine disaster.

It would appear that Mr. J. McIntyre, of Onehunga, was the first to arrive at the correct solution of the morning's disturbance. At about seven a.m. he informed one of the *Herald* reporters that at about half-past two a.m. he was awakened by the noise as of guns firing, and getting out of bed, he dressed and went on to the verandah of his house, and then was able to hear the sounds more distinctly. After listening awhile, he arrived at the conclusion that the noise did not proceed from guns, but was from some fearful volcanic eruption, and he could distinctly see the reflection of the flashes of fire and lightning, and they appeared to him as if someone was waving a lighted torch to and fro. He believed that when the news would come in, it would be found that an eruption had occurred somewhere in the direction of Opotiki. How true Mr. McIntyre's predictions were are now only too well-known. Everyone spoken to at Onehunga about the matter firmly believed that the noise was of the guns of some vessel in distress, the idea of a thunderstorm or volcanic disturbance being ridiculed.

At about eight-thirty a.m., however, it began to be circulated about town that a catastrophe, far surpassing in horror even the most terrible of shipwrecks, had taken place; that a great volcanic upheaval had occurred in the Lake district, the whole country between Tauranga and Taupo being involved in the danger, and that a loss of life, all the more terrible in that its extent was unknown, had occurred, and that all the surviving inhabitants were fleeing for Tauranga. There was at once a rush for the *Herald* publishing office, and throughout the day the office and the street in its vicinity was crowded with people anxiously awaiting the receipt of the successive telegrams which arrived from the seat of the disaster. Never even during the sharpest crises of the war was a deeper interest manifested. Tens of thousands of copies of extras, issued on receipt of each fresh telegram from Rotorua, were eagerly contested for by an excited crowd of numbers of individuals.

Charles discussed the noise with several of his friends, all waiting eagerly for any news of what had actually occurred, and then at eight-thirty a.m. the notice went up outside the *Herald* office, that it had in fact been an eruption in the Lake District. Poor Charles! This was even worse than his wildest fears. Tarawera had erupted. What could have happened to the Haszard family, with whom he had often stayed, living at Te Wairoa, right under the mountain? And what about the Pink and White Terraces?

Then he remembered his own family, and his new-born son. He walked quickly to the *Evening Star* office and inserted a birth notice in the evening edition. Then he trudged up the hill to his home at 40 Wood Street, and told the family the news.

Before long, he returned to Queen Street, to obtain the latest information as soon as it came to hand. Every bulletin seemed to be worse than the last. In fact, for the next two weeks, he was so unhappy that it seemed no one could comfort him.

Ellen was terribly upset. First Bessie had not liked her baby brother, and now her dear Charles was so despondent about the eruption that he scarcely had any time either for her or her new-born son.

However, help was at hand. Her beloved pastor, Tom Spurgeon, came to visit her.

"What a lovely boy you have there, Mrs Blomfield," he said. "Charlie must be very proud of you both."

"Charles is so concerned about the Tarawera eruption that he has scarcely taken any notice at all of the boy," she replied, and she confided to him all her disappointments.

"I'll speak to him," he said, and asked how the girls were getting on at school.

When he had gone, Ellen felt much better. "Dear Mr Spurgeon," she thought, "I shall call the baby 'Thomas' after him." He had been a true friend to Charles and herself ever since he had arrived from England.

"Charlie," Tom said, next time he saw Charles. "You must be a very proud man, with such a good wife and a fine son, too. To say nothing of your three sweet little girls."

Charles smiled, but answered: "But Tom, do you realise the Pink and White Terraces have been destroyed?"

"You know," said Tom, "I think you have been ordained by God to leave a lasting memorial of the Eighth Wonder of the World. What a good thing you listened to me when I suggested that you go down there and stay for a while! You will be able to paint lots of copies of those sketches you have already done, and if you sell them to the tourists, they will go back all over the world."

Charles felt that a great burden had lifted from him. He ran up to Ellen's room, and said as he kissed her, "You know, I've thought of a good name for the boy. Let's call him 'Thomas' after Spurgeon. He has been such a good friend to us."

He walked out on to the top verandah and into his Cubby House — a small room which he had built on to the end of the verandah. It was here that he painted, or spent his time stuffing the birds he had found in the bush, and even slept when he wanted to retire early and make an early start for a sunrise painting. "Have I really been ordained?" he wondered. The despair he felt about the lost terraces was relieved by the knowledge that he, Charles Blomfield, could show posterity by way of his paintings the glory he had seen.

Births

BLOMFIELD.—On June 10. at her residence, Wood-street, Auckland, the wife of Mr Chas. Blomfield of a son ; both doing well.

Marriages

FOGARTY - McCORMICK.—On June 2 at the Roman Catholic Church. Parnell. by the Rev. Monsignore Fynes. V.G., Patrick Joseph, eldest son of the late Martin Fogarty, Gort, County Galway, Ireland, to Elizabeth, eldest daughter of John McCormick, Wairoa South. Both of Auckland.

PRIME—ADAMS —At the residence of the bride's father, by the Rev. J. Robertson, B.A., William Arthur, third son of J. W. Prime, to Jessie eldest daughter of W. Adams, Esq., Grey-street, Auckland.

The Evening Star :

WITH WHICH ARE INCORPORATED

The Evening News, Morning News, and Echo.

For the cause that lacks assistance,
For the wrong that needs resistance,
For the future in the distance,
And the good that we can do.

THURSDAY. JUNE 10, 1886.

THURSDAY, the 10th of June, 1886, will be memorable in the annals of New Zealand as the date of the most disastrous outbreak of volcanic forces that has occurred on these shores within the historic period. The telegrams which we publish to-day from Rotorua and Tauranga, while describing a scene of terrific grandeur unparalleled in the history of New Zealand, will recall to the minds of readers the graphic accounts of the destruction of Pompeii and Herculaneum, as well as the records of minor calamities of that kind. Though happily unparalleled in New Zealand in the memory of man, the eruption of this morning, extending as it did over a wide extent of country and spreading ruin and desolation in its path is but a faint reflex of the scenes of horror which must have been enacted in that pre-historic period, when the scores of extinct volcanoes in Auckland district were in a state of activity, and belching forth fiery lava, flames and smoke in all directions. At that time the land would be uninhabitable, and probably there was no one to witness the terribly beautiful display of pyrotechnics ; consequently no human beings would be involved in suffering or death. Such is not the case now, and the tale (just partly told) of the hardships endured and fiery deaths suffered by the unfortunate inhabitants of the Rotorua district, is sad and harrowing in the extreme. Already steps are being taken to relieve the survivors of the calamity, and when detailed accounts are forwarded by our special reporters despatched to different points, public sympathy will assume a more definite and decided shape. Thanks to the activity of our correspondents and the energy and courtesy of the officials of the telegraph department we are enabled to-day to give full particulars regarding the sudden and alarming eruption of this morning, which has laid many miles of country waste, and caused a human sacrifice which must be of vast extent, though possibly the full loss of life will never be ascertained.

10. Desolation

The news that Charles had been fearing finally reached Auckland. His friend Mr Haszard, and three of his five children, had been killed. Charles was heartbroken. But it was with deep relief and delight that he read how Mrs Haszard and her two remaining daughters, Clara and Ina, had been saved. Clara's account ran as follows:

We were all in bed at eleven o'clock. At a quarter past one I was awakened by a rumbling noise, and father asked me if I felt the earthquake. I said "Yes" and it kept on a long time. Mr Blythe, the surveyor, was awakened, and father said, "It is the most wonderful sight I have seen," and we went on the verandah to see it. There was a large inky black cloud hovering over the truncated cone of Tarawera, with lightning and balls of fire shooting out of it. Mr Blythe said it was a cloud charged with electricity. We all dressed and went into the sitting room, thinking it was the safest part of the building, as it was constructed of corrugated iron. We lit a fire in the stove, and mother sat down in the middle of the room, with all her children around her.

Looking out of the window, it was like a great sheet of fire. Father and Lundius and Blythe were looking out of the window. I sat down at the organ and played and sang hymns. At three o'clock we heard a rattling as of stones falling on the top of the house. The noise was so great that we could not hear each other speak. We afterwards found it to be caused by falling lava. When that came on, father went out into the middle of the room, leaning on mother's chair. Mr Lundius picked up a piece of the lava, when we all came to the conclusion that Tarawera had broken out into a state of eruption. The volcanic shower continued to pour on the house for about an hour. A tremendous gale of wind arose, and then came down the chimney with such force that we were nearly suffocated with the smoke, and had to cover the stove with a mat, and pour all the water we could get on it. This not being sufficient to put out the fire, my father took the pipe off the stove.

At about four o'clock we were all, excepting Messrs Blythe and Lundius, assembled in the middle of the room, believing it to be the safest place, as the walls were bulging and threatening to come in. I walked over to the door, seeing it bulging, to lean against it. Messrs Blythe and Lundius were standing at the same place, when suddenly there came a tremendous crash, and all was dark, the roof falling on top of us. I put out my hands, and grasped on one side Mr Blythe's hand, and on the other Mr Lundius's, instinctively, for protection.

Meanwhile quantities of lava fell on our heads. Mr Lundius jumped up and smashed the windows, cutting his hand very much. Finding he could not do it so well with his hand, he used his foot and got out. He then said: "I'm out. Come out, Miss Haszard," and he pulled me out. Mr Blythe followed, but on getting into the open air we were struck about the head and body by lumps of lava. We shut the door, but finding the roof bulging down, and being unable to get into some of the other rooms, we opened the door and stood in the doorway, so as to be ready to escape. I was perishing with cold, and Mr Blythe got some blankets to protect me from the cold. Just then the house appeared to be struck with lightning and burning lava, and it took fire.

We all rushed out into the garden. When the portion of the building in which we were took fire and burst into flames, we endeavoured to find some other shelter, and got into the paddocks, stumbling over some uprooted trees in the darkness.

Seeing by the light of the burning apartment that the henhouse was standing, we went there for shelter, and remained there until daylight watching the principal buildings burning. The corrugated iron building remained untouched, owing to the quantity of volcanic mud around and above it. We waited there in great anxiety, being under the apprehension that all the house was on fire.

When daylight arrived, Mr McRae and the two Birds, his brothers-in-law, came up from the hotel to see how we had fared, and we all went down to the corrugated portion of the dwelling house to see about the rest, and found a Maori woman, Mary of the Mu, with my sister Ina. It appears that when the building fell in, Mary snatched my sister into the bedroom, and they had crawled under the washstand; after a while, finding no more mud fell on them, they endeavoured to push away the stuff which was covering them. In this they succeeded, and raised themselves upright, waiting their fate, and continued there, in the dark, till half-past six in the morning.

At daylight we were re-united through Mr Lundius breaking the window, and getting the native woman and my sister out. The whole party, including Mr McRae's people, listened for any sound to show that any of the rest of the family were alive in the collapsed corrugated building, but hearing none, and seeing at least eight and a half feet of mud on the debris of the fallen roof, we all went down toward Ohine-mutu, everybody leaving the settlement.

When we got inside of Tikitapu bush, we met Mr Robertson's coach, which brought us to Mrs Brent's boarding house at Rotorua. Mr Blythe and Mr Lundius went back to Wairoa.

Mr Blythe continued the story:

After seeing Miss Haszard and her sister consigned in safety to Mr Robertson's care, Mr Lundius and myself returned to Wairoa. Mr McRae and Mr Humphries returned with us.

When we got back to the native village Mr McRae got some spades out of his store, and we started to dig among the ruins of Mr Haszard's house for the inmates. Constable Maroney and Mr Merritt joined, and after digging through three and a half feet of mud, Mr Humphries, who before had said he had heard some sound, saw a hand, and the fingers moved. It proved to be Mrs Haszard, who called out to us. After considerable labour, owing to the fallen timber, he managed to extricate her, and removed her to the whare of Sophia, the native female guide.

We continued digging until about three o'clock from that time, when Messrs Johnston and Robertson came from Rotorua and saw what we were doing, and advised us to give up, as there were no hopes of saving any more alive, as the debris appeared to be level all over the floor. As to ourselves, we were quite knocked up, the excitement alone sustaining us. We left for Ohinemutu, taking Mrs Haszard with us, everybody kindly rendering help.

Mr Haszard's brother, Mr A. J. Haszard, went with a rescue party to Rotorua, and met Mrs Haszard at Brent's boarding house where she was receiving medical attention. When she was well enough to talk, she told him her story:

My two daughters, Clara and Ina, escaped into a detached portion of the house. While sitting in my chair, with my three remaining children around me, I was pinned to the floor by the leg through the roof falling in, and I believe that it was at that time my husband was killed. I had my youngest child, Mona, a girl aged four, in my arms, a boy aged ten, Adolphus, on my right, and a younger child, a girl aged six, on my left. Mona, who was in my arms, cried to me to give her more room, as I was pressing her against the beam, but the load of volcanic mud pouring down on me prevented me from being able to render any assistance, and the child was crushed, and smothered in my arms, and died. Adolphus said to me, "Mamma, I will die with you," and I think he did shortly after, as he did not answer again. The little girl, I think, died shortly after, as she said "Oh my head" as the mud was beating down on her, and she spoke no more.

During my entombment I thought a search party would come to search the room. I 'cooeed' to the first people I heard about the place. Mr Blythe and others got me out, on hearing my call, after being entombed for several hours. My injuries consist of bruises and cuts about the head and limbs, and the leg which was jammed by the beam has not had the circulation restored to it yet. Many of the injuries were sustained by endeavouring to protect my head from the falling lava.

Later Mrs Haszard told Ellen: "When they were trying to get me out, the beam was so heavy it seemed impossible for them to move it. It suddenly came to me, and I called out: 'Why don't you cut the legs off the chair?' They then got a saw and cut away the legs of the chair, and were able to pull me out."

Help was given to the survivors from the most unexpected quarters. Mr Robertson, who owned the coach at Rotorua, could have secured a large sum by taking fleeing residents to Tauranga. He declined to do so, but went on to Wairoa without fee or reward to render any assistance in his power to those who most urgently needed his help; and in Auckland,

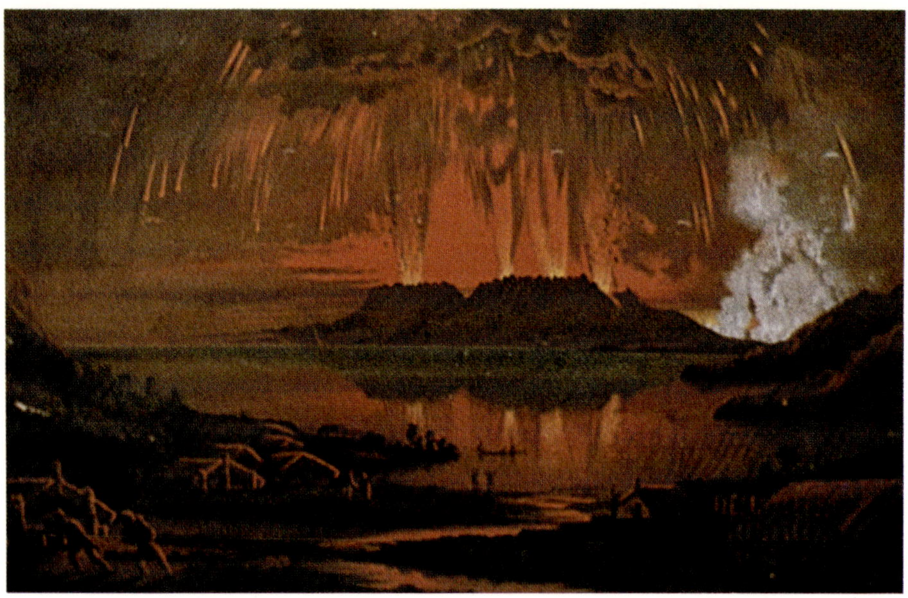

Eruption viewed from village of Waitangi, 1886. Lithograph by A. D. Willis taken from original painting.

Mr George Rignold staged a play, *Called Back*, to a full attendance at the Opera House, and gave the entire proceeds of the performance to the sufferers of the Tarawera eruption. Many others, too numerous to mention, gave their assistance in many and varied ways.

By this time Charles's nephew, Blo, was working for the *Herald*. He was sent to Tarawera to see if the Terraces had been destroyed, and tells his own story:

The Saturday morning immediately after the big eruption of Tarawera when every man, woman and child was shocked and stunned by the great volcanic outburst and loss of life, Willie Wilson and Manager Day came to our cubicle and called me aside. They excitedly explained that I was to catch the coming train and get to Ohinemutu (Rotorua) as quickly as possible. Day put into my hands £12.0.0. for expenses and bustled me off.

Willie Wilson said, "Now above all, boy, I want you to ascertain if the Terraces are gone," and he shook my hand with a "Don't forget now."

I grabbed a sketch book and pencils and without overcoat or other necessaries, made a bolt for the train and just got it.

The train only went as far as Hamilton. As it was a bitterly cold June night, I hired a horse to carry me to Oxford (Tirau) and left early next morning, reaching Oxford that Sunday night.

The only travellers I met on the road were two Maoris, riding to their native camp. They were good company, and wanted to buy my hired pony, and urged me strongly to bunk in that night with them.

I got to Oxford Hotel and found great excitement there. A party of refugees from Ohinemutu had just come in by coach. The late Harry Kerr had brought the first coach through since the eruption.

Joseph Howard Witheford, an active Auckland citizen, who was responsible for Auckland's Calliope Docks, through working for the Admiralty at home, was amongst the passengers, and gave a graphic description of affairs at Rotorua, and his full conviction that the whole district would go up "in the air". He told of the horrible experiences the travellers had had, coming through the bush that night. He warned me not to go on.

I hired a trap and driver and did go on early next morning. Arriving at Ohinemutu that afternoon, I found plenty of excitement for a growing lad of twenty years.

There were three hotels in Ohinemutu. Rotorua as it is now, did not go beyond Ohinemutu. Tamatekapua, the big Maori meeting house or *wharepuni*, was on its outskirts; a few scattered bath buildings and the Post Office and the teatree and a track to Whakarewarewa.

Every hotel was full of press-men and Government officials. The Palace Hotel was the home of the *Auckland Star* staff. The late T. W. Leys, and Jim Philp, reporter, and the late G. W. Read and a reporter for the *Evening Bell*, a rival Auckland evening paper. The late William Berry, editor and George Main, reporter, were housed in an old wooden structure known as Robertson's Hotel, at the foot of the hill, opposite Tamatekapua Wharepuni. Both hotels have since been removed.

George Main was pained and irritated at my appearance, and put it very plainly to me, that there was no hope of my getting any sketches or getting anywhere near the Rotomahana Lake where the Terraces were situated. Mr Berry was more kindly and explained that the Wairoa Valley was choked up with ash and debris, and the road impassable.

Things looked pretty bad for me, so I took a stroll around the Maori village and saw steaming and bubbling *ngawhas* (hot pools) and open baths and cooking places of hot or boiling water. I chanced across a young Maori of my own age, who became very friendly, toting me around.

The Maoris were in a very troubled state; every now and then an earthquake shook the ground. Tamatekapua was full of refugees, men, women and children, from the ash strewn lands, crying and praying every time the bell was rung on the *marae* as an earthquake shook.

When the young Maori, Mita, learned of my mission, he was greatly interested, and hit on a means of my getting to the scene of the eruption. His brother Hingawaka the native policeman, possessed a horse, and he would pinch it for me, if I could start early next morning.

With a haversack and sketch materials, I started off early next morning. It was bitterly cold, but a fine day. The horse, a piebald pony, with an old saddle, and mixed rope and leather bridle, reins, stirrups, spurs without rowels, and a strap for a horse whip, away I went on my adventure, with a vague idea as to my line of travel!

After travelling about a mile on my road to Wairoa, a party of horsemen overtook me. They were well horsed and provided, so I reckoned they were off on the same job as myself. I tried to prick my pony with the spurs, but found he ignored them, but a cut with the strap and off he cantered.

I found and lost that party time after time, but kept steadily on their tracks, until coming to a swollen muddy river, I found one of the party, a Mr Churchward, stuck in the middle of the stream and his mates on the far shore, shouting advice. My pony ignored the lot, cantered about a chain or two lower down, and crossed easily. I got back on the track and was not passed until over a mile away on my journey.

It was known as the old Galatea track, and the party was testing the road to Rotomahana, as the Wairoa track was impassable.

Mile after mile, I rode on, keeping the other party in view until I came to an old Maori settlement, where the first signs of dust appeared. The tracks through the fine volcanic dust from the eruption led me through the village to a range of hills, where the dust became deeper and deeper, until the pony found it difficult to proceed.

Then on turning, I found the party's horses, tied to the top of *tutu* bushes. I tied up my pony, tying my raincoat over the saddle and following the tracks, ploughed knee deep. The dust was very fine, and every step sent up a cloud of fine particles that choked the nostrils and mouth.

Earthquakes were frequent. The surrounding hills were beautifully rounded off with fine dust.

Suddenly, a Maori, with eye-balls poking from his head like a crayfish, burst on me from around a hillock, going for his life. Seeing me, he yelled "*Taipo! Taipo!*" (Devil!), and fled on. He was found afterwards, a Maori guide of the party, with Captain Steele from Hamilton.

I came across the party on top of a cliff overlooking Rotomahana. It was a grand sight, but awful. To the right, were two erupting hills, one throwing up an immense volume of black mud and steam; the other a vast column of steam, roaring to the sky.

In front was Tarawera; the mountain that had erupted. Its side towards us was one big jagged vent, throwing up smoke and steam like a bull roaring. Below, Rotomahana Lake was one mass of steam.

The party I had met included Dr. Hector, who had several instruments with him for some purpose. The party didn't seem to take much notice of me until Captain Steele, a Waikato man, saw my sketching, and asked my business. I told him I was the *Herald* artist, and would be glad to know if the Terraces were destroyed. He said the only way to ascertain that was by going to see, and that could only be done by going down the cliff to the edge of Rotomahana. He pointed out the Pink Terrace site. Acting on impulse, I slipped down the face of the cliff, an easy thing in that dust. Steele followed me, saying it was a foolish thing, but guided me on; down several plateaux to the edge of Rotomahana Lake.

What a scene it was of fierce action. The whole lake bed was one mass of boiling, snarling, bubbling action; jets of mud were being cast into the air in all directions; the steam, blown by the wind, revealing new horrors every minute.

Steele explained to me that the place we were standing on was just above the site of the Pink Terrace, and without any doubt they were blown to atoms.

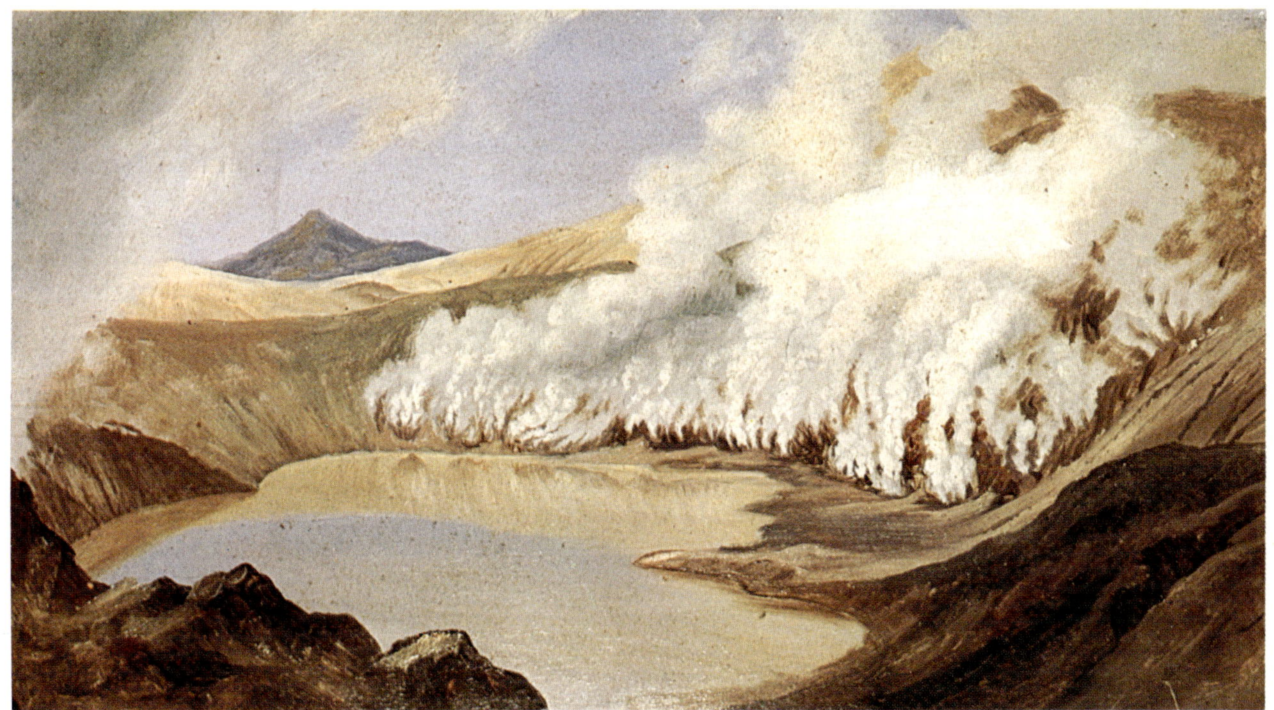

*Site of destroyed Terrace,
October 1886. Oil on card,
19 × 12 in.*

This was proved by masses of salmon-coloured silicous rock lying around us. We proceeded around the lake edge to get a view of the White Terrace site, through the steam. Awaiting a chance, Steele pointed to a spot under Tarawera, as a breath of wind blew the steam apart and said: "There you are, the White Terraces have gone too."

We trudged back through the dust. As we got back to our Pink Terraces' position, Steele pointed to where our tracks over the lake had been broken off, where the bank had fallen in. We were lucky not to have delayed there.

Arriving at the cliff face, what had been easy to descend was a terror to climb. The dust made it almost impossible, and like Bruce's spider, we climbed and climbed only to slip back. Steele then took off his boots and dug his toes in, and reached the top. I did the same, but not with the ease he did. When I reached the top, the party had left.

My eyes, mouth, nose, and ears were one mass of volcanic dust, and thirsty — I could have drunk a river dry. The party had left a soda bottle, half full of water. It didn't go far.

Then I made for my pony. Rain started to fall, the dust became sticky, and when I reached my pony, the poor beast had rolled in the dust to free itself. My raincoat was one mass of mud. I put it on, and made for home.

When I reached the old Maori village, I came to a fence, where the party had put up the slip rails. Thinking there was reason for closing the gate I released the reins while putting up the rails, and my pony,

evidently hungry, trotted off and left me. As evening was coming on,
it was raining, and I was miles from anywhere, I got a shock and felt
unhappy, but the pony, finding nothing but dust, stopped. On mounting I left the opposite rails open and made for home.

Mile after mile, in the rain, cold and hungry, my pony carried me
through that dark night; through Earthquake Flat and over the river
without mishap, until the lights of Rotorua appeared.

When I got to the Post Office, there was a group with Mr. Berry and
Geordy Main; worried and getting up a party to find me, knowing
where I had been, what I had, and what I'd seen, they were pleased
to see me.

Old George Main got my story and was eager to telegraph it off.
In order to keep me away from brothers of rival papers, he locked me
in a side room of the Telegraph Office. As I was hungry, cold and tired,
I kicked hell out of the door. Mr Dansey, the Postmaster, came and let
me out.

As it was hours after meal time at the little old pub, nobody took any
interest in my wants. I had no change of clothes, so I took the pony
across to my Maori boy friend's people's whare. The Maoris were all
up and about, howling and praying, so I was well looked after. Stripped,
I got into a *ngawha*, was fed, and had a 'flea' sleep.

In the morning, I got more descriptive sketches of Warbrick's boat
attempt across the volcanic erupted zone. Carts loaded with furniture
and belongings of refugee families with the women and children aboard,
came into Ohinemutu. The place hummed with excitement. Journalists
jumped into action every time a newcomer appeared from the erupted
country.

I was enjoying myself, when George Main came to me and told me
to go home. He had by some means hired an old bus-horse, saddled and

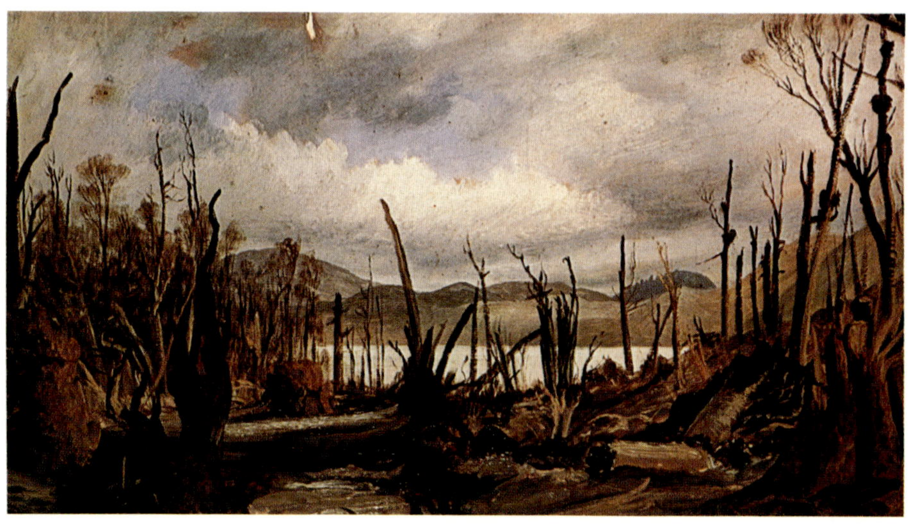

*Destruction at Tikitapu,
October 1886. Oil on card,
19 × 12 in.*

94

bridged, and as I had no effects to gather together, he pushed me off in the afternoon on my way home.

The old fleabitten grey bus-horse went fairly well, until we reached a stretch of road covered with mullocky sandstone repairing. As it had begun to rain again, this stuff made a sticky surface that my prod went lame in. The darkness came on and I was far from home, cold and utterly miserable. A Maori *korowai* mat that my friend Mita's people had given me, I put around my loins to try and keep some warmth in my legs.

Once I came across a couple of little tents lit up inside, belonging to the road menders. In my misery, I called out to them. A head poked out of one of the little nests, a surly voice asked my trouble, listened and popped back.

Mile after mile through the soaking dark bush, I plodded on. At last a point of light appeared as I topped a hill, and disappeared as I dipped into a hollow. It heartened me, coming nearer very slowly. At last I came to the Oxford Hotel, banged on the verandah post, and brought out Mr Rose, the proprietor. He told me to take my horse to the stable at the back. I went there, and banged on the top of an iron shed, bringing out a surly little rouse-about. I was so cold my legs were numbed; I slid off the horse to the ground.

I remembered little, until I found myself stripped and before a fire in the parlour of the pub, with kindly Mrs Rose, who had blanketed me, and put me there to warm out. Mr Rose, Harry Kerr, the coach driver, and a couple of other men were deep in a game of poker. I slept like a top, until daylight, when I took the train. The train didn't go beyond Oxford then.

Arriving in Auckland city, a mass of muddy clothes, sketches and lumps of the destroyed Terraces.

As telegraphed stuff had been published about my little bit, I was hero for a day in the *Herald* office, but that didn't last long.

Mr Willie Wilson got his piece of Pink Terrace; Mr Berry, the editor, who was a good friend to me, wangled the firm for a suit of clothes for me. I got that and Willie Wilson's lasting friendship, for my part in the game.

My friendship with the boy Mita continued for many years. I became friendly not only with all of Mita's family, but also the Te Tuparas and many others at Ohinemutu. Rotorua was a much more interesting place then, than it is today.

A little incident in the Pink Terrace specimen deal; Mr Cobb, the head of the litho department, a dear old soul, with beautifully curled white whiskers, pink-cheeked, and a churchman, begged me for a piece of the Terraces for his museum. As I had parted with the last lump, we in the artist's department decided to manufacture one (we were brick bare in those days). Digging out a bit of the *Herald*'s walls, we coated the bit of brick with slime from the litho stone bath, and when it was dried, the piece of Pink Terrace was presented to the delighted Mr Cobb.

Some years after, attending the wedding supper of Mr Cobb's daughter, my mate Hunt drew my attention to the old father, exhibiting proudly a piece of the Pink Terrace, under a glass case, to his party.

News from the stricken thermal regions almost filled the columns of the newspapers after the Tarawera eruption. Early reports that the Pink and White Terraces did not seem to be seriously damaged were followed by an item in the *New Zealand Herald* of June 16th, 1886, in which it was stated that the Terraces definitely were destroyed. The item continued:

A party of six who left Rotorua for Rotomahana by dray road have just returned. They advanced to the hill at the back of the Pink Terrace, this being the most accessible side. Smoke was blowing up the valley, a quarter of a mile from the crater. At the back of the terrace, four of the party halted, declining to go further, but a son of Captain Steele of Hamilton, and Mr William Blomfield, artist of the *New Zealand Herald* staff, pushed on to the very edge of the crater and peered down. They watched one mud volcano and counted four seconds until the mud fell. Blomfield started his sketch, when Steele called him back and they had only retired about fifty yards when the place where they had been standing slipped into a crater.

As soon as Mrs Haszard was well enough to travel, she and her two daughters journeyed to Auckland, wearing clothing which had been given to them by wellwishers, as they had lost all their possessions in the eruption. They looked quite smart, all wearing Salvation Army bonnets! Clara soon received a teaching position in the country, but Mrs Haszard and Ina lived in Auckland, and after a while they managed to occupy a house at 27 Wood Street, and were constant visitors at the Blomfield home.

From the descriptions they gave him, Charles painted a picture of the mountain in eruption, taken from the ill-fated village of Waitangi, a few miles around the shore of the lake from Te Wairoa. Only one Maori lady escaped from this village, so aptly named "Weeping water" by the early Maoris, and she was rescued by a surveying party headed by Mr Percy Smith. She was reported as "progressing favourably, although she was six days without food".

In 1889 Mr Willis published a book written by Edward Wakefield, named *New Zealand Illustrated — The Story of New Zealand*, in which he included a large reproduction of Charles' sketch of the eruption, and mentioned that the picture was not imaginary, as Mr Blomfield had some months previously painted the view from Waitangi and only put in the eruption from the descriptions given to him by eye witnesses, who all testified to their accuracy.

Many years later, Ina Haszard, now Mrs Hobbs, wrote:

I am now the only survivor of the Haszard family of Wairoa. My mother and sister, who were survivors, passed away some years ago. Painful as the subject is to me I have felt it a duty to my native home, New Zealand, to leave a brief record of my experience, and being an artist, I have also used my best efforts in producing a painting — "Mount Tarawera in Eruption". To live again in memory that terrible drama, for the purpose of creating this picture, has proved a trying ordeal, but I hope my efforts have not been in vain.

Ina's picture of the eruption shows the black cloud over the mountain, with the moonlight shining on the lake, and balls of fire shooting across the sky.

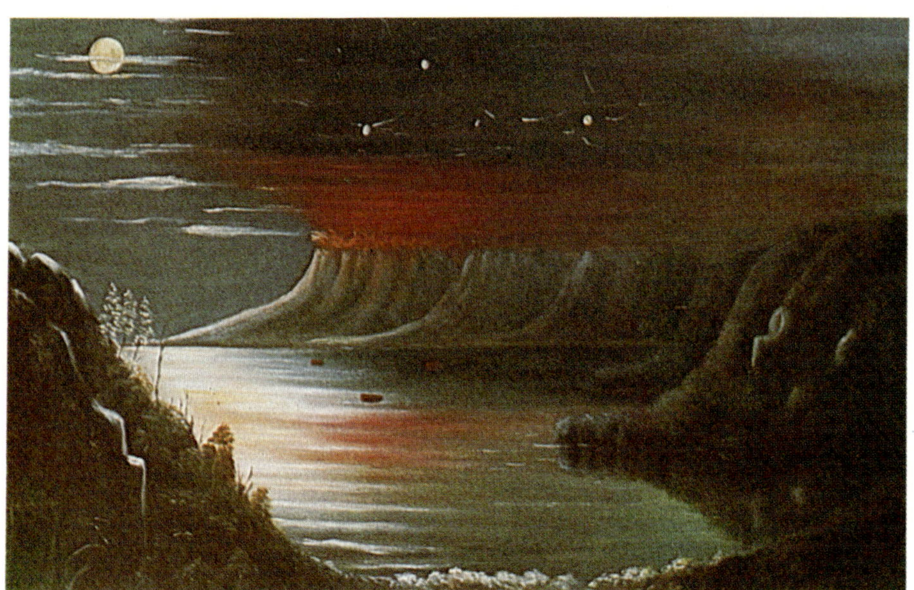

Tarawera Eruption, by Ina Hobbs (née Haszard), 1935. Oil on canvas, 36×24 in.

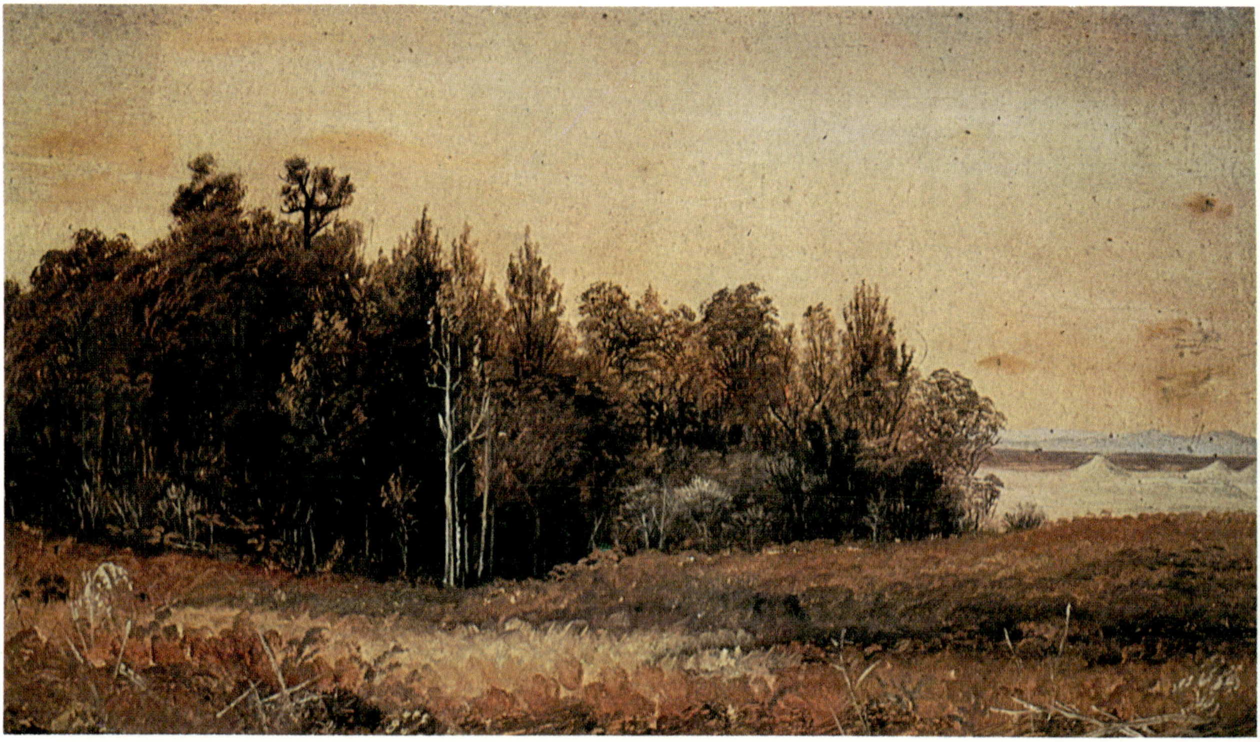

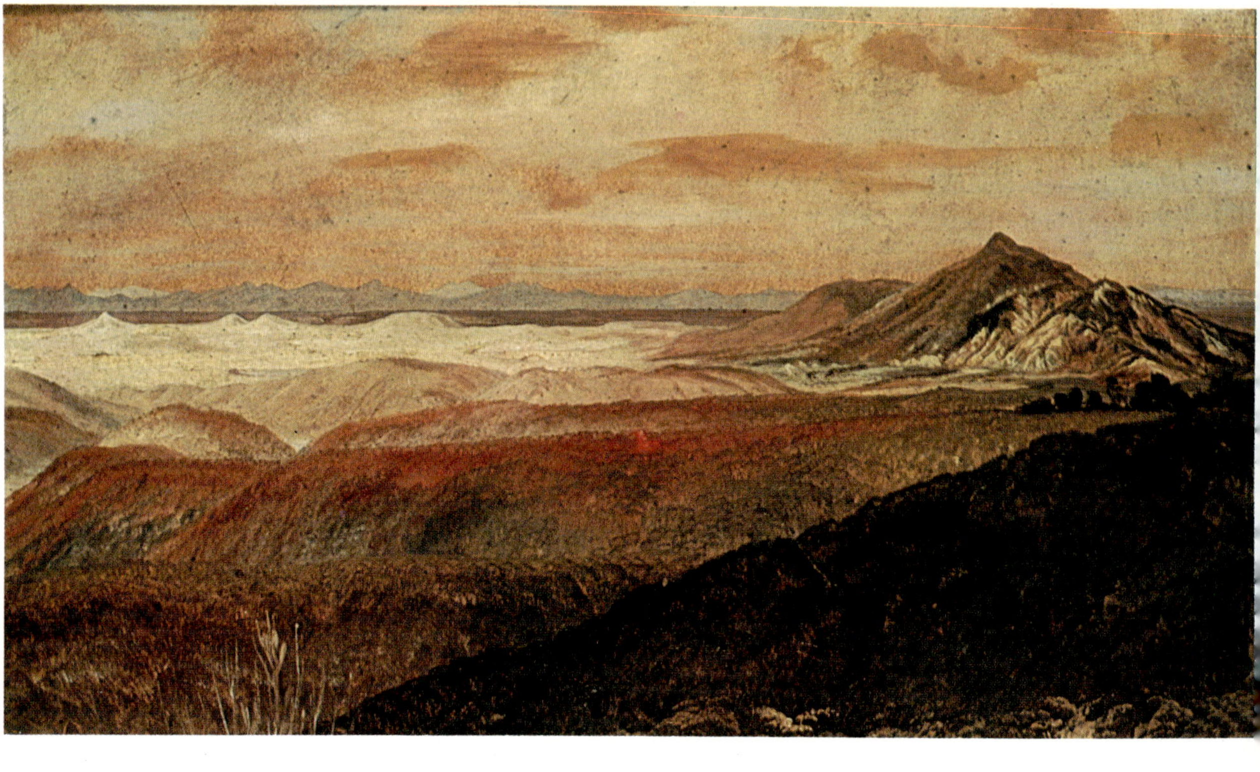

11. Aftermath

By October, Charles decided he must go back to Rotomahana and see for himself what had happened there, and take more pictures to show to his friends and relations.

Once again, he wrote regularly to his wife:

I have been this morning to the volcanoes at Rotomahana, a tramp of about four miles over the mud-covered hills (the mud is hard now and you can get along fine). The sight was very grand and awful. What must it have been when the geysers were all playing up mud and stones hundreds of feet high.

I am writing a diary every night so I will send you extracts from that describing the scenes just as they struck me first. One thing dear, you may be sure of, there is no danger where I am going. I only want to paint the scenes and I see plainly that I must not get too close or the effect will be lost. I got two very good scenes today. Scenes you must see to understand, for surely never before was there anything like this except perhaps in the Moon.

The one I got this afternoon is from the edge of the devastated country showing the dead bush and dead fern in the background, then gradually getting whiter and whiter till the country is one mass of oatmeal coloured hills and valleys. As I came back today I had a splendid view of Tongariro covered a long way down with snow. It looked just lovely. Tomorrow I am going to the Kakaramea Mountain close by here, and get a picture of it before the snow melts away.

Saturday night. Yesterday I went to the Waiotapu Valley and Kakaramea, and today I have been again to the volcanoes and got two splendid sketches. I feel tired tonight but very well. I find it a fine thing to take some cold porridge in the billy with me when I am travelling over the mud-covered country, then when I feel thirsty a few spoonfuls of cold porridge is so refreshing, and I believe strengthening likewise. I have not seen a soul since I came here. The tourists go now by Wairoa and do not come this way. I think they miss a great deal by so doing, and Mr Blythe has not showed up yet, so I am Monarch of all I survey.

Sunday night. This has been a dull day in more senses than one. I have been wishing Fred could have come with me, for I feel as though it would be nice to have a companion. Better still I wish I had you and the children. Oh Ellen my heart turns to thee. How I love thee you don't know how much. I can pray for you though I am far away, and so I do and will and all the children. God bless them. I hope I shall be a better father to them when I get back again. I feel different this time somehow, I don't seem so willing to leave you all. I feel that I love you

Destroyed bush, Rotomahana, October 1886. Oil on card, 19 × 12 in.

Vaiotapu after eruption, October 1886. Oil on card, 9 × 12 in.

all so much and that you all love me so much and the dear little boy too, he forms another link to bind me to home. May he grow up to be a blessing and comfort to his mother. Well I can't have you here, so I must be content to make myself happy in my loneliness. I have had a good rest today and shall feel all the better for it tomorrow, for I expect I shall have to work hard this week. It is getting cold, so I will turn in. Is it not a good thing I can keep warm in bed. Goodnight dearest, partner of my joys and sorrows (I think I ought to write the JOYS large and the sorrows small) don't you think so? Goodnight.

Rhyme without reason.

Strictly private

1. The day is long without Thee
   My darlingest of Pets
   The day is long without Thee
   Ere yet the red sun sets.

2. The hours move very slowly
   One hour seems really two
   And yet they move so sweetly
   For I ever think of you

3. The night seems long without Thee
   Thou lamp of sweet delight
   The night seems long without Thee
   I'd have thee if I might

4. For when awake reclining
   Upon my ferny bed
   I miss thine arms entwining
   And the nearness of thine head.

Composed on the road to Ohinemutu Monday morning.

Charles's brother Fred came down to join him for a few days and Charles wrote again:

We have had a busy time of it. Last Monday we left here early for the top of Tarawera and intended to stay out two nights. We got as far as the base by twelve o'clock with our swags, and then left our things and climbed the mountain, getting to the top about three o'clock. We found out a very easy way up; there was only a short piece at all difficult and steep. We saw the craters and a grand sight it is, the rich colours and metallic hues are wonderful. We got down and camped under the shelter of a small hill and lit a roaring fire of the driftwood and made ourselves very warm and comfortable in the little tent.

The ground was rather hard, the mud was baked pretty dry, but we slept well and then started off back to Rotomahana and got back to the tent by moonlight about eight o'clock, very tired. The next day, Wednesday, we stayed at Pareheru resting ourselves, and I sketched from there and then on Thursday we left for Orakei Korako, but took the wrong track and got over to the Waiotapu district and got some fine sketches of the mud geysers and a beautiful clear lake, the Opouri, where we found a canoe and paddles and had a sail across and back again.

We slept there that night and the next day crossed the country to those whares by the hot spring where we slept when we made that ever memorable journey to Orakei Korako, where you had the bathe, you know. We stayed there Friday night and I got a fine sketch of the Boiling River which we traced to its source, a beautiful clear pool surrounded by the most wonderfully beautiful rocks and ferns.

Then yesterday afternoon we came back here. Tomorrow we hope to get into Ohinemutu early and then go to Wairoa. Fred is coming home on Wednesday. He seems to have enjoyed himself and it has done him good, and I have been very glad of his company. I can tell you he has also helped me a great deal. He will bring the specimens of stone, etc., we have picked up.

And now I think I have given you a sketch of our movements this far. You may depend I have been and am often thinking of you dear, and the darling little ones. I am very well and happy. The time seems to have gone by so quickly that I have hardly noticed it flying by. I hope you too have been well, and happy and enjoyed yourself. As to my future movements, I don't know for certain. It depends first upon what news the letters bring me, and secondly upon whether Mr Horne is prepared to send me to Wairakei on the cheap. He half promised to do so. I shall see when I get into Rotorua. If not, I may stay a week at Whakarewarewa and then I shall come home. I will keep this open till I get the letters. And now dear little wife, may God bless you and keep you safe from all harm and sorrow. I need not tell you how I love you, for you know I do, don't you dear. xxxxx Good bye.

Monday night. I got your nice long letters today and eagerly devoured the news and messages of love they contained.

Whakarewarewa. October 23rd, 1886.

Dearest of Loves,

As soon as one letter is posted I begin another. I went into Ohinemutu today and got your loving epistle and posted one to you. Mr Horne can't get away to go with me to Wairakei but advises me to go by coach and he would wire to the manager and get him to meet me with a horse to take my things on. So I thought it best to take the opportunity to go, which might never occur again. I shall have to pay the coach fare, and then shall be quite free of expense and shall come home direct from there to Lichfield, where the coach meets the train, so it will only cost me about £5.0.0. more altogether. If you write any more direct to Wairakei, Taupo, I expect they get a mail there sometimes. I go on Wednesday morning early from Ohinemutu.

I shall go in on Tuesday night and sleep there. I could spend another week or two here as there are many spots of interest, but then I can come here anytime. I have already got some good pictures here. The weather has been very wet. Yesterday it rained all day but today has been very fine. There is a young man staying with me in the boarding house today. He has come to try the baths for sciatica. He has been two months at the Government baths and got no good, so he will try this for a month. He seems a quiet young fellow.

Reading your letter over again, I am so glad that little son is keeping so well and making you so happy with his laughing ways. Keep Frank as long as you like, but make him do something for you, chop the wood, and weed the garden or something. It will do him good both ways.

Whatever Fred may have been in Ohinemutu I was well enough. We had been without meat for two or three days, and then we ate a loaf and a tin of salmon and just afterward Mr Horne would have us come into lunch and we ate some stewed steak and kidney. Don't you think I must have been well to stand that?

About the pictures, I think there is one small white terrace at home, but I think it is the Tattooed Basins. However, I would send it down if you can find it. Don't send anything unfinished down.

We are having a great lot of rain here. I wish it would settle fine. I wanted to do a lot here tomorrow, but if it is wet I can't do it. Well, it is all ordered for the best, and we must make the best of it.

"Come wet come shine, we murmur not
All's for the best
Let's do our part what e'er our lot
Leave Him the rest.
C.B.

You see the poetic spirit has not left me yet. Your love has inspired me and this came into my head all in a minute as I wrote:

When loving hearts still think of us
The day seems bright
And fond affection gives to us
Songs in the night.

Tuesday afternoon. I have just walked in from Whakarewarewa and am going to stay at Lake House tonight, and tomorrow at six o'clock I start for Wairakei. Good bye dearest.

Ohinemutu. Tuesday night.

Dearest Ellen,

I posted you a letter today, as the mail goes out early tomorrow, but as I am going early tomorrow myself and I may not have an opportunity of writing again, I thought I would just let you know the latest news. Mr Horne has been very kind. He is to give me a letter to the manager at Wairakei and I am to stay there quite free. I pay my own coach fare, and he has been kind enough to charge me nothing for my stay here, nor for the horses to Pareheru, so you see I am getting off very easy. A fine thing, isn't it, to be able to do it so cheaply. I shall be home in about three weeks' time now, I expect on a Friday. I have got some very good sketches at Whakarewarewa, and feel now in just the right humour to make a real good job of the Wairakei pictures which I shall do on canvases direct and finish there. I am taking the little tent so that I can pitch it over me if the weather gets hot, or if it rains. I think I am in for three jolly weeks and mean to make the most of it.

I hope you will keep your spirits up and don't fret after me dear. I shall be all the better for another three weeks of this kind of life. It will quite set me up. I feel so well now.

I camped last night in the little tent as the Maoris wanted 10/- to let me stay another night at the house, so I crossed the creek and camped on the other side and took sketches from that side today, and so dodged them grandly. I must have camped right over the line, as I felt the ground bumping and throbbing every now and then as I lay down, but I spent a very comfortable night and slept well.

Goodbye sweetheart, goodbye. God bless you and the dear children. I would write to them only I haven't time,

C. Blomfield.

Wairakei, October 31st, 1886.

Dearest Wife,

It seems quite an age since I had your last letter (yesterday week) and here I am almost as lonely as at Rotomahana. I am the only visitor, and have the large whare where the visitors are put up all to myself, a large comfortable bedroom, and my meals are brought in to me in the diningroom where a good fire is lit in the evening. The things are brought in by a boy and sometimes Mr Callum comes in in the evening after tea and has a yarn. Mrs Callum does not show herself much, so you see I have not much company.

I have breakfast at half past six and get away at seven o'clock, and then am all alone till four o'clock at night, when I come back again, but although I should prefer company, I must not complain as I am very comfortable and feel very well indeed, and this is really a wonderful place, and I am getting some good pictures. The geysers are far better than anything I have expected, and after Rotomahana are the finest things I have seen yet. Fancy the gully below the waterfall at Wairoa near the Haszards all among those rocks, but the water hot and on either side of the creek great geysers throwing up boiling water from strange fantastic looking basins of different colours, the whole half hidden in clouds of steam making it more strange and mysterious. The Geyser Valley alone is a sight worth coming thousands of miles to see, and should prove in course of time a great attraction. It only wants to be known, and I hope to make it better known when I get back. I am painting on the canvases here, and I don't see how I can get home before Friday night, November 19th. I shall post this on Wednesday as there is only one mail a week here. Perhaps by that time I may be more sure.

Today, Sunday, is gloriously fine and sunny, a very sharp frost last night and ice this morning. I am on the bank of the Waikato River now, writing this not far from the house. The river is very beautiful here, so deep, so clean, and wooded on either side, but I think it is time I went back to lunch.

Sunday afternoon. I have just been up a little hill close by and seen Tongariro. It is steaming away at the top and covered a long way down with snow. Ruapehu was hidden by cloud.

I have been reading all your letters over again today, such nice loving letters, quite love letters in fact. I am longing for Wednesday night to come when I shall get another I expect, perhaps two. It seems as if you were not so far away, dearest, when I can read your letters and write to you. God bless you.

When is the little pastor coming back? Will he be home before I am? I do wish he could have been here with me a week or two. This is just the place for him to rest himself in, so quiet and homelike, but I suppose he is enjoying himself in another way. I have written to him from here, but I don't know whether he will get it before he leaves Dunedin. Tell him this if he comes back first.

The weather seems now quite settled, fine today, has been glorious — up till yesterday it was very wet. I am so glad I brought the little tent as I pitch that and work under it even if it does rain.

Tomorrow I am going to pitch it in the Geyser Valley, and I expect I shall be there a week or more as there is a great deal there to paint and I am the first and only one who has attempted it in colour. I must do justice to it. From what I see of it, it will be the hardest job I have ever had, but I mean to take my time and do my best.

And now dear Ellen my own sweet wife, I must say goodbye once more for today. May the peace of God which passeth all understanding keep your heart and mind in Christ Jesus. From your loving husband,
Charles Blomfield.

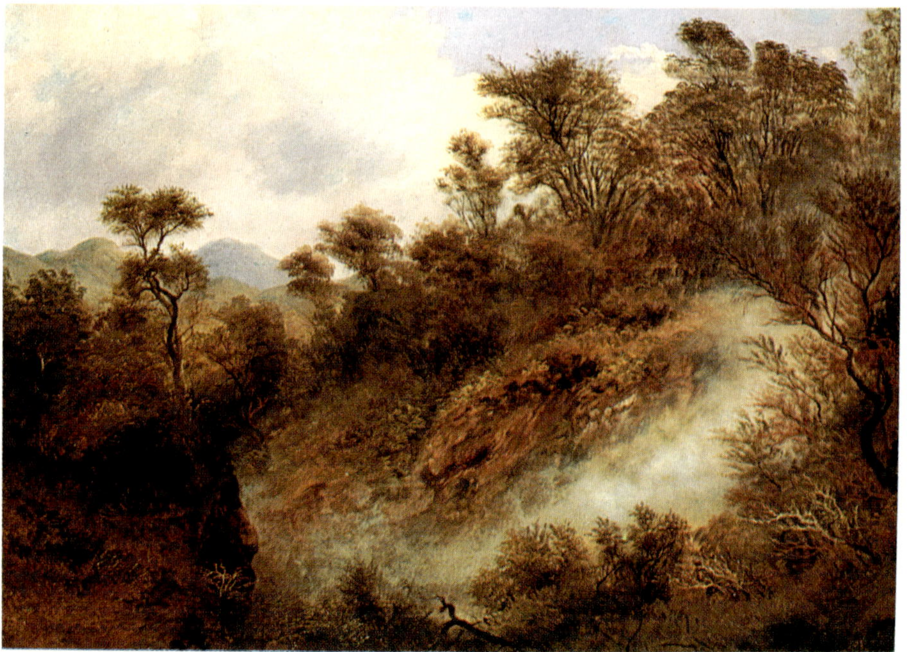

Geyser Valley, Wairakei, 1885. Oil on canvas, 24 × 18 in.

Champagne Pool, Wairakei, undated. Oil on card, 10 × 14 in.

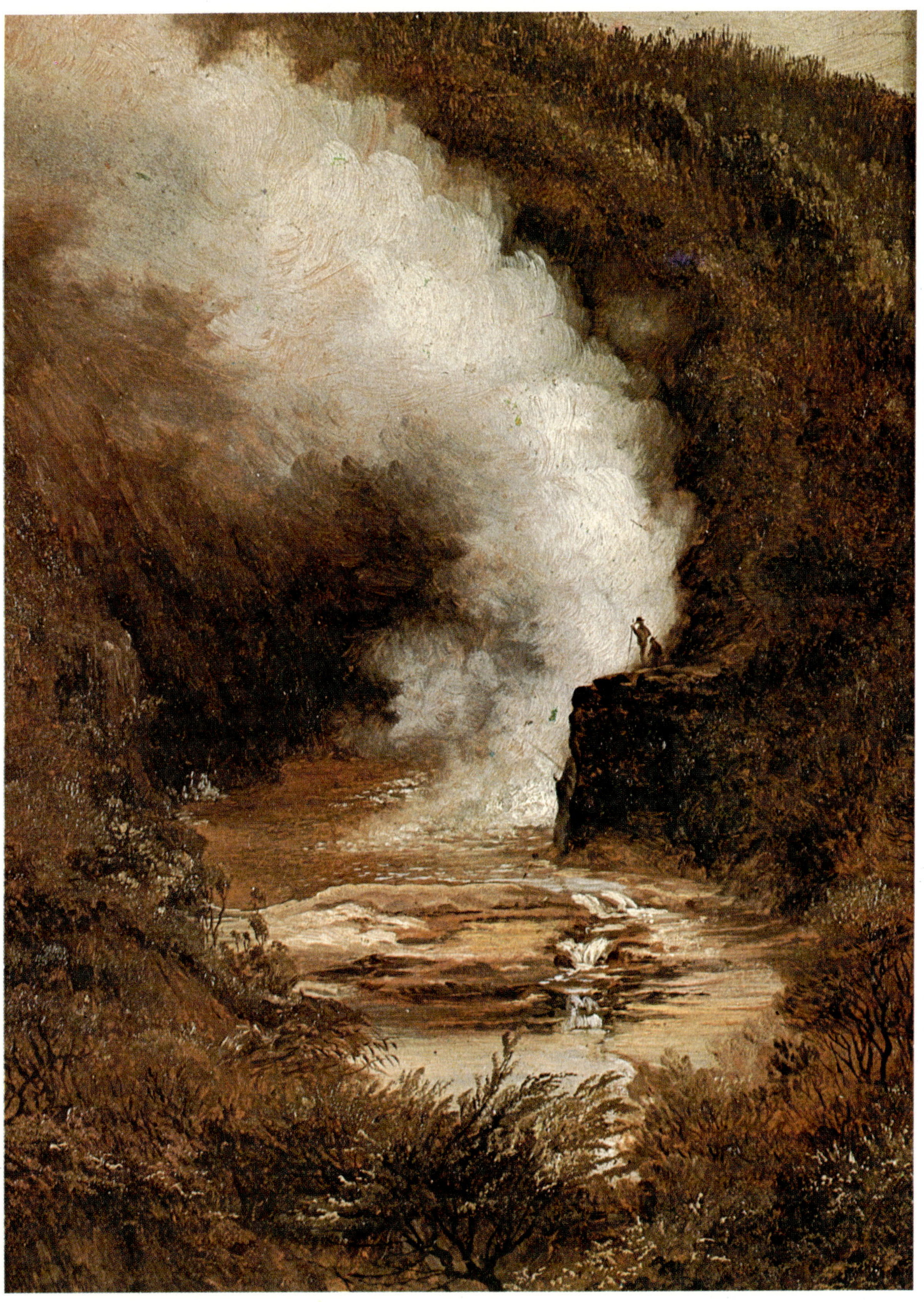

Not only did Charles love to paint nature as he saw it, he also liked to write to the newspapers about his trips, as follows:

After a look at the desolated country, and bidding the Maori goodbye I pitched my tent, and started to look for water. The camp being on the top of a hill it seemed a hopeless task to try, especially as the hills are all pumice, through which the water runs as a sieve. However, I took the billy and travelled down a gully, which seemed a likely place. It was joined by other gullies, proving that a considerable extent of country was drained by it, still while the marks of copious rain were everywhere apparent, the soil had let it all through, and the surface was dry and disappointing.

After about a mile of this the valley was hemmed in by masses of rock, and just below the welcome sight of rushes and reeds. Just a little further at the foot of a rock which blocked the drainage, there was a pool of cold clear water.

The mud is now quite hard, except near the lakes in the valley, which are fast drying up. The valleys prove the best walking, as the rain has consolidated the deposit, and you avoid the fissures which scar the hills in every direction. From close to Pareheru camp a valley leads down to the first lake, and you can travel down this gully right on to the craters, passing on the way a stream of good fresh water, which has worked its way out of the hillside. The grass sown by Mr Percy Smith, where the rain has not washed it quite away, is growing very luxuriantly. Some of it is quite six inches high, and very healthy looking.

I am camped at Pareheru, all alone. The visitors seem to all go by way of Wairoa and over Tarawera lake in Warbrick's boat, and up the mountain. I think they miss a great deal by not coming this way, as the southeast end of Rotomahana is still showing signs of violent energy, and the high pressure steam issuing from a thousand vents among jagged masses of piled up rock, and the boiling, seething water at the bottom of the great crater, is a sight not to be compared to the view from the top of Tarawera, which mountain is now perfectly quiet. My opinion is that the volcanoes are quieting down, and when the crust gets cool enough, a large lake will take the place of the existing craters, with perhaps some geysers and boiling pools at its margin.

4

New Landscapes
1887 - 1893

12. Lake Taupo

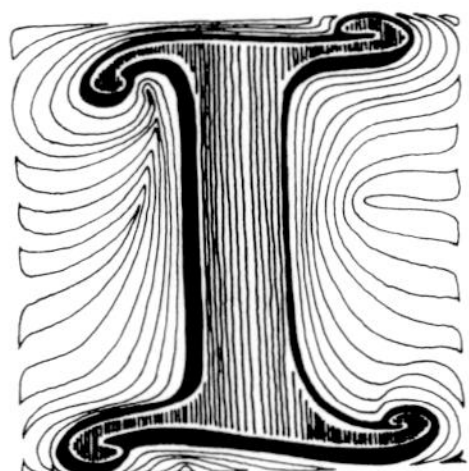N 1887, CHARLES persuaded his brother-in-law, John Graham, to go with him to Taupo and explore the distant shores. They took a rowboat stocked with a month's provisions, and set off to travel around the great lake.

"We have passed some beautiful places," Charles wrote to Ellen, "tall cliffs rising sheer up from the water two hundred feet, clothed here and there with trees and shrubs, and have had some fine views of the mountains covered a long way down with snow. We have some idea now of how long it will take us to go round the lake, as we can see the extent of it and the different places we want to stay at. It does seem a great sea from here."

Charles obtained letters of introduction to the chiefs of Waihaha and Wanganui, the two Maori settlements on the lake, and the two men proceeded on to Waihaha, right in the centre of the western bay of the lake.

"There are a few Maoris here and some whares," Charles wrote, "but oh how changed to what they were a few years back, everything in the way of carvings and picturesque buildings gone to ruin. The natives themselves are all right. I got two sketches of men in the old flax mats, those that fray out like hair. . . . When I commenced painting them, all the settlement wanted to be taken and the women went and dressed up in their best finery. They were so disappointed when I could not draw them all. I did one woman side face, but that did not satisfy her at all. She wanted to know why I did not show her other eye, and they strongly objected to the dark side of the face caused by the shadow.

"We found a cave at the end of the beach today, among some bush, and when we climbed up to it we found four coffins piled up there, and in another place we found old decayed mats, canoes, bones, and masses of Maori hair and a skull, but we are very careful not to touch anything as the natives would know who did it, and might make it awkward for us."

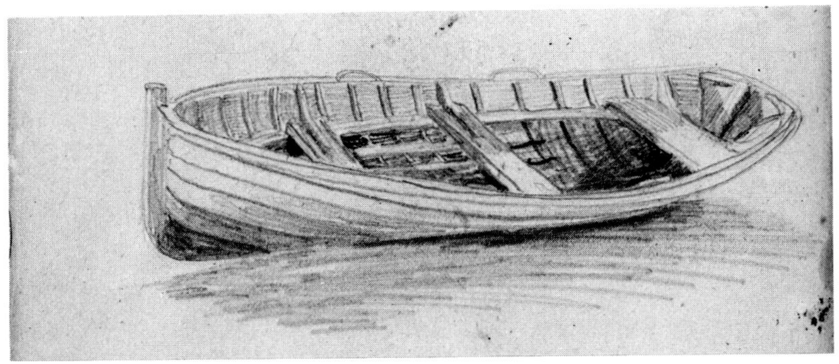

Once again Charles wrote about his adventures to the *Herald*:

There is something fascinating in the very name of Lake Taupo —
Te Moana as the Maoris call it, "The Sea" — with its wide bays and
bluff headlands, storms and calms, ocean billows and currents, its
historical associations and romance. When pulling or sailing round
some towering cliff or skirting some wide bay, it seems hard to realise
that the real old sea is far away, and that there is no brine in the spray
as the long rollers dash on its pebbly shore. Not long ago every bay had
its native *hapu* (sub-tribe); canoes plied across laden with the products
of peace, or crowded with painted warriors; they might be seen
> Tearing through the tortured water,
> Eager for the vengeful slaughter.

Now alas, with few exceptions, all that is left of them are a few
whitened bones in some lone cave, or perhaps, a deserted hut tottering
in decay. It has its romance too, legendary tales of witchcraft and
terror, of monster taniwhas rising from the water to destroy the inmates
of some illfated canoe, tales of Maori braves incited by love or hatred
to deeds of heroism or cruelty. There is a fascination also in its physical
features, 600 square miles of fresh water, with a coastline of over 150
miles, surrounded by high mountains, bush-covered cliffs and frowning
precipices, over which the rivers leap in snowy foam.
The very water has a charm; clear as crystal, of immense depth and
lovely colour, rising amid the snows of Ruapehu, fed by the hot streams
and geysers of Tokaanu, it pauses and gathers in this huge reservoir a
water supply for nations, and then rushes headlong down the Waikato
Valley, leaps over the Huka Falls, past the wonders of Wairakei, foams
and dashes through the Aratiatia gorge, gathers strength from the hot
waters of Ohake and the Waiotapu Valley, the boiling fountains of
Orakei Korako, dashes along its rocky course, till far below at Cambridge
it becomes a broad navigable river to the sea.
But there is another feature which, perhaps more than all these
(especially to those who have seen the devastating influences of the late
outburst at Tarawera) adds interest to the scene, and fascinates the
mind — the evidences of its volcanic origin. There it is, a huge crater,
its rocky sides still torn and scarred by earthquake shocks, and its shores
still strewn for scores of miles with pumice, the snowy cone of Tongariro
still smoking in the distance. One's thoughts go back to the time when
this great rift was formed, when explosion after explosion convulsed the
air, when clouds of hot pumice darkened the sky, and the island was
shaken from end to end. What a sight might that have been after the
eruption! A yawning abyss, twenty-five miles across its steaming sides,
over one thousand feet high, the bottom below the level of the sea!
And then the conflict between the two elements fire and water before
the present lake began to fill! Surely, apart from its beauty, there are
associations connected with Lake Taupo sufficient to make it unique
and famous.

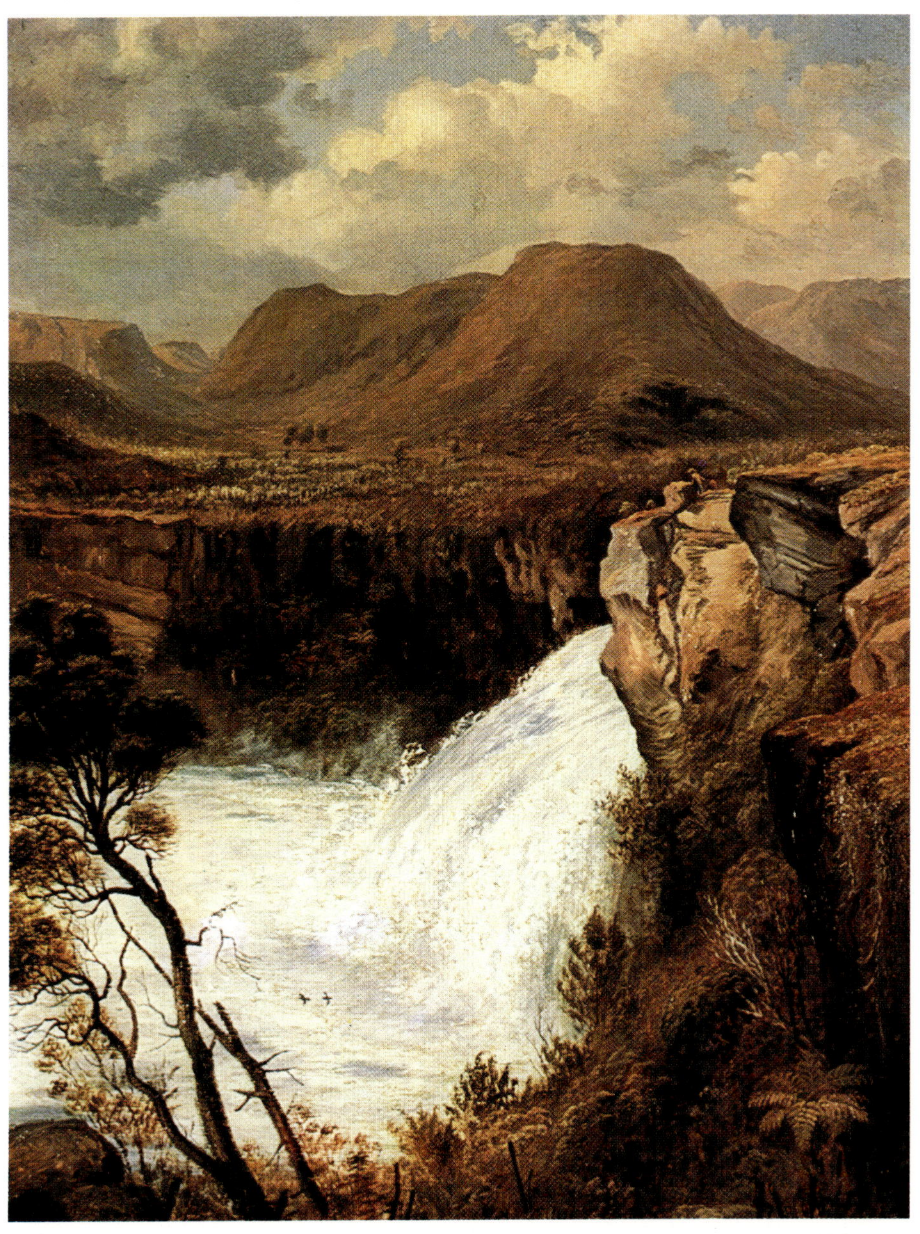

Huka Falls, 1887. Oil on canvas, 20 × 24 in.

Having arranged for an extended excursion round this lake, I arrived there the first week in October in company with a friend, hired a boat from Dan Ferny, the Taupo boatman, and we were soon fairly launched upon our voyage. It is true people said we were too early, that the lake would be rough and the weather cold; but we had a safe boat, a comfortable tent, a month's provisions and plenty of warm rugs, and could defy the weather. To us it was, indeed, a voyage of discovery; and the love of adventure disdains a few slight inconveniences.

Tapuaeharuru, where the Waikato leaves the lake, is perhaps the least interesting part of it, as the shores are low and tame. It is after passing the long, low point which stretches out upon the right, that the great western bay opens to view, and bold bluff headlands, reaching far into the lake, form a noble scene. On the extreme end of this point are some interesting caves; a flat rock makes a good landing place, and a piece of fern-covered ground in front of the cave makes a good camping place. A large ngaio tree grows at the entrance of the principal cave, and from the inside a grand view is obtained across the lake of the great Tongariro group of mountains, covered with snow, framed as it were, by the rocky walls of the cave.

A mile or two further on rises one of those rocky bluffs which are so characteristic of the western bay. It is a bold headland, for behind it stretches a deep bay, and then another headland, rising higher still, its precipitous sides going straight down into the water, every nook and cranny covered with dark green foliage. Then we pass Whangamata Bay, a long deep inlet, and soon come to a very interesting point — Te Kauae — where the perpendicular face of the riven rock rises far above our heads, a great massive wall of dark grey stone. This rocky wall runs a long way inland, making a sheltered corner, where we camped for a few days. A long sandy beach runs round a wide bay here for some miles, and the scenery is most enchanting. White cliffs, peeping out of the dark native shrubbery, border the smooth sandy beach, on which the water now ripples with a faint murmur and now breaks with angry roar. There are several fine echoes on the lake, but the finest of all is here. From the water on a still day three separate echoes give back the voice — so plainly, indeed, that the answer seems to be human.

From this long beach, which forms the north-western corner of the lake, we took advantage of a favourable wind, and sailed right across to Waihaha — a distance of about twelve miles — passing several places of interest on the way. One point is exceedingly beautiful. Great masses of detached rock rise from the water in picturesque confusion, clothed with a luxuriant growth of trees, mosses, and ferns. The wonder is how large trees — manuka and pohutukawa — manage to find root on these bare rocks; in some places you see thin roots clinging to the bare face of a rock, while the tree is waving its branches fifty feet above you. Then we passed another fine bay, where the Waihora river comes down into the lake, and some green willows mark the site of a deserted settlement. Then a large body of water comes tumbling over the rocky precipice into the lake, making a fine cascade.

This shore of the lake is one long line of high cliffs, very precipitous, with only one or two breaks where the rivers come down — in some places clothed with bush, and in others sheer precipice 200 feet high. The water is so clear you can see a long way down; but the bottom is far away out of sight; and when the wind is hushed and the water still, each rock and tree, and moss-grown stem, is imaged forth in richer tints below.

At Waihaha a large stream runs into the lake, and the cliffs open and form a frowning wall on either side of a sheltered valley prized by the Maoris for growing fine potatoes. The river is deep and navigable for some distance inland. There has once been a large settlement here, but all that now remains are some ruined patakas and dilapidated whares. The river, as it runs through the settlement, overhung with great weeping willows, peach and cherry trees, is very beautiful, and if it were not for the native huts and the rugged background of massive rocks, might pass for an English stream.

The natives were all away planting potatoes except an old man and woman, who emerged from the darkness of a smoke-stained hut, almost in a state of nature, as we appeared upon the scene. But the news of our arrival soon spread, and before long we had the whole tribe down upon us, and I was soon busy painting the "Maori at home".

We have some artists in Auckland who take a pride in painting the figure, and are accustomed to paint from a well-posed model warranted not to move, with the light adjusted to a nicety and every other convenience of a well-appointed studio. Some of these gentlemen should come to Waihaha and paint the Maoris there. To be hemmed in and jostled by a motley crowd all anxious to get the best view, and all jabbering away in a language you don't understand; to have your seat shaken or your elbow jolted just as you are going to make a hair stroke, would, I fancy, be a new sensation for them, and then your discomfiture is complete, when some half dozen dusky damsels crowded out from behind, peer over your canvas in front, and shut out all your view.

About a mile or so up the Waihaha river there is a very fine waterfall. It may be approached either by road or boat; in fact, we were foolish enough to pull our boat right up to the fall and enjoy the novel sensation of being rocked and tossed about in the large basin below, and gaze up at the mass of water foaming over the rock. It does not seem so much to fall over as to tear and writhe in agony, leaping and plunging hither and thither, altering its form every second with a horrible din of crashing and tearing as though whole forests were being shattered with hurricane force; a noise which may be heard miles away.

If the visitor is fond of adventure, and does not mind a little hard work, it is possible to climb the steep rocky bank to the right, and stand immediately above the fall, when we find ourselves between high perpendicular rocks in a narrow defile or canyon through which the river rushes, disappearing at our feet down a narrow corkscrew-like crevice in the rock, through which it hisses and boils, emerging below a mass of tortured water, to make the final leap. It is evidently this narrow tortuous channel which gives the fall its strange character, as the water gets jammed, and backs in this passage and dashes out in spurts and billows in a most eccentric fashion. A broad white beach surrounds the lakelet which receives the fall, and the view from this beach is very fine, the dark rocks towering high above the massive foliage, making a fitting setting to the sparkling water.

Leaving Waihaha, the next place that arrests attention is a high bluff, covered, from the water's edge to the summit, wherever they can find a footing, with magnificent birch trees, the only place on the lake where this tree is found. With its handsomely marked trunk and cedar-like foliage, it seems the very tree to suit the rugged scenery, and we can almost fancy we see the summit crowned with that 'craggy keep',

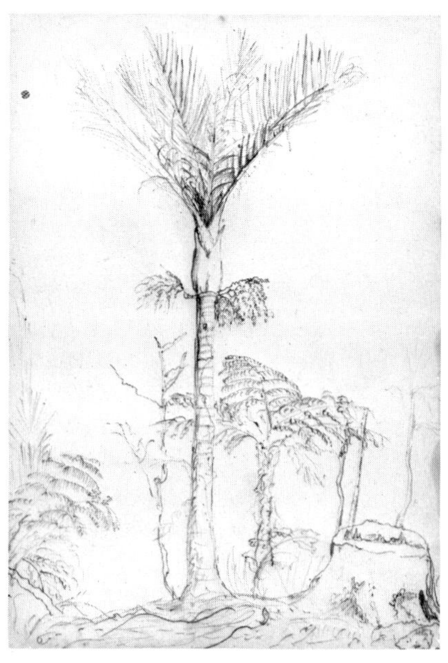

Which, like an eagle's nest,
Perched on a rock's basaltic crest,
And girdled with the shaggy pine,
That robes the rugged Apennine,
Seemed in its awful site and form,
A fitting cradle for the storm . . .

We pass this point with the feeling that it is a pity the birch does not extend all round the western bay, and soon find ourselves at another river, the Whanganui.

No signs of Maoris here, everything is in a state of nature, so we creep along the shore till we find the entrance of the river, and after passing over a shoal or two and running foul of a snag, we are fairly in and pulling up between wooded banks. The river is narrow and soon divides into two, so we take the largest branch, that to the right, and after a few turns, suddenly find ourselves right in front of another magnificent waterfall, which comes leaping down between high banks and massive foliage.

A narrow strip of sand borders the deep basin which receives the fall, and here we pitch our tent and make our home for four days. Such a quaint nook! Walled in all round by high hills. We could see the clouds passing over the sky, but could feel none of the wind — a sylvan retreat where one might hide away from the world's noise and care for months and never be disturbed, with only one means of egress, the creek; the boat the only connecting link with outside life.

This fall is very similar to the one at Waihaha, but there being less water it lacks that dash and hurry the other has. To make amends, however, it spreads out more gracefully, fanlike and symmetrical.

I said there was but one way of egress from this secluded dell, but when we had been there a day or two we found a narrow track, all

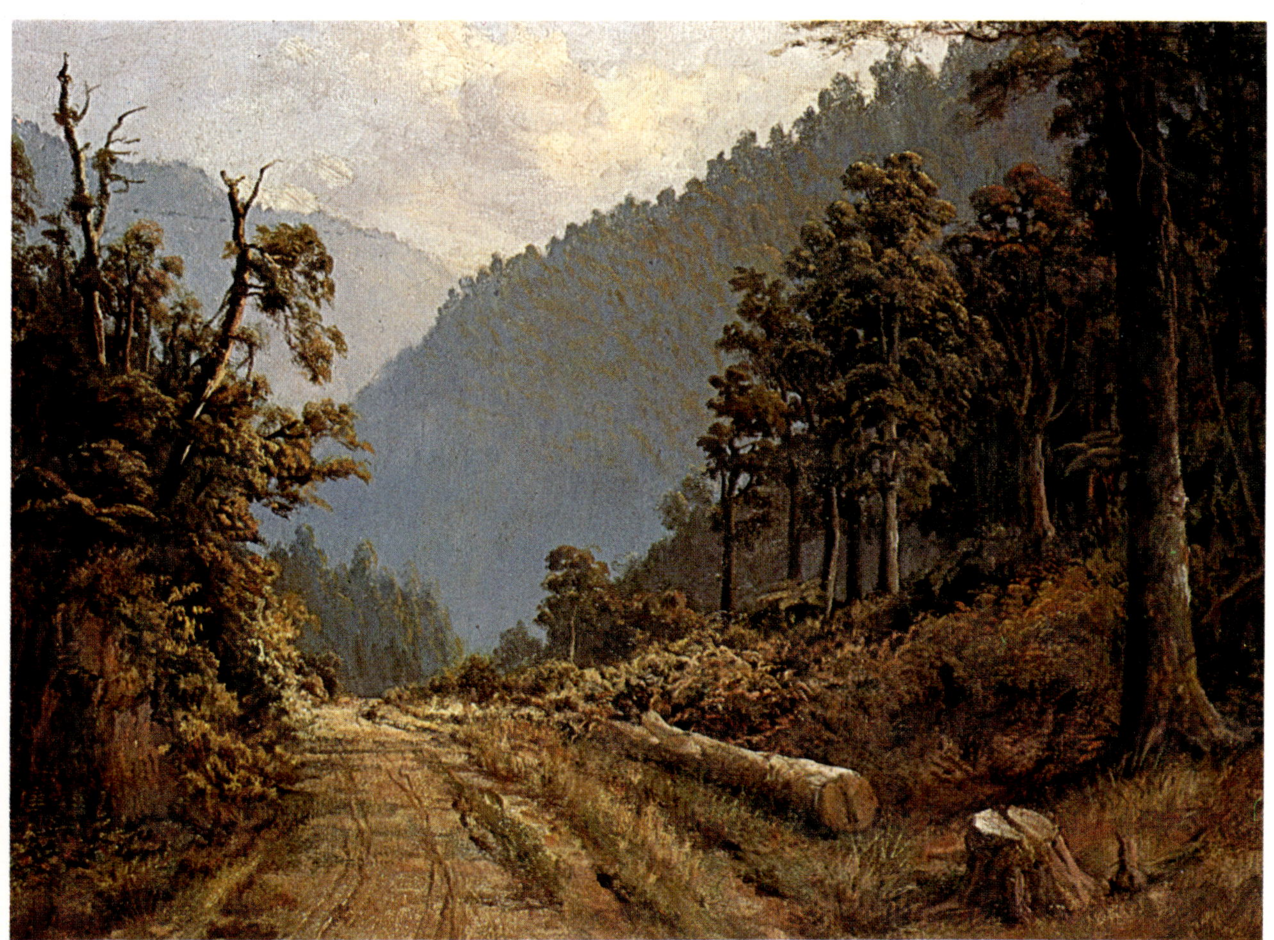

*King Country, undated. Oil
on canvas, 25 × 19 in.*

overgrown, which led to a pass up the cliffs. It was just possible to get up, and that was all. Steps had been cut in some places, and the remains of a flax rope hung down, which had evidently assisted in the ascent. The discovery of this track led to an amusing adventure, which might have been attended with very serious consequences, and which I will here relate, as illustrating what may occur to an artist in search of the picturesque.

We had a letter of introduction to the chief of these parts, and thinking this track might lead us to his whereabouts, we started one afternoon to explore. When up the steep rock, the track led through a bush gully, and on to the plains at the top. We followed it some four miles, till we came to a cultivation at the edge of the bush. Here we found some natives, but the chief we wanted was away. Being short of fresh meat, we bargained with them for a little pig to take back with us, and at length agreed to pay five shillings for one on condition that the Maori would kill and clean it. When you have to deal with Maoris you must never be in a hurry, and when the pig was caught, killed, and cleaned, it was getting late, so leaving the animal's head behind, we started off, one of us carrying the carcass on his back. We had not gone

115

more than half way when we took the wrong track, and while we were hunting about for the right one the sun went down and darkness began to gather. However, the moon was in her first quarter, so there was a little light. Up one hill and down another we tramped for an hour or more, vainly endeavouring to find the ravine we came up by, until we came to a place where in the darkness it seemed impossible to proceed further, as we were overlooking a deep chasm, and could just make out the tops of trees far below us, but could see no way of reaching them. Things now began to look serious, as we had neither food nor blankets and the nights were very cold, and to be stuck out all night on the side of a barren fern hill was anything but a cheering prospect. However, thinking this must be the gully we came up by, we determined at all hazards to find our way down into it, and so retraced our steps some distance, and at last found a place where the sides of the ravine were not quite straight up and down, and here we managed to scramble down, when to our great delight we found the right track at the bottom.

Now, we thought, our troubles are ended; we shall soon be at our camp; but the worst yet lay before us, for soon we were in the bush where the feeble moonlight could not penetrate, and where we had to grope our way more by instinct than by sight. At length we found our way out of this, and on the top of the cliffs, but in the dim and uncertain light, we could not find the pass down the rock.

In vain we searched every inch of ground, scrambling over great boulders, and forcing our way through high fern — now climbing higher up the hill, and now feeling carefully along the edge of abrupt precipices, we could not find the exact spot where we came up. Knowing well that to attempt to descend anywhere else would be foolishly risking our necks, we were reluctantly obliged to give up the thought of reaching our tent before morning. This was the more annoying as we were within cooee of it, and could hear the sound of the waterfall quite close by.

What was to be done? We could not stay where we were, for there was scarcely room to stand up, much less to lie down and spend the night, so we decided to try and regain the bush. This was a matter of no small difficulty, as the moon's faint beams, which had helped us a little hitherto, now disappeared behind the hill. However, feeling our way cautiously along, we had just reached the shelter of the trees when suddenly I heard a cry, apparently from the earth beneath me. It was from my companion, who was following me closely.

"I've fallen down a deep hole," he shouted. "But I'm all right"; and sure enough his foot had slipped or a stone had given way beneath him, and he had fallen down about twenty feet and landed on his head on some soft earth. He was afraid to move, not knowing how far it might be to the bottom. So striking a match, I reached down to him with a branch of a tree, and managed to fish him up from his precarious position.

This opened our eyes to the danger we were in, and we were very glad when we had gained a piece of level ground in the middle of the bush. We were both very tired and hungry by this time, so we lit a big fire, cut some steaks off the little pig, which my companion had stuck to bravely all the while, grilled them over the embers, and succeeded in taking off the keen edge of our appetites, and then lay down and tried to sleep. But as soon as we began to doze the cold crept round and woke us up again, so we resolved to keep up a roaring fire and watch for the morning.

When the first grey light of dawn was brightening the east, it took us a very few minutes to find what we had been searching some three hours for in the darkness, the path down the rock, and in half an hour we were safe at home. A sorry figure we cut that early Sunday morning as we came into camp, seedy and travel-stained, one of us with the mutilated pig, all begrimed with earth and broken fern, strapped upon his shoulders — the poor little pig that had cost us so dear.

From Whanganui it is but a few miles to the Karangahape Cliffs, and we had been looking forward to rounding this promontory as the most adventurous, as well as the most interesting part of our journey. For some eight or nine miles there is no landing place, the cliffs rising perpendicularly from the water, in some places to the height of 800 feet, exposed to the full fury of the north-east, north, and north-west winds. It is here the dreaded taniwha lives; the low island lying just off the highest part has a great rock at one end shaped like a whare. This is his house; from under here he rises when winds are piping and waves are dashing against the basaltic rocks, and woe to the ill-fated canoe that comes within his reach; neither it nor its occupants are ever seen again.

The Maori who gave us this information was evidently in earnest; his eyes flashed and voice trembled as he told the story; adding for our comfort that it was only the Maori who was afraid of him; he never came to hurt the Pakeha.

We had a head wind and nasty sea passing round this fearful place, but our boat was a good one, and an hour's hard pulling brought us round so far that the wind was in our favour. It certainly looks a giddy height, looking up from the water, with crowds of wild fowl wheeling about its beetling brow.

Passing these majestic towers which form the southern extremity of the western bay, the lake narrows, and the shore becomes less interesting, but the lake is redeemed from anything approaching the commonplace by the lofty mountains at its southern end. Tongariro is now lost to view, but rising with a grand sweep and graceful outline are Pihanga and Kakaramea, 4200 feet high, their sides clothed with dense forest, backed by the rugged Kaimanawa range, streaked with snow.

As we approach the head of the lake, numerous jets of steam issuing high up on the slopes of Kakaramea mark the position of the great landslip which buried Te Heu Heu and all his tribe; and just below, nestling among a luxuriant growth of English fruit trees and native shrubs, lies the lovely village of Waihi.

Here the scenery loses all its rugged wildness, and all nature seems

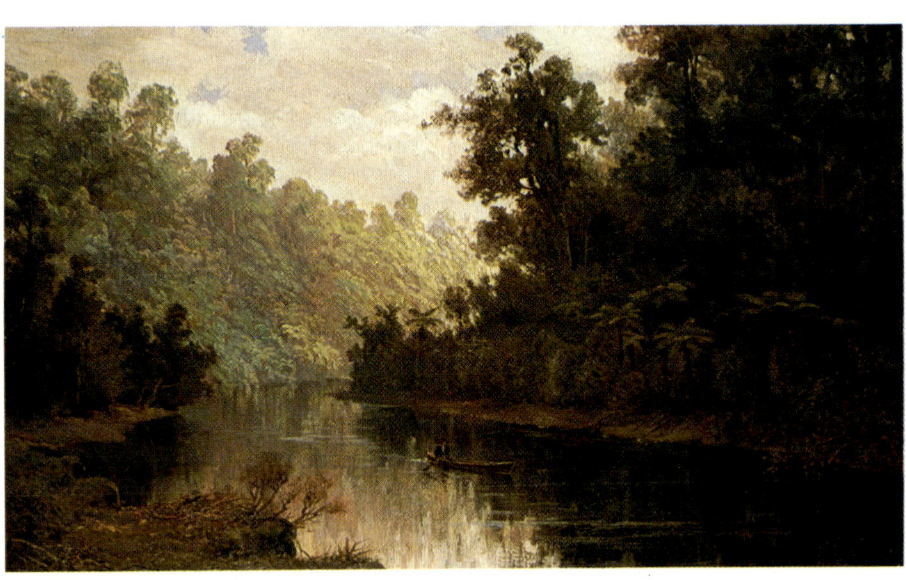

to smile. Sheltered from every cold wind, and open to the warm sunshine, the prolific soil brings forth in abundance; hot springs bubble out
all along the shore; cherry, peach, and gooseberry trees promise an
abundance of fruit; the ground is carpeted with strawberry plants, the
sweet briar and hawthorn blossom perfume the air, and the graceful
denizens of the soil move about and gather into picturesque groups as
they fetch water from the spring, or sit in happy leisure at the wharepuna
door to smoke or chat and pass the time away. What a lovely place for
a sanitarium! — where the healing waters, pure mountain air, and
delightful scenery would all conspire to restore nature's wasted energies.

Tokaanu is situated about two miles from Waihi, on a wide delta
formed by the Waikato river, which rising among the snows of Ruapehu
runs into Lake Taupo just here. It has once been a large and thriving
Maori pah and settlement, but all the whares and fortifications have
now disappeared except a carved post here and there and some half
dozen tumbledown huts. Large willows and yellow broom, cultivated
fields and weatherboard houses, give the place an English air. The most
interesting things here are the hot baths and geysers, which are well
worth a visit.

The eastern shore of the lake is comparatively flat, and void of
interest, but the island Motu Taiko, which lies near the eastern shore,
although it looks small and insignificant compared with the great
expanse of water, is in reality a gigantic column of lava six hundred feet
high, more than half under water, crowned with pohutukawa trees.
It is supposed to have been the core or neck of an immense crater, the
sides having been washed away by the water.

I have thus endeavoured to bring before your readers some of the
leading features of Lake Taupo. To those in search of health or pleasure
I can imagine nothing more enjoyable than a camping tour round the

118

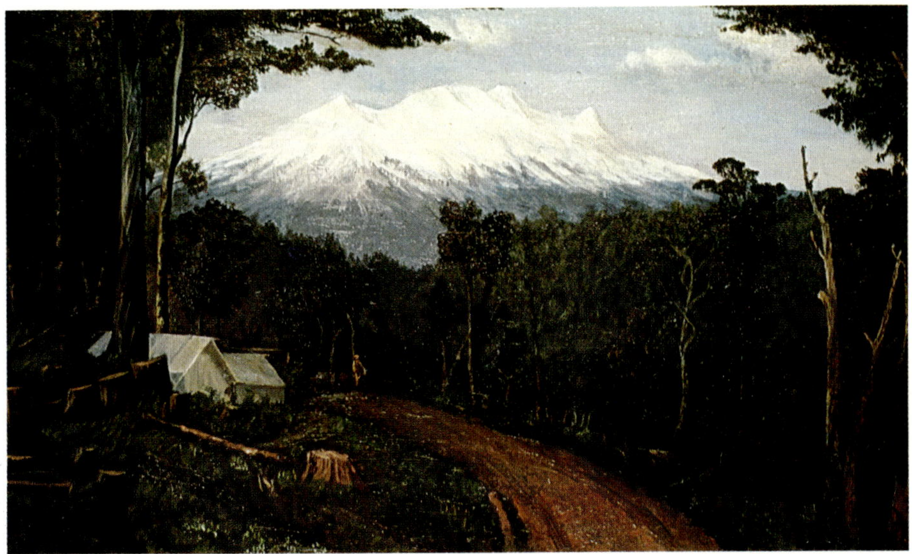

Mt Ruapehu, undated. Oil on card, 18 × 12 in.

western bay, especially during the summer months when the fruit is ripe. Cherries, grapes, strawberries, gooseberries, etc., abound. Wild fowl are very numerous, ducks seem literally to swarm on the rivers and quiet bays; pheasants, too, are plentiful, and the sportsman used never fear an empty larder. The air is dry and bracing, and the climate wonderfully healthy. Two steamers are now plying upon the lake, and at Tapuaeharuru, the visitor may obtain all he needs in the way of stores for the trip.

When Charles returned home, he exhibited his best painting in his studio, which by now was situated in Victoria Arcade, and received the following report in the local newspaper:

Our local artist, Mr Charles Blomfield, has just completed a fine painting of Lake Taupo from the Tapuaeharuru end. In the foreground the Waikato as it emerges from the lake reflects the glowing colours of the evening sky, while far away in the hazy distance, across the deep blue lake, the towering masses of Tongariro and Ruapehu are seen framed as it were by the dark trees on the river's banks. The sky is evidently a New Zealand one, perhaps we ought to say a Taupo one, for Taupo is famous for its gorgeous sunsets, and altogether the effect is a pleasing harmony of warm tones. The painting will well repay inspection, and may be seen by anyone calling at Mr Blomfield's studio, Victoria Arcade. We understand this picture is being engraved for the Picturesque Atlas of Australia.

Again, in 1888, he sent several of his pictures to the Art Exhibition and received the following commentary in the *Herald*:

Mr Blomfield sends ten oil paintings, five of them the result of his recent trip to Taupo and Tongariro. Although they do not arrest attention on account of their size, these pictures are well worthy of close inspection. Most of them, we understand, were painted on the spot direct from nature. While there are disadvantages and drawbacks to painting a finished picture out of doors, such a practice conduces, no doubt, to a faithful style.

The best of the Taupo ones to our mind is "The Waihaha River and Settlement", that represents a scene on one of the rivers running into the western bay of Lake Taupo, a part of the country rarely visited, but soon to be recognised as one of the most beautiful spots in the North Island. The river is gliding slowly past, reflecting the dripping foliage of the overhanging willows, which are just putting on their spring dress of delicate green; some Maori whares and figures give life to the scene.

"Lake Taupo from the Bridge" is a picture favourably noticed in these columns a short time ago. Another picture represents a Maori Runanga house, richly ornamented with those grotesque carvings now becoming so scarce. The background is boldly painted, showing heavy rainclouds hanging about the high mountains, bringing out by contrast the bright colouring of the whares in the foreground.

"The Whanganui Falls" and "Tongariro and Ruapehu" seen across the Lake from the inside of a cave, are both very characteristic of the scenery of the western shores of Lake Taupo.

Perhaps there is no place outside of Auckland better known than Waiwera and in two of Mr Blomfield's pictures everyone will recognise familiar scenes — the well-known form of the Bastion Rock, the *Rose Casey* landing her passengers, and the cart waiting to run them up upon the beach. And in the view from the rocks looking towards the Kawau we recognise the Little Barrier rising behind the Kawau and the Mahurangi Heads.

"Christmas Time at Takapuna Beach" is a fine study of a grand old pohutakawa tree in full bloom.

"A Moonlight Scene" is evidently a new departure for Mr Blomfield, a composition inspired by some lines in Cowper's *Task* —

> At eve
> The moonbeam, sliding softly in between
> The sleeping leaves

The subject chosen is a difficult one, a bush creek overhung with ferns and trees. The queen of night is rising; her pale face partly hidden by fern leaves and creepers; her bright beams reflected in the rushing waters below. The artist has avoided the common mistake in moonlight scenes in making everything black and white, for here we have the mellow radiance of real moonlight, and in the deep gloom of the distance a quantity of rich mysterious colour. The effect is charmingly poetical, and the painting may be regarded as Mr Blomfield's happiest effort at the present exhibition.

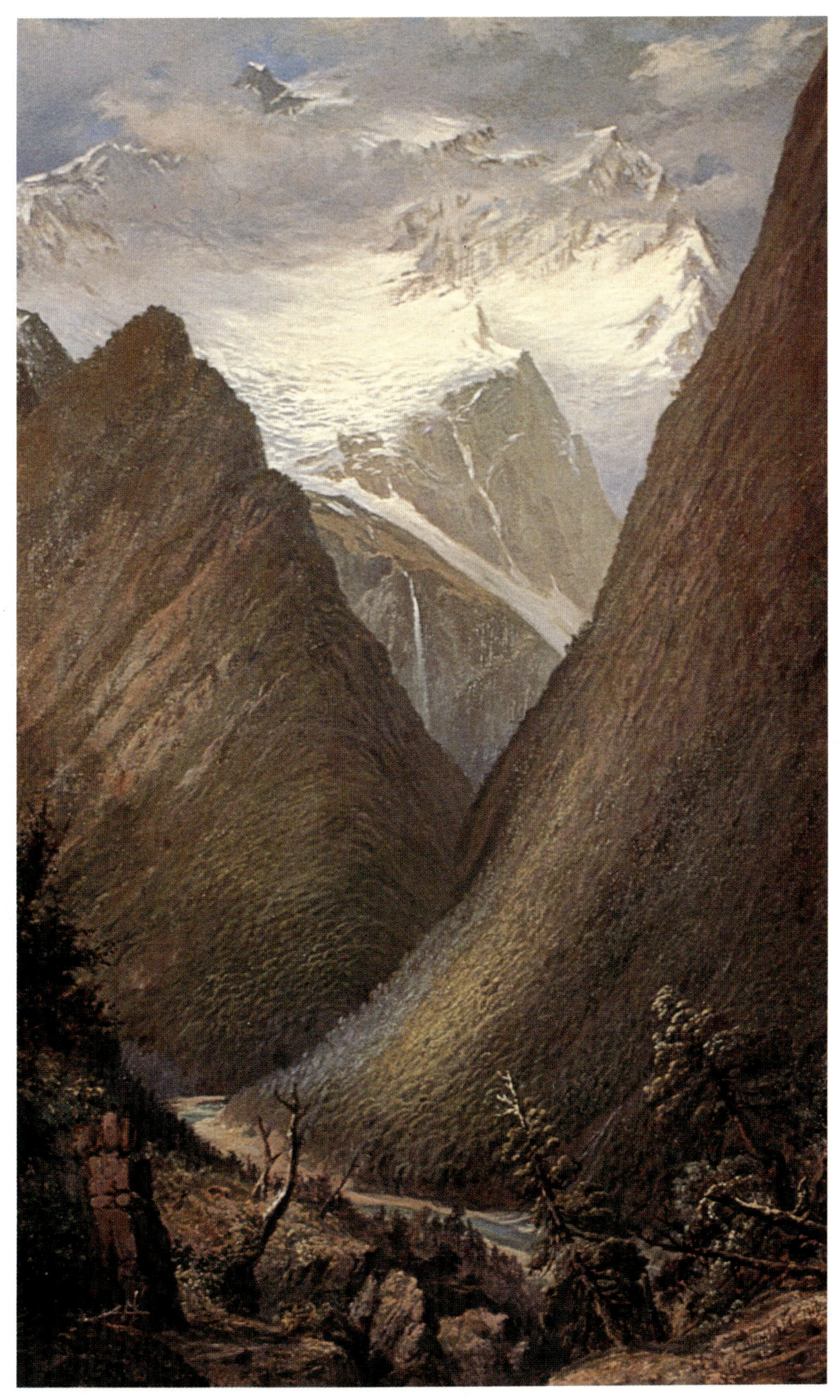

Mt Aspiring, 1912. Oil on canvas, 22 × 34 in. (Editor's note: this is more probably a view of Mt Avalanche.)

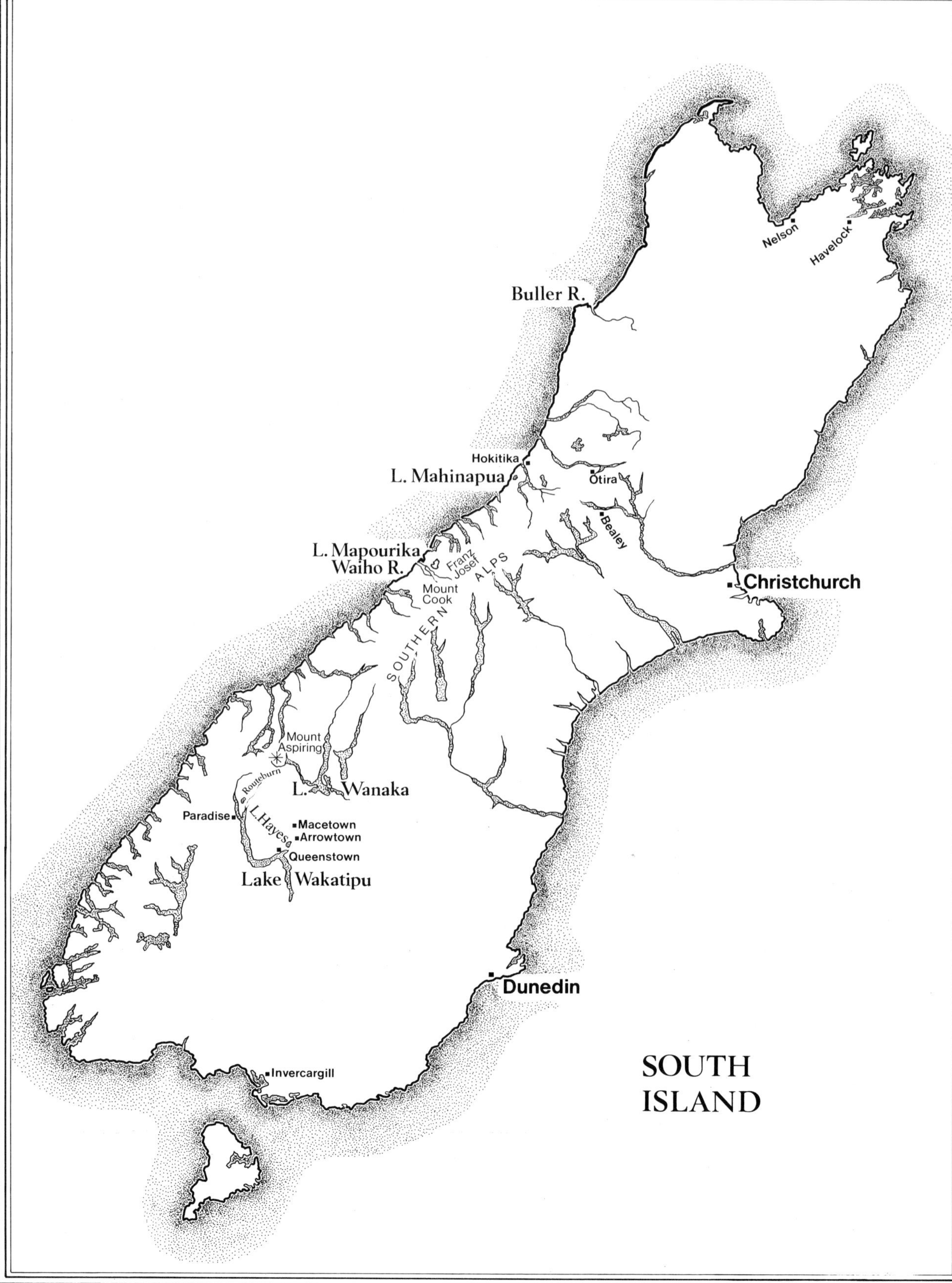

Nelson
Havelock
Buller R.
Hokitika
L. Mahinapua
Otira
Bealey
L. Mapourika
Waiho R.
Franz Josef
ALPS
Christchurch
Mount Cook
SOUTHERN
Mount Aspiring
Routeburn
L. Wanaka
Paradise
L. Hayes
Macetown
Arrowtown
Queenstown
Lake Wakatipu
Dunedin
Invercargill
SOUTH ISLAND

13. Impressions of Westland

During the next year, Charles stayed at home, working at his studio and painting and decorating more houses and shops. He had become expert at putting gold leaf lettering on shop windows, and received many orders for this type of work. Then, on November 26th, 1888, a second son was born to Charles and Ellen. He was a beautiful bonny boy — so different

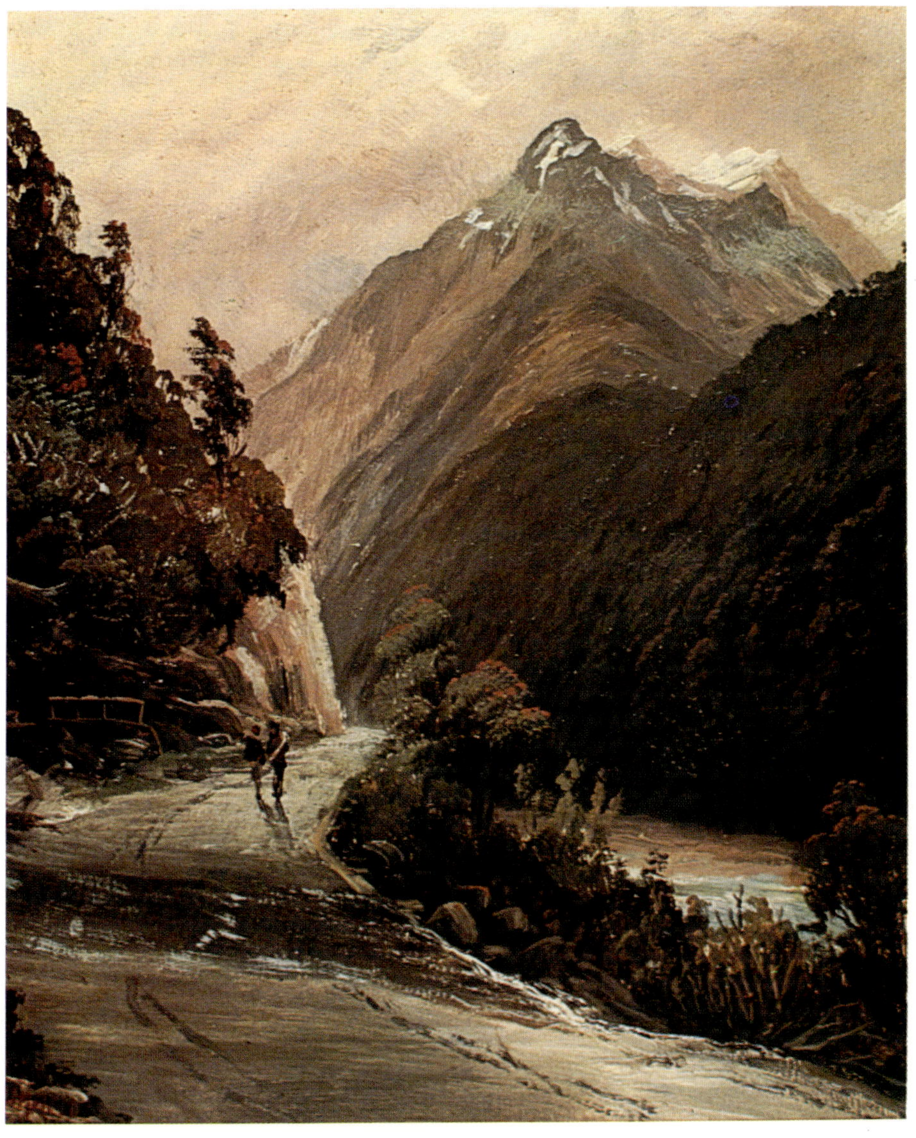

Otira Gorge, 1892. Oil on card, $11\frac{1}{2} \times 9\frac{1}{2}$ in.

from the ugly baby Tom had been two years earlier — and the family loved him on sight. They called him Charles Reginald, but he was always known as Reggie, and he brought great joy to his parents, sisters and older brother.

But despite Reggie's arrival, Charles was still restless and anxious to explore his beloved country. He could not forget a trip he had made some years before to the South Island, and wished to return to the beauty he had seen there. In particular, he wished to return to the lakes; he had described Wanaka and the Matukituki Valley as "one of the grandest sights . . . in the way of rugged gorges, high snowy peaks, grand waterfalls and fearful glaciers, that it is possible to conceive."

While Charles was considering retracing his tracks of 1884, his good friend Thomas Spurgeon was also planning a shift. He had never really settled in New Zealand, and wanted now to return to his native land, hoping to be called one day as pastor to his father's Metropolitan Tabernacle. Just before he left, Charles gave him a painting of the New Zealand bush. Tom was thrilled, and by way of saying thanks, wrote this poem to Charles:

O Charley Wag, O Charley Wag
You are quite too, too kind,
To favour me with such a view
In such a frame of mind.

No better gift could you devise
Howe'er you thought I'm sure
For you have kindly furnished me
With ferny furniture.

Nor could you find an apter scene
(At least I've not seen one)
To picture forth the natal day
Of C.H.S's son

His Temp'rance views are there portrayed
By stream and bit o' blue
The distance represents the home
From which this seagull flew

And in the foreground stands the fern
Of son — Tom's history
The pendant fronds his byegone years
The verdant ones the new

And lest I should be proud, to count
On many full-monthed years
Not all its foliage is seen
But only part appears.

Yet that which cuts it off I see
Is just a line of gold
Type of the bliss awaiting me
When life's short tale is told

The brook that says that your love flows on
In streams as fresh and free
The fern-tree leaves no doubt but that
Love's furnace glows for me

That picture, Charles, will be to me
A picture of yourself
Alas that I must hang you then
Or put you on the shelf.

Thanks, thanks, a thousand thanks dear friend
With kindness so imbued
Accept the best return I have
Your Pastor's gratitude.

Thomas Spurgeon.

Finally, by 1891, all arrangements were made for Charles to make two or three trips to the South Island, and thus try to cover as much of the scenery as possible. His first letter to Ellen came from the Otira Gorge, and described a meeting with the Dutch artist, Van der Velden.

I was told he was here taking pictures, and that he was one of the best artists in the world, so I wanted to see him, and yet I was rather shy of meeting such a great man. The day I camped here I heard that he was coming to see me the next day. That was Sunday. So about eleven o'clock two gentlemen came along, one carrying a large sketching box, and the other a box of colours. The elder of the two was Mr Van der Velden. He came into the tent and lay down on the stretcher, and seemed to enjoy it immensely. He can only speak a little English. He has been living in Christchurch some months, and has some large pictures there on exhibition.

He was going up the river a little above my tent to paint a picture of a waterfall, so after a bit I went to see how he was getting on. He has a very strange style of painting — all broad touches, and when you look close in there is nothing but careless drawing, but give it the right distance and the effect is very fine. So he asked us down to see his studies. . . . We saw all his pictures and some of them were very good, and then we stayed and had tea with him. He is a jolly old fellow with such a pleasant laugh, and very clever, but of course not one of the best artists in the world. . . . His wife does all her own work, so that shows he can't be very famous.

Like Charles, Van der Velden considered New Zealand an ideal place for artists to visit, being new and as yet unspoiled.

"He finds so much to paint here," Charles wrote, "that life is too short to paint it all. It will soon be, as I have often said, we will have artists coming from all parts of the world to paint and the local artists will have no show at all."

Charles's letter from the Otira Gorge continued:
Sunday night. I have had a pretty fine day but cold. I went down to the bottom of the gorge this afternoon to get a little sunning. It is warmer there, past the hotel. The photographer was there from the Bealey. He showed me a proof of me and my camp which he took at the Bealey. It comes out well. He is going to give me one of it. I saw down there also, two gentlemen from Christchurch who are going through and camping, having their own horses and trap. One of them is a maker of electric appliances for curing diseases, and he can supply a machine and all etceteras for £3.10.0. I should like to have one, if we could afford it. Perhaps I could exchange a picture for one.

Now goodnight dear. May the angel of God be round you all this night to watch and guard from all harm. May God himself send down his richest love and blessing on my dear loves for his blessing maketh thee rich and he addeth no sorrow to it."

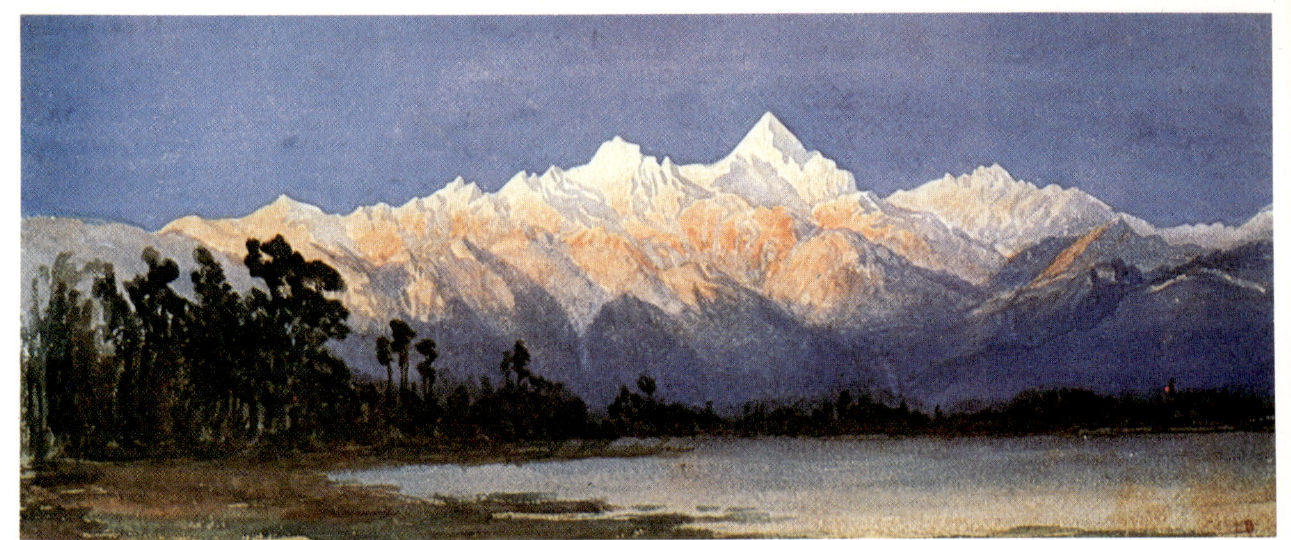

From the Otira Gorge, Charles Blomfield travelled to Hokitika, and from there set out to visit Mt Cook, hoping to capture on canvas some of the views that he had seen in photographs of the grand Mt Cook scenery. Once again he wrote an account for the newspaper:

Not much is known about the coast of Westland. It is rather out of the way; the difficulties and dangers of travelling are too great for the ordinary tourist to include it in his pleasure trip. And yet it is a land of great and varied beauty; a land of mountains crowned with snow and glacier; a land of magnificent forests, dizzy precipices and rocky gorges, gemlike lakes, rushing torrents, and broad lagoons. A land of gold too.

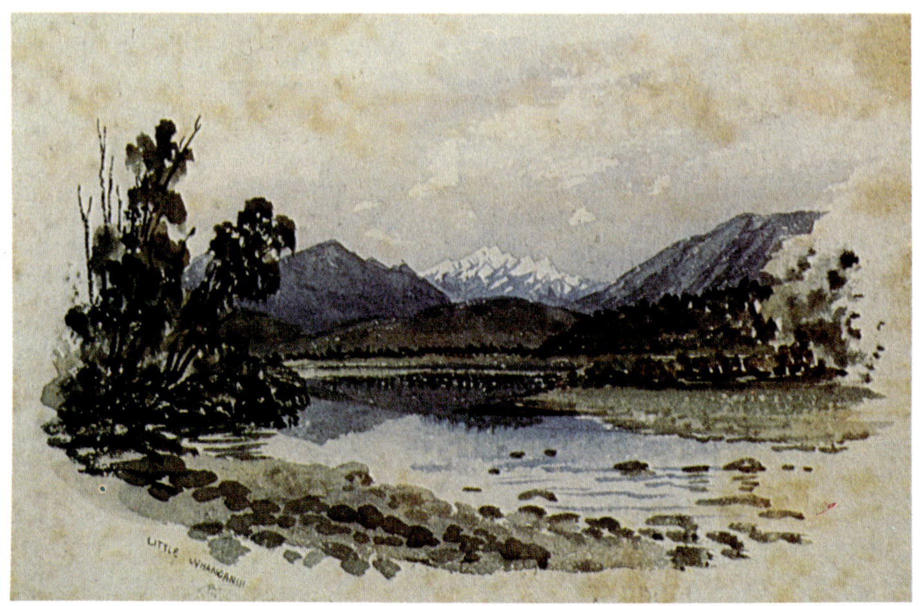

Its ocean beaches were once the scene of busy industry, but long since deserted, save for a few old diggers who still fossick a bare living from the ocean sand.

One of the busiest places in the old mining days was Okarito, near Mount Cook, a long sandy beach backed by an extensive lagoon. These lagoons are peculiar to the district. A warm ocean current washes the western shore of the South Island, bringing with it a warm moisture-laden air; this is chilled by the ice-covered peaks and causes an enormous rainfall; as much as twelve feet in a year sometimes, and the flooded rivers bring down a vast amount of water to the sea. In many places the westerly gales block up the outlets of these rivers with sand, the waters gather behind, cover the low-lying land, and form shallow lakes, some of considerable extent.

The Okarito lagoon is ten miles long. The water gradually rises until the pressure overcomes the resistance, when it forces a passage through the sand, and the accumulated waters rush out for days or weeks, until another gale piles up the sand and again blocks the entrance. Woe to the horseman who tries to ford the stream just after one of these outbreaks. Many a man has been washed out to sea in the attempt. There is always a large sheet of water behind.

The dense forest crowds to the edge of this, forming a belt of dark verdure between the shining waters and the huge mountains beyond, while on the ocean side the forest straggles out, individual pines and rimus standing out singly, close to the beach, taking on the most grotesque shapes and vivid colours. Torn and twisted, they stand silent witnesses to the fury of the western storms.

The scenery of this coast is very fine. The lofty snow peaks of Cook and Tasman, and a hundred lesser giants, rise boldly from the dark forest which clothes their scarred shoulders right up to the snow line. The sombre green, broken here and there by the dazzling white of a giant glacier, which, like a foaming torrent, fills the deep ravines. The placid waters, mirror-like, repeat again mountain, bush, and sky. The reflections, broken perhaps by the flapping wings of a black swan, or it may be reflecting the graceful image of a tall white heron, motionless as the rock it stands on. And here in the foreground, just where an artist would place them, the picture is completed by a group of stately pines.

When I made my acquaintance with these parts, the only means of communication was by a narrow horse track. Travellers had to ford the rivers or cross in a boat, while the horses swam. The mailman provided me with a horse and a packhorse for my camping gear. We travelled down the coast, now along a sandy beach, now over rocks and stones, now climbing across a jutting point, or racing round a headland to escape the rising tide. Our speed was limited to the gait of the packhorse, something between a walk and a trot, and gave us plenty of time to admire the scenery, but was rather tedious going.

We reached Okarito one day about noon, and I at once set about finding a suitable place for a studio. This was to be my headquarters for some weeks. The township which once extended for a mile along the beach, was reduced to half a dozen dilapidated houses clustering round the landing place, for Okarito boasts a small harbour and jetty. Seeing a cobbler at work in a little shop, I asked him if he knew of any place I could rent.

"Yes," he said, "I can show you the very place. Come with me."

So I followed him beyond some tall trees, and there was a two-storey house, empty and out of repair.

"This," he said, "is where the minister lived."

"What is the rent of it?" I asked him.

"Half a crown a week," he replied.

So I soon completed the bargain.

I had just settled down after tea when a knock came at the door. On opening it, there stood a group of children of all ages from four to fourteen — all the children in the place, I believe.

"If you please, may we see your pictures?" they said.

So I had them in and showed them what few sketches I had already taken. It was pathetic to witness the delight of those poor children. It was evidently quite an event in their monotonous lives.

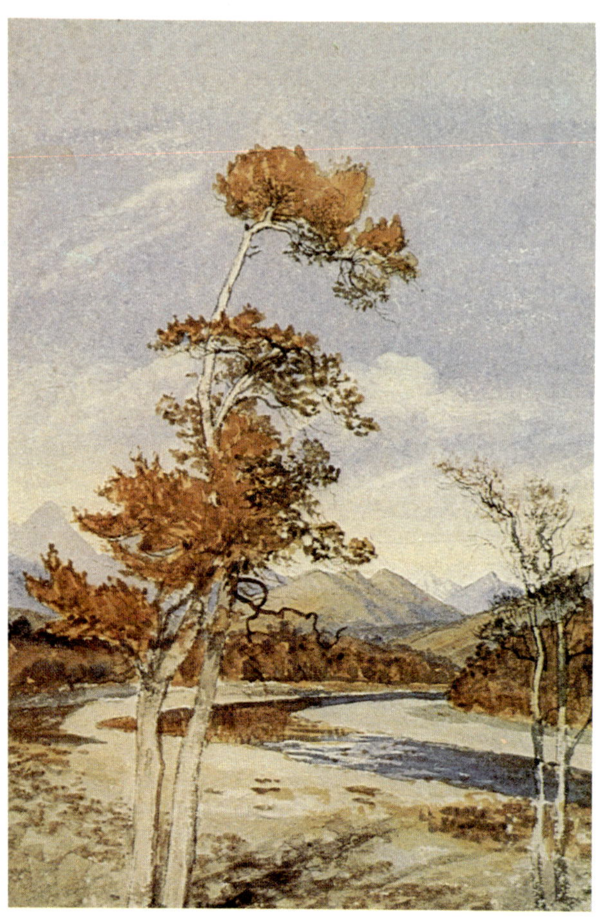

South Island river, Rakaia, undated. Watercolour, 8 × 11 in.

The whole population for miles around was dependent for their supplies on a small steamer which came down from Hokitika every three months. They were then out of flour, and were awaiting the advent of the supply boat anxiously. I happened to be there when she came in. When I came outside in the morning, it was evident something unusual was happening. The whole village was down on the beach dressed in their Sunday best, the children had a holiday from school, and when it was reported the steamer was in sight they were all excitement. The state of the weather, the tide, and other conditions had to be favourable or she could not enter. Now we saw her lying two miles off waiting for the tide. An old man'o'warsman, dressed for the occasion — he was the harbour master — mounted a small hill and signalled the boat from a rude flagstaff. Now she begins to move. The crowd on the beach watched with breathless interest. Would she make it, or must they starve until a more favourable opportunity? Now she is near the bar; the pilot, all excitement, guides her safely over, and people begin to breathe freely as she enters the little basin; but, alas, it was not to be — as she nears the last turning, she grounded on a sandbank. Frantic efforts are made to get her off; kedges are run out and a rope brought ashore and manned by all the men, women, and children in the place; but the rope suddenly parted in the centre and sent the crowd head over heels in the sand. It was no use, the boat remaining immovable, and they had to wait till low tide and unload the cargo into drays.

One of the finest scenes of the district is the great Franz Josef Glacier. It alone is worth travelling any distance to see. As viewed from the coast, it presents the appearance of a torrent of sparkling foam, filling up a wide ravine, its whiteness enhanced by the contrast of the dark green of the surrounding bush. On a nearer view the torrent is seen to consist of glacier ice, crushed and torn into a thousand peaks and spires, its interstices gleaming a lovely turquoise hue. But it is when the visitor gets right up to its terminal face that he realises the stupendous character of this frozen river. The mind is overawed in gazing up at high cliffs and precipices of solid ice, spires and monuments of a hundred strange shapes, dark blue caverns leading to unknown depths below, while beyond, hemmed in by rocky walls, are miles and miles of ice, mounting higher and higher till at the elevation of two miles above the sea, its starting point is seen among the eternal snows of the Southern Alps.

When we consider that Westland consists of a narrow strip of land between the mountains and the sea, often not more than twelve miles wide, it is remarkable what a wealth of romantic and picturesque scenery it contains. The endless succession of icy peaks, dazzling snow fields, and giant glaciers, the numerous rivers wandering over wide shingle beds, or rushing through rocky gorges; the ever-present bush, clothing mountains, hills and plain in living green; the glorious ocean beaches and bold headlands, are surely enough to make the place unique, but bountiful nature not only endows the spot with these, but throws in a half-dozen lakes of singular beauty.

If I were asked to name the most beautiful lake in Westland, I should

unhesitatingly give the palm to the Kaniere Lake, near Hokitika. It has
not the breadth of Lake Brunner, nor the stately splendour of Mapourika,
but it has an enchanting beauty all its own. Its charm, I think, is partly
due to its setting. Lying some twelve miles from the coast, it nestles
directly under lofty mountains, well away from the haunts of man, and
its forest fringes still retains its primeval grandeur. Its charm is also due
to the noble forms of the high peaks, which sentinel round it. Cairn
Peak is especially beautiful and worthy to take its place with Mitre
Peak, in Milford Sound, and Walter Peak, at Lake Wakatipu, for
beauty of outline.

• The surveyors had a terrible time triangulating this country. They
tell thrilling tales of hardship and adventure. One of the trig stations
was on Cairn Peak, hence its name. Everything; food, camping gear,
and instruments, had to be carried up the steep mountain side on the
men's backs. When they ran short of food, one of the men would be
sent back for a bag of flour. Sometimes he would be stuck up for days
between two flooded rivers, and the flour would be half-eaten before
he reached his party. They had nearly finished their work and were
anxious to get away as food was short, when it came on to blow a gale,
and the wind made the instruments unsteady. They had already built
a cairn of stones for shelter, and now they added to it and built right
round the instrument, leaving only one little peep hole. Still the
theodolite quivered. At last they were forced to the conclusion that the
mountain peak itself was moving with the wind.

In my visit to this lake, I met with a curious adventure, illustrating
as it does the varied experiences encountered by an artist in search of
the picturesque. Hearing there was a hut at the lake, I packed some
food and my blankets on my back and walked there. The road, which
is fairly good, ends at the lake, the last few miles being cut through
dense bush. Reaching the place in the afternoon, I found the hut, but
the walls had been used to keep the fire going. I set to work fixing things
up and gathered a stock of firewood, and just about dusk went to start
the fire and cook my tea, but judge at my consternation! I had no
matches. I searched my pockets in vain; for the first and only time, I
had forgotten the matches. I could not cook without a fire, and as it
was late in the autumn, the nights were frosty.

I was at my wits' end, when suddenly I remembered passing a little
digger's hut about four miles back. I retraced my steps, and after an
hour's hard walking, came to the place, only to find it all in darkness,
the man was out! It opened to my touch, and feeling inside the first
thing my fingers came in contact with was a box of matches. The man
had left them handy just inside the door. Helping myself to a few, I was
soon back at the hut, where a good supper and a cheerful fire quickly
banished fatigue and hunger.

The next morning, finding an old canoe, I paddled out on the lake,
and just round a point came across an example of the devastating forces
of Nature. An immense landslip had fallen from the side of a mountain
a mile away, leaving an ugly scar. From high up it had started, and

coming down had cleared a broad roadway through the bush right into the lake, carrying everything before it except a clump of large pines, which were left like an island in a river of debris.

I have very pleasant memories of the Mahinapua Lake. I camped there three weeks in a snug little shooting ranch, kindly lent me by some Hokitika residents. They were great canoeists, and came out on Saturdays for the week-end in their canoes, and kept me supplied with game. I had kaka stew, pigeon and roast swan. The latter does not make a bad table bird, but it takes a terrible lot of stuffing. The lake is reached by the lovely Mahinapua Creek, which drains the lake and enters the Hokitika River close to the sea. It has not the scenic magnificence of the other lakes, the mountains being more distant, but it has a sylvan beauty which is very fascinating. Tall pines and rimus grow close to the water's edge, sometimes right in the water. Trailing creepers hang from projecting limbs, bright with white clematis, or the scarlet rata blossom. Pushing the boat through these, you find yourself in a veritable fairy bower, a Naiad's cave, the softened sunlight tinted by the greenery.

One characteristic of this region in the autumn months is a calm atmosphere. Day after day the air is absolutely motionless, the reflections perfect; every twig and leaf has its replica below, and it is a weird experience at night to watch the moon rise over the distant bush. Every star is imaged in the dark water, and as the moon rises, two moons appear, which gradually separate, further and further apart, until one is overhead and the other seemingly at an infinite distance below.

Southern Alps, undated. Oil on card, 14 × 9 in.

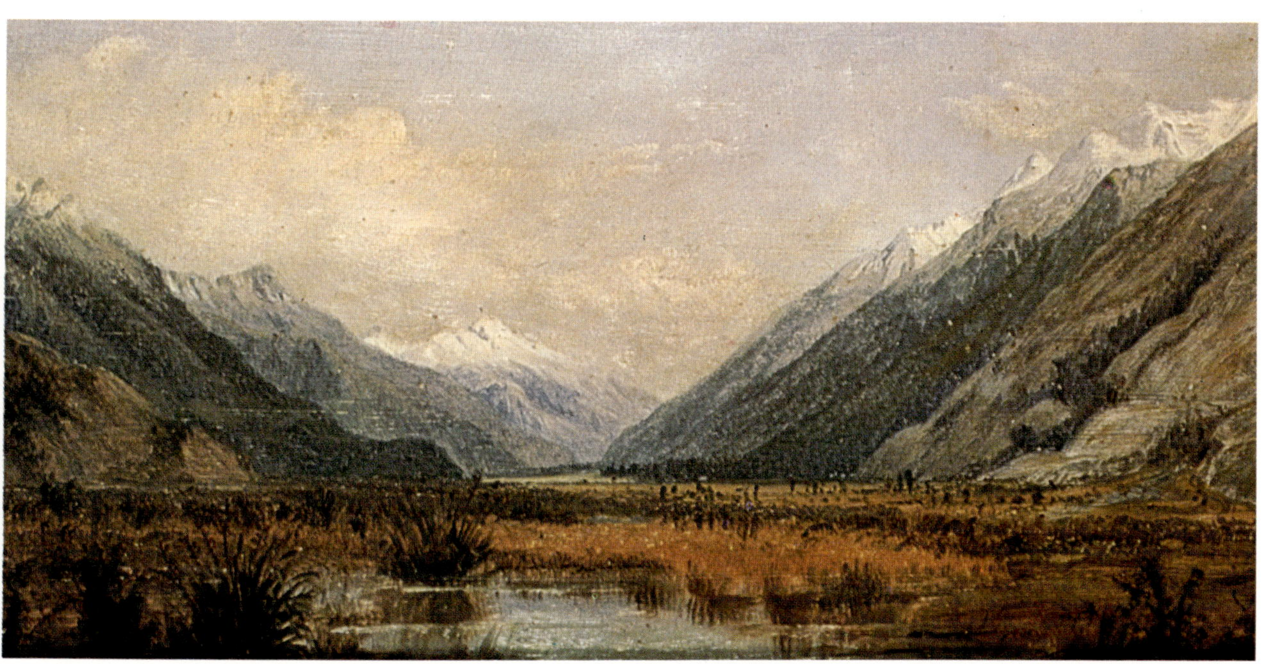

The Mapourika Lake is approached from Okarito. It is larger than the Kaniere Lake, but the mountains do not take so fine a form. But what they lack in beauty they make up in height and grandeur. The loftiest mountains in the alpine chain look down upon this lake, Mounts Cook, Tasman, De La Beeche, and a dozen other giants, the famous Franz Josef glacier filling a wide gorge in the centre. It is a lake of many moods.

There is a solemn grace when the clouds are partly veiling the mountain tops and casting dark shadows on the silent waters. Every sunrise has its glory. Every sunset its special display. But now and then, perhaps after a day of storm and gloom, the sun, as though to atone for the sombre day, will break through the clouds and light up the scene with an unearthly radiance. The torn shreds of cloud will be turned to gold and amber. The craggy heights glow with crimson fire, while the snowfield, blushing with the tenderest rose, seems too ethereal for this common world. I don't know how others are affected by these sights, but when I gaze on a scene like this, and watch the mysterious shades go green gradually up the mountain side until the evanescent pageant fades away, my mind is filled with an unutterable longing, the soul seems to yearn for something it knows not what, and with the exquisite delight, is mingled a shade of darkness.

14. The Southern Lakes

Charles returned home in 1891, but October of the same year found him travelling again, this time in Nelson and Blenheim. On this second trip he took his second daughter, Nellie, with him. He was to be grateful for her company, for he soon became ill with what he diagnosed as "acute rheumatism of the bowels".

I awoke with a nasty pain in my right side and had to get up, and before six I was in great agony and started applying hot flannels to my side and bowels. Little Nellie got up and did what she could for me, but the intense pains lasted till nearly two, and then I got much better, and on Monday we came into Havelock, and in here on Tuesday we got this cottage and got fixed up a bit. Wednesday morning the pains returned and were very bad till about ten, but I was able to work a little in the afternoon and went out to the town after that, but Thursday it started again, and that was the worst from early Thursday morning till two or three on Friday; I had no relief. The pains were so bad that I could not stand, if I wanted to move I had to shuffle along in a stooping posture, trembling like a leaf. All night I could not lie down properly and only slept for a little while at the time, and then had to make for the fire and get some fresh hot flannels. All the time I was in such pain nothing passed my lips but hot water and the juice of two lemons, and you can guess how tired and helpless I got.

I was on the point of wiring for you to come down several times, and should have sent for a doctor if it had lasted much longer.

I did not like to tell you about it before as I know it would make you uneasy, but I thought now I ought to tell you. Dear little Nellie, I don't know what I could have done without her I am sure, she was so brave. Some children would have been so frightened, and she has helped me so much you can't tell, and you should have heard how sweetly she prayed for me that Jesus would take the pain away and make me well again.

Yet there has been mercy mixed even with the affliction, for if it had come on the Monday instead of Sunday, how ever should we have got to Havelock, and then it kept off until we were safely fixed up in this comfortable little cottage, where we can keep a good fire and have the water laid on and everything handy. I feel much better today, but oh so weak. I went for a little walk this afternoon and it seemed so strange to have to walk so slowly and feebly.

Tomorrow is Sunday, so I hope to be better and able to work by Monday. I have bought a new body bandage today, and some cayenne pepper and mustard. I don't think the doctors could do me much good, do you?

I hope and pray I may be able to get home before I get bad again.
I don't like leaving here without giving it a trial and selling something.
If I had only known the pictures would have sold at Wellington, I
would have come right home from Nelson, but I acted for the best as I
thought. Now good-night dear for the present, God bless you xxxxxx

Blenheim, October 14th, 1891.

Dearest Wife,

You will be anxious to hear how I am getting on. I am very much
better and have had no return of the attack, and am getting strong
again slowly. I have been wearing the bandage night and day. At night
I dip it in weak hot mustard water and take half a spoonful of cayenne
pepper in hot water.

Yesterday we were driven out to Mr Rose's place, Mrs Hooper going
too. They have a large family and a nice large farm house. They were
not all at home, so we are going again on Saturday evening when the
others will be home, and are to have a musical evening. We came home
early in the evening.

Today there was to be a garden party at one of the leading Wesleyans'
houses. We were going, but it came on wet just at this time, so I did not
venture. I hope they did not suffer much, the money was in aid of the
church. It has cleared up beautifully now. There was to be a concert
tonight.

I have taken a large empty shop and am to have my show on Friday
and Saturday, and hope to get away next week if possible.

Nellie is very well, but will be glad to get home again, I am sure.
I think you will see a difference in her for the better.

I have been able to do some work today. The last week has seemed
like lost time to me, but then I could not work when I was so bad,
could I? I feel very thankful I am so much better.

This is such a queer little place. There are some nice shops in it,
large drapers with good windows, but no nice paint shops like there are
in Nelson, or Westport, or even Hokitika, and no place where you can
buy vegetables. I have not seen a cabbage or turnip, or anything like
that all over the town. Certainly nearly everybody here has a nice
garden, but it is a wonder no-one wants to sell them. I should like some
celery, but it seems impossible to get it. I have been having lemons, and
they seem to do me good.

Now Ellen dear, goodbye once more. May God bless you and me
and bring us once more together again, with much love from yours ever,

Charliexxxxxxx

The local newspapers described his exhibitions:
Mr Charles Blomfield, a well known artist of Auckland, is at present
in Nelson, having just returned from an artistic tour on the West Coast
and the neighbourhood of Mount Cook. He has with him a large
number of sketches and pictures in oils, of remarkable merit. His colour
is excellent, and the finish of his outdoor work deserves very high praise.

In addition, he has the special faculty of representing New Zealand foliage truthfully. There are so many pictures that it is impossible to give a detailed criticism, but several hours could be exceedingly pleasantly spent by lovers of art in examining them. Mr Blomfield proposes to give the public an opportunity of seeing his work, and we can confidently recommend all who are fond of pictures not to miss the opportunity.

Mr Charles Blomfield, of Auckland, an artist of colonial reputation, who has now painted the scenery of most portions of the North and South Islands, is at present in Blenheim, after having camped for a month in the Pelorus district, taking sketches of the beautiful scenery to be found there. He has been nine months touring the Nelson and Westland districts, camping on the Buller river, Christchurch overland road, the Southern lakes, and the West Coast as far down as Mount Cook. At present Mr Blomfield is laid up with rheumatics, but he hopes in a short time to be able to get about, and hold an exhibition of his large collection of new studies in Blenheim. From a personal inspection of his work elsewhere, we can assert without fear of contradiction that Mr Blomfield's views are about the best oil paintings of New Zealand scenery to be found, and are well worth the prices asked for them.

"Franz Josef Glacier from the Waiho River" by Mr C. Blomfield, gives us an admirable idea of the grandeur of the Alpine scenery in the Middle Island. When Lord Onslow, a few weeks since, was travelling down the West Coast, he was very much struck with the grandeur of the scenery as he neared Mount Cook, and especially the great Franz Josef glacier, a sight in his estimation quite unique, and likely when better known to attract thousands of visitors to this colony. It is a view of this glacier, taken from the Waiho River, which Mr Blomfield has made the subject for his brush. The view is good and well selected, and a choice illustration of Alpine scenery. Sir William Fox, in one of his sketching tours years ago, also chose the same locality for his pencil. Mr Blomfield has succeeded admirably in giving us a good idea of the wild rugged grandeur of the scene. The foreground is powerfully treated, though some of the boulders on the right are peculiar looking; but the torrent flowing from the melted snow of the glacier, rushing over and around the boulders is a very fine piece of work, the transparency of the water and its life and motion being very realistic. The foliage on the margin of the gorge on either side is well put in, and carefully treated. The greatest attention has been paid to illustrating the majesty of the towering peaks on the right of the gorge, about which the rain clouds and mists are hovering, and which give a sense of loneliness which is oppressive. The highest peak is excellently treated with the exception perhaps of a slight hardness on the inner point of the mountain. As to the glacier itself, rent and crushed into a thousand peaks and crevasses, it gleams white beyond the dark foliage of the middle distance, and is remarkably realistic. The perspective is good and gives the requisite impression of distance and depth. The sky is well painted and Mr Blomfield has rarely been more happy in this respect than in the present picture. He has made the Southern Alpine scenery almost as much a specialty as he formerly made the Hot Lakes scenery. Those who have not seen the Southern Alps would do well to inspect the picture, and others of his in the exhibition, as giving an excellent conception of the grand and beautiful works of Nature almost at our doors.

At last, in 1893, Charles managed to reach the Southern Lakes again, and as usual, kept in touch with Ellen:

Arrowtown, January 28th, Saturday

Dearest Ellen,

I got your last letter today and I think it must be the last, but I think I must have missed one for you speak of Mrs Haszard's accident and tell me nothing about it, as though you had told me about it before.

I am glad you got the money all right. I only wish it was more. I sent another £5 last week — did you get that? Don't forget to let me have word each time you get any money, so I may know if it is all right. I know you must want it badly and only wish I could get more to send you, but I am sending it as fast as I get it, only keeping enough by me to let me get back from here if I get no more — in fact I have hardly kept enough by me as I don't know how I may get on. I think I shall be able to send you another £5 next week, as I have got an order for a picture for that Mr Baird. Do you remember last time I was down here an old gentleman who has a most beautiful place at Lake Hayes asking me in and giving me a lodging for some paintings? Well, he lives between the Arrow and Queenstown, nearer here than there, and yesterday I took the whole day and went over to Lake Hayes and got two pictures and then about twelve o'clock I went up to see the old fellow and of course he asked me to stay to dinner and I showed him the pictures I had done, and he took a great fancy to one of them and after a bit of talk and showing me all round his place, he agreed to buy it for £2.2.0 and afterwards asked what a painting of his house would cost. I offered to do it for £10.10.0., but he said it was too much, he did not care to spend all that on it, and at last we agreed that he should have the sketch and a picture of his house framed for £8.8.0. It is too little, but I was so glad to get it, for I have a frame the size I want to get rid of, as it is rather too heavy for carrying about.

So after I have finished with my pupils here, I am to go to his place and stay there two or three days and paint the place. In the evening I got another sketch from his garden and he liked that so much he took that instead of the first one.

He has a beautiful place, and no mistake — the air is all perfumed with the scent of flowers, the verandah overgrown with creepers and honeysuckle and such a large orchard — a nicely furnished house and

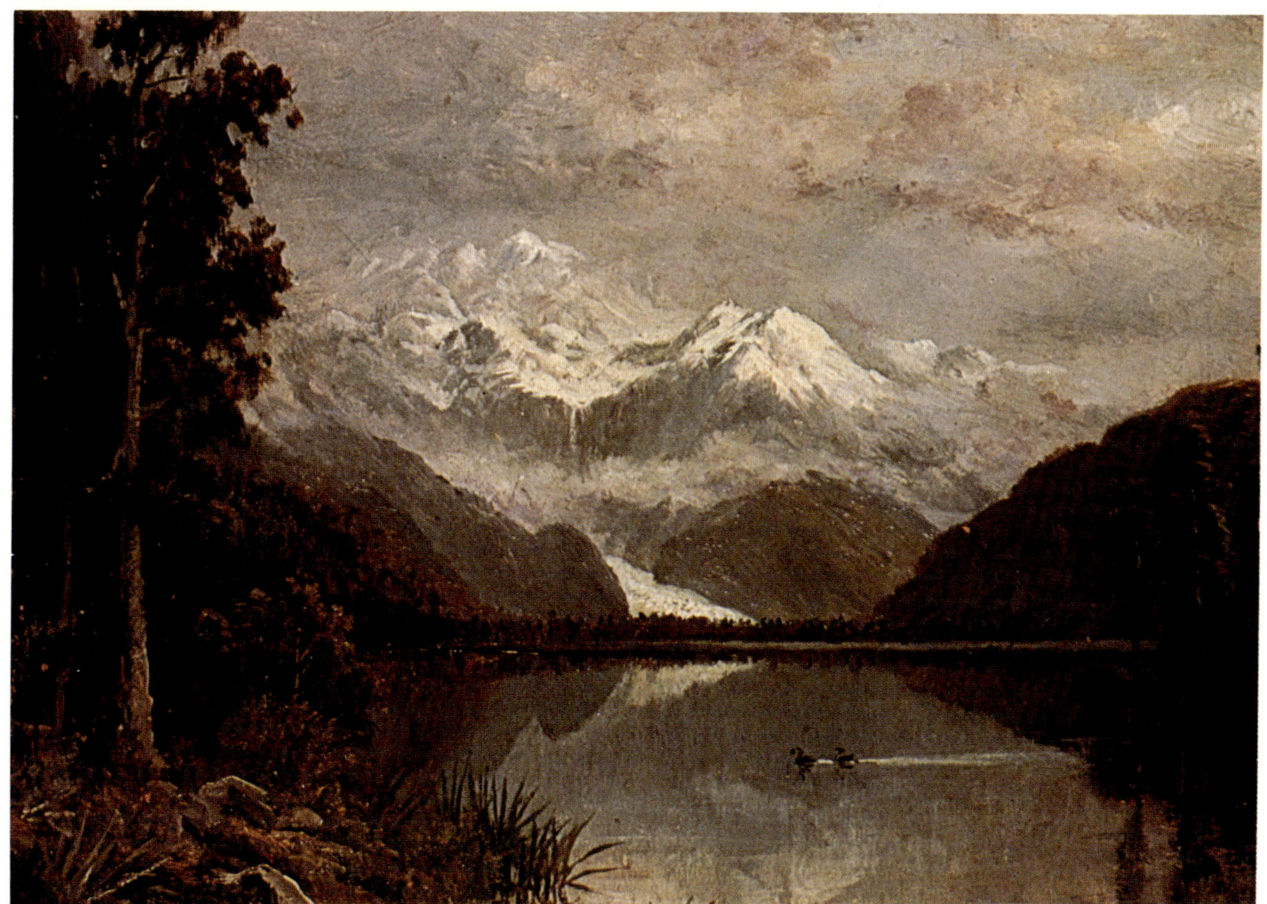

Franz Josef Glacier from Lake Mapourika, 1892. Oil on card, 15 × 11 in.

two servants, a gardener and boy, and then the manager and farm servants. He is said to be very near with his money and it is a wonder how I got so much out of him, but he is that sort of a man. Anything he has you are perfectly welcome to, and if you and I were to go there in the winter or the summer for that matter, we could stay there as long as we liked and be perfectly welcome.

A lady from Dunedin has been staying there six weeks and yesterday two ladies and a gentleman drove out from Queenstown to see the place, and he makes them perfectly at home, and we all had tea together in fine style. I shall enjoy my stay there I am sure, and he likes to see and talk with anyone from another place.

The money is not much is it, yet I felt so thankful for even small sums like that.

There are beautiful raspberries and apricots there, and the grapes are just getting ripe. This is a cheap place for me to live. I get rabbits for the asking. The father of one of my pupils presses me to take peas and beans and fruit. I got about seven pounds of ripe plums and a lot of apricots for one shilling and gooseberries — why, there are long hedges of them, and a lot of fruit on still.

The Arrow is such a queer place, and up the Arrow river where the gold digging is going on, it puts me in mind of the Tarawera Eruption, such desolate rugged scenery, towering rocks, bare and gaunt, and such queer colours, and the road built up for three hundred feet above the river in some places. Look over the wall and there is the creek at the base of a rocky precipice.

I am staying in a nice comfortable cottage of the Rev. Mr York's, the Church parson, and am more comfortable than I would be at Queenstown. I hear there are a great many tourists there this week. I hope they may buy something. Address the letters, Queenstown, still. I shall be leaving here on Tuesday, I expect, if no other pupils turn up.

Sunday afternoon. Dearest wife, it is such a hot day again. I have been to the Presbyterian Church this morning, and heard a Mr Paulin, the minister from Queenstown preach. He speaks very well, an earnest Christian man. His text was 'Behold I stand at the door and knock, etc.' He drives from Queenstown here and back again to preach there tonight. Mr York came out here yesterday afternoon and on to Macetown, another ten miles, to preach there this morning and comes to preach here this afternoon and back to Queenstown to preach this evening, so you see the ministers have plenty to do. I have had dinner with Mrs Lawton. Her daughter is one of the pupils I have here — such nice people, used to live at Tauranga and know Captain and Mrs Way and all about Rotomahana.

I am sending a present for our dear son, Tom. My old Waterbury! I can't get it to go properly. It stops at most inconvenient times and when you have teaching engagements, it is very awkward, so I have invested in a new one and send him the old one. He will be able to wear it occasionally, and if he winds it up carefully and minds how he moves the hands, it might go for a good while. I can fancy how he will strut

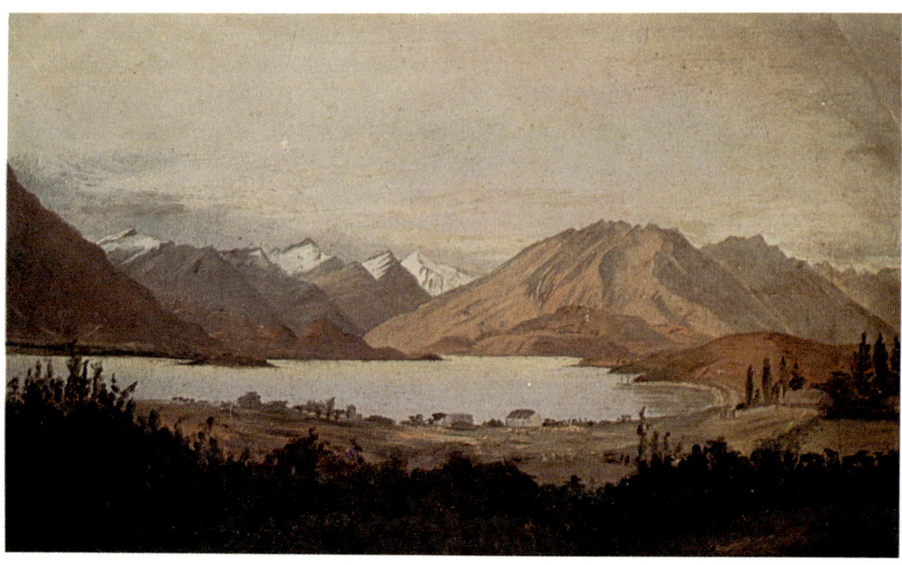

Lake Wanaka, undated. Oil on card, 17 × 11 in.

about with a real watch of his own on. God bless him. It has done me good service and lasted two years and more. I got another, chain and all, for fourteen shillings.

Mr York has just come back from Macetown and the bells are ringing for church, so goodbye, Ellen dear. May God bless you and all of us, and lead and guide and provide for us in his own way, from your loving husband,

Charles Blomfield.   xxxxxx

Monday night. The day has been very hot again, and as the heat comes I get that tired and worn out feeling again, but when the day is cooler and the cold wind blows I feel better. One thing, the days are getting shorter now. When the days were so long and the sunset effects so fine, my mind seemed to be kept on the work so to speak, trying to take it in. Even if I was not sketching, the mind and memory were busy, and when this lasts till nine o'clock at night, as it often does, it takes it out of me, but it will soon be dark at eight now, and then I shall get more rest. The sunsets are fine from here, such a grand outlook across diversified country, backed by forested hills and mountains, and then the grand mountain forms and peaks in the far distance, and as the sun is going down and the warm orange glow is over all the sky, those distant mountains take on what Ruskin calls 'One Royal Robe of Kingly Purple'. Every evening the effect is different and all beautiful. 'Thou makest the outgoings of the evenings to rejoice.'

While Charles was away, Ellen was having troubles of her own. It was not easy keeping a family of five growing children clothed and fed when the money did not come in very often. At last the day came, when she did

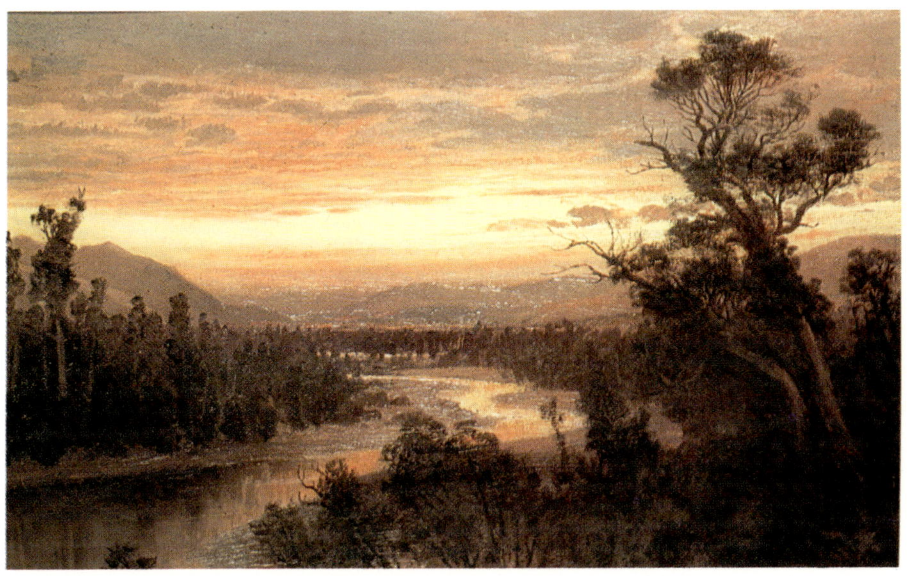

Fox River sunset, undated.
Oil on card, 21 × 15 in.

not know how she was going to buy them any food for their evening meal.
She prayed that God would look after her, but this was not easy to believe
when there was no money and no food in the house.

Suddenly there was a knock on the front door. This was unusual, as she
was not expecting any guests, and the tradesmen always came to the back.
She hurried down the hall and opened the door to find a complete stranger
standing on the doorstep.

"Mrs Blomfield?" he asked.

"Yes," she replied.

"Good," he answered, "I wish to pay you the £15.0.0. which I owe
your husband for some work he did for me at the end of last year. I am
sorry I have been so long in bringing it."

Ellen clapped her hands in joy. She could not believe that her prayers
had been answered so quickly; now they could live in comfort again until
she received some more money from the South Island.

Charles recognised his family's difficult situation, with his perpetual
absences, and their lack of a steady income. He wrote to Ellen:

> You say that you would like me to get something to do so that we could
> be all together. I am sure I do wish I could, but I do not see how, unless
> we could sell the house and then you could all come down to Wellington,
> and I feel pretty certain I could make a living there for a year or two,
> and then we could go to some other place and I would work at my trade
> or anything, so as to be at home with you all. How would it be to
> advertise the place for sale and if a good customer turned up, we could
> take it as a good sign that we were doing the right thing moving, and if
> nothing came of it, well this would be no harm done? What do you say
> to trying it while I am down here. Somebody might be looking for just
> such a place as ours.
>
> About Nellie and the typewriting. I do not know anyone who teaches
> it, but no doubt when the time comes she could learn from somebody.
> I did not think of her earning her living for a time yet. Only if she would
> like to do that she must keep it in view and learn all she can at school,
> especially grammar and *spelling*. It might not even be necessary to go
> to anyone to learn. The way would be to get a machine and practise
> so many hours a day until she was proficient. It would be as easy as
> learning to play the piano and much more profitable. An expert at it
> would be sure of good paying employment either for another or on their
> own book. If she started a business, she would require another with her,
> perhaps Bessie might do. I suppose one reads and the other prints. The
> machines are expensive, about £9.0.0. I think, but what is that if a good
> living depends upon it, and it would always be worth the money to
> sell again.
>
> I am glad Mr Blakie liked my letter. I have had none from him, yet
> I sent that description of the sunset to the *Southland Times* and today I
> got six papers with it in. I will send you one. I am rather proud of it.
> I think it is a good piece of writing, and it almost all came into my head
> and only wanted licking into shape. I have sent an advertisement to
> their paper saying I am coming there to teach in March so that the Art
> Students can get ready to take advantage of such a well known Artist

as your better self. The *Otago Witness* of February 2nd has a grand piece about my visit to Arrowtown and what a fine teacher I am; I must try and send you one.

That £5.0.0. seems to have come in the nick of time, as you were so short. I sent £10.0.0. with my last letter, did you get that all right? What a pity it is the money is so hard to get and you should be so short and have to make such shifts. I have been painting some sketches for the Christchurch sale. I have done ten in three days, and he will mount and sell them. I hope it may fetch £12.0.0. or £14.0.0. I will tell him to send the money to you direct; and then the Auckland Exhibition will be coming on next month and perhaps something will sell there. I wish I could send up something from here, but I am afraid I can't in time. I am camping in a lovely piece of bush on the Diamond Lake and there is so much to see about here I might stay a month.

I am living on rabbit. They are so nice and suit me better than butcher's meat and cost nothing. Mr Haines gave me two. He catches about twenty or thirty every day in traps and he showed me how to catch them, so I shan't be short. It costs me very little to live here, and the travelling doesn't come expensive. If I was putting up at hotels all this time I should be quite stumped up long ago.

Friday night. Today has been a disappointment. I started at half past five and meant to get as far as I could up the Dart River, but when I got there to the river bed a strong north wind began to blow and clouds of dust or fine sand came from the river bed and obscured the view and covered my palette with sand and a little cloud began to gather on the glaciers. This soon spread and soon the tops were covered and the wind was very unpleasant, so I came back and have been sketching near the tent all day, and now the sky is quite overcast and it is raining hard, so I have left off work sooner than usual and have time for some writing.

In your last letter you spoke of Mr Blakie wanting you to take Andelia's class in Sunday school. I think you were quite right in declining, as the girls are pretty big and they would notice a mistake so readily. I think it is a pity you could not do it at some other time. In this work of course there are many other ways of doing good and you are doing the Lord's work when you teach and train our children in His ways. Yet I often think the Sunday is spent in a very lazy way when we just go to Chapel and get all the good we can and do nothing. Don't you think you might do a lot of good if you were to go and visit some poor old or sick body on Sunday afternoon and cheer them up.

What makes me think of this was last Sunday I went up to Mr McKenzie's home to dinner and after dinner he asked me to go with him to see a poor old blind lady named Mrs Oliver. She is eighty-four years old and quite blind this eight years. She is such a dear old soul and so resigned, submissive, and full of earnest Christian love. Mr McKenzie read and talked with her, and then a Mrs Perryman, sister to the Wesleyan Minister, came in and spoke to her a little, and then we all prayed for her and she prayed too and joined in singing a hymn. It was such a privilege to see one so ripe for the kingdom and so ready to be translated to the better world. She seemed so grateful too, for our visit, and I thought she was never going to let go my hand.

And now, Dear Ellen, Goodbye. May God bless you all and keep you safe.

From your loving husband, Charles.

The *Otago Witness* was certainly lavish in its praises of Charles:
Mr Blomfield, who ranks with our foremost painters in oils, is at present on a professional visit to these parts, and has been favoured with the finest weather imaginable for his purpose. At the recent excursion to Rere Lake, Mr Blomfield secured quite a budget of pictures — gems all of them — and he has yet the head of the lake to do. His pictures do full justice to our scenery, and will go a long way to make it known far and wide.

At Queenstown as well as at Arrowtown a number of art students have taken advantages of Mr Blomfield's visit by attending his classes, and so rare a chance of receiving instruction from a master in the art may not occur again in a decade. Personally, I cannot speak too highly of the clear and intelligible manner in which Mr Blomfield conveys his instructions, and the student, if at all an apt one, must benefit by his teachings to an extent that is surprising to the learner himself.

Mr Blomfield had occasion the other day to call attention in the *Wakatipu Mail* to the carelessness with which fires are lit and left burning by the thoughtless. While at Rere Lake, where he stayed for a week, he found a stump on fire, the fire defying all his efforts to put it out, and he fears that it may be the means of destroying a gem in the shape of a grove of ferns. Mr Blomfield suggests that something in the shape of the Australian Bush Act should be introduced into Parliament. This

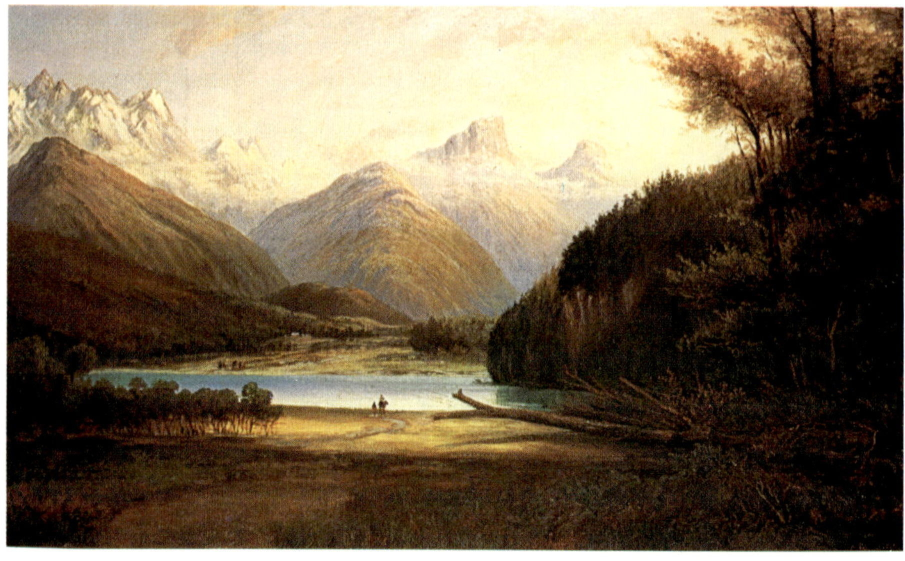

Diamond Lake, Chaos and Cosmos, 1909. Oil on canvas, 35 × 23 in.

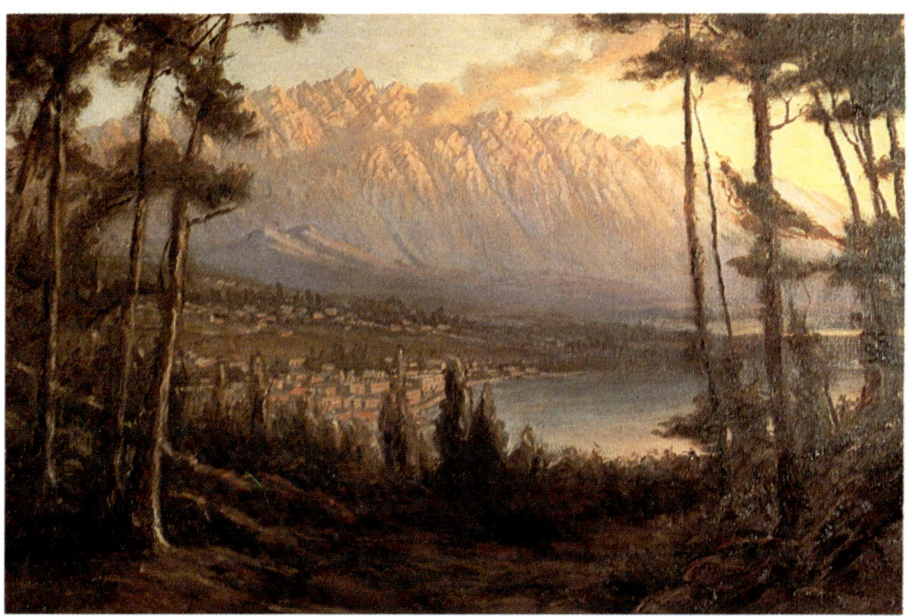

The Remarkables, undated.
Oil on canvas, $26\frac{1}{2} \times 19$ in.

is to the effect that anyone who intends to light a fire must erect a chimney or wall first, to prevent the fire from spreading. The wall may be of sods or stones, but must be three feet high.

And in the *Southland Times*:

Mr C. Blomfield, an artist who is now sojourning for the purposes of his profession and who intimates elsewhere that he will visit Invercargill in March — on the shores of Lake Wakatipu, sends us the following description of some sunsets he has witnessed in that romantic region. Mr Blomfield seems to have been singularly fortunate as to the time of his visit to Wakatipu, which he reached after a journey down the West Coast. He says:

The sunsets at Lake Wakatipu have been for the last week or so phenomenally beautiful; it seemed as if some master painter were trying combination after combination of colour on a mighty scale, flinging glorious arrangements of purple and gold, green and scarlet over the vault of heaven. Now it was a blaze of orange, reaching far towards the zenith, saturating the flying flakes of vapour through and through with gold; now a dark stormy effect, the lower edges of the heavy cloud masses lit up with a ruddy glow and the mountain peaks standing up like dusky sentinels around a lake of pitch. Then again it was as though the heavens were mourning over some deed of murder, and were vainly trying to hide in sable shroud the crimson stain. Next evening a soft pearly sky, gold and green with hazy crimson streamers like angels' wings, a sky to muse and dream over. It seemed each evening the utmost limit of gorgeous effect was reached and the mind, satiated with beauty, cried 'Hold, enough', when the next evening produced something totally different and more glorious, culminating on the evening of Friday, January 20th, in a spectacle so magnificent, that the very memory of it haunts the mind like a heavenly vision. The day had been dark and stormy, the lake chafed restlessly between its rocky walls, black clouds hung threateningly over Walter and Cecil Peaks, when suddenly the western sky was lit up by a blaze of crimson fire, the splintered edges of the distant peaks outlined in deepest purple, while the dying sun sent one horizontal ray of coloured light across the sky to the summit of Walter Peak, making its grey old crags and precipices glow with a bloody stain, while the lake below, from out of the gloom, was throwing wave after wave of liquid fire."

A short time later, Charles wrote this article for the newspaper:

Visiting the Head of Lake Wakatipu, after an absence of nearly eight years, I have been struck with the evident marks of progress made in that part of the district. Good roads, smiling pastures, snug homesteads and cultivations have taken the place of what was then little else but tussock and fern. Certainly the feeling is not all one of pleasure, for the miles of burnt and blackened forest on the Kinloch side are a great eyesore. Certain improvements also might be suggested. One is a good horse track to Sylvan Lake, and then that charming little lake will take its rightful place among the Lions of the district. A track through the bush from this lake to the Routeburn might easily be made, and thus save the necessity of having to go all round by the Routeburn station to it. A few gaps in the bush going up the Routeburn gorge would also be an improvement.

By way of information, I might be allowed to give intending visitors the benefit of my experience. There is so much to be seen at the Head of the Lake that time may be saved by knowing exactly how to go about it. Perhaps the most convenient and central place to make one's head-quarters is Paradise, at Diamond Lake, a lovely quiet retreat, where one may study nature in all her many moods, and where, when the eye gets tired gazing at rugged peaks and dazzling ice, one may turn to the softer charms of sylvan glade and moss-grown stump, and study the Creator's handiwork in little things; may sit and watch the wild fowl skimming the surface of the silent lakelet, or make friends with the ubiquitous little robin; or listen to the musical call of the Tui or Cuckoo. A place so charming in which to dream away the happy hours of a honeymoon, that one would almost run the risk of marriage over again! It is no wonder our esteemed friends, Mr and Mrs Mason, fell in love with this spot some nine years ago, and built the present accommodation house and lived there in happy retirement several years.

So many fine excursions can be made from this spot too. Just behind the house is Mt. Alfred, of easy access and ascent, affording those who do not care for higher climbing, a charming view of the surrounding region, while for those who are more athletic or more ambitious, there is Mt. Earnslaw, its dark craggy peaks towering up into the region of the clouds.

An excursion to the Chinaman's hut, about ten miles up the valley of the Dart, will well repay anyone; the scenery is quite unique in its grandeur and the journey is quite easy on horseback, even for ladies.

Then, on the other side of the Dart, which is easily forded, there is the Sylvan Lake, a spot that deserves to be better known. From Paradise it may be reached in two hours — a lovely little lake, like Rere Lake, entirely shut in by dense birch forest and grand mountain peaks, with little rocky islets overgrown by the moss and shrubs. And last, but not least, there are tributaries of the Dart. The Rockburn, the Beanburn and the Routeburn, all of easy access from Paradise. The Routeburn is a perfect gem in its way. I question if the far-famed Otira Gorge can compare with it in some respects. The advantage the Otira Gorge possesses is a wide open road, from which the river and the mountains are visible at every step, while the Routeburn has to be negotiated along a narrow horse track, shut in by dense bush, through which here and there you get a tantalizing glimpse of stupendous precipices, towering peaks, dashing waterfalls and dark ravines. But Oh! the beauty of that forest of silver birch, the witching charm of the scattered sunlight falling through the delicate tracery of the leaves — the fairy forms of branch and stream, bejewelled by fungus and lichen — the carpet of lovely moss and hymenophyllum.

These and a hundred other beauties in addition to the glorious view

Mt Earnslaw, Wakatipu, undated. Oil on canvas, 22 × 14 in.

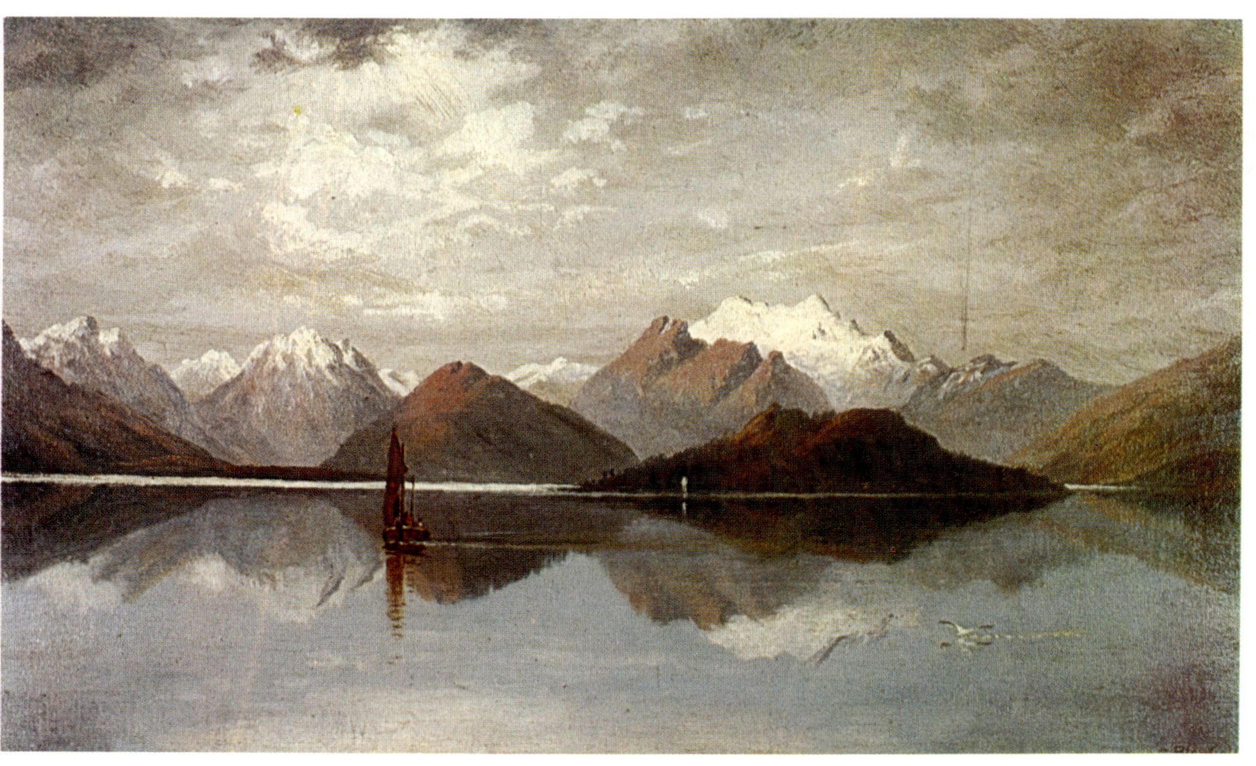

from Lake Harris saddle, will make the Routeburn a favourite route for
tourists. But won't someone come with an axe or a saw and clear away
the trees here and there, where the best points of view are; so that
.visitors may realize the grandeur of the Routeburn Gorge? I am, etc.
                              Charles Blomfield
                              Queenstown, March 8th, 1893.

While he was staying at Paradise, he was seen painting the countryside
so often, that the local inhabitants called one of the hills "Blomfield
Mountain" and it is still known by that name in his memory.

*Mitre Peak, undated. Oil
on canvas, 36 × 18 in.*

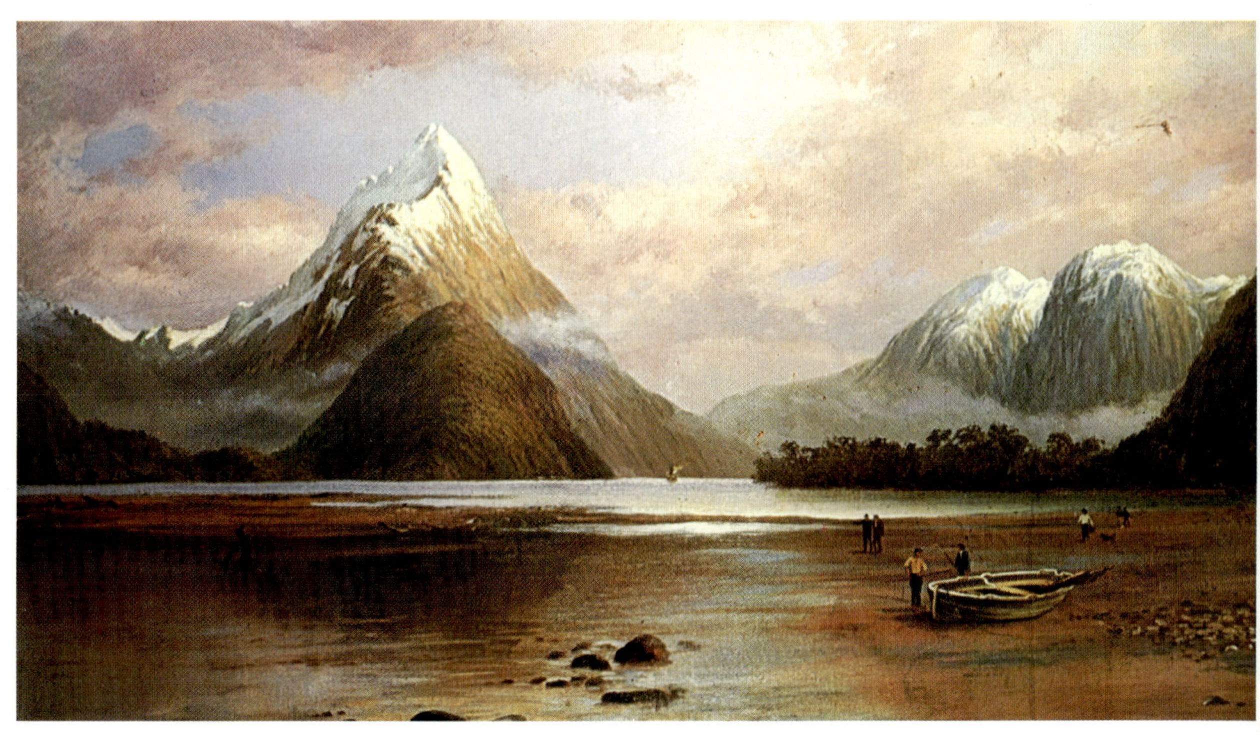

5

The Autumn Years
1893 - 1926

15. Father and Daughter

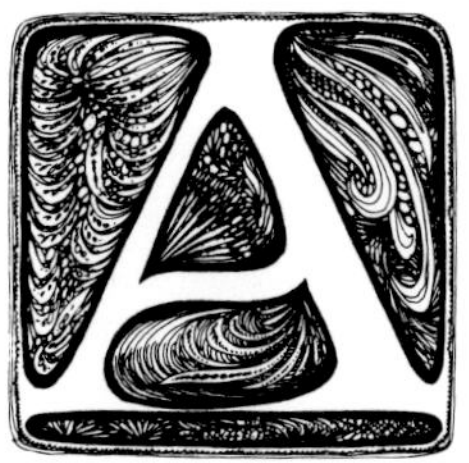

LTHOUGH HIS WORK was generally well received, Charles was not earning enough money to keep his family in the comfortable surroundings he wished for them. In 1893 he decided to take an exhibition to Australia and try his luck over there. In Ballarat, Victoria, he held an auction of his work, but was disappointed by the results — only managing to sell his smaller paintings, and raising less than £30 from the whole sale. But although Charles was becoming despondent about his lack of achievement, newspapers on both sides of the Tasman continued to praise his work.

An Australian newspaper printed the following critique:

The fine collection of oil paintings of New Zealand landscapes, from the brush of Mr Chas. Blomfield, now on exhibition in Retallack's buildings, at the corner of Bridge and Grenville Streets, comprise pictures of the most remarkable scenery in the Nelson and Westland districts, the West Coast Road, Otira Gorge, Mount Cook, and the great glaciers of the Southern Alps, Otago Lakes, etc. The Franz Josef Glacier is the largest, and undoubtedly the most important picture in the exhibition. The scene represented is unique.

The artist has realised the wild, desolate grandeur of the scene, the movement of water in the foreground, the fallen timber, and shingle bed of the river giving character to the subject. The group of dark pines in the middle distance is very skilfully introduced, and serves to give tone to the greys of the mountains. The lines of the riverbed and distant forest lead the eye naturally to the distance, which is treated with great delicacy, the atmospheric effect being delightfully rendered.

There are two large paintings of the Kaniere Lake, Westland, that command attention. This picturesque district is rich in wild scenery — noble mountain peaks and luxuriant bush. The still waters of the lake, in which form and colour are repeated, and the beautiful surroundings combine to make an attractive pair of pictures. A brilliant sunset effect on Lake Wakatipu is also worthy of notice. The rays of the declining sun are lighting up the icy peaks of Mount Earnslaw, whilst the lower hills are shrouded in purple haze. The dark birch trees in the foreground are just sufficiently brought out to give force and atmosphere to the distance.

Amongst the smaller sketches are several deserving of mention. "Sunrise at Mount Cook", "Mount Cook" and "Hooker Glacier at Sunset" are rich in colour and tone. Several views of the Westland Lakes, Otira Gorge, Routeburn Valley, and Buller River are pretty bits of composition, and these together with a number of weird scenes from the Hot Lake region in the North Island, will give visitors to the exhibition a vivid impression of that wonderful country. No charge is made for admission.

Another newspaper commented:
Mr Blomfield . . . is evidently in love with Nature in all her moods, and is thoroughly capable of reproducing them on canvas. Several of his views are characterised by a vigour and dash that at once compel admiration, while others are as attractive from the attention paid to detail and the care and taste with which the colours are blended and contrasted.

But despite such favourable interest, Charles still found himself unable to send sufficient money home to Ellen. In Bendigo he decided to look for work painting shop signs, and managed to get a job doing a sign for a Chinese launderer — a far cry from painting the beauties of New Zealand's South Island.

Eventually Charles returned to New Zealand and set up a studio in Wellington. He expected to have his sixteen-year-old daughter Mary to look after him, but Ellen had other ideas. Mary and Nellie had both been away on painting trips with their father, so Ellen considered it was now young Bessie's turn.

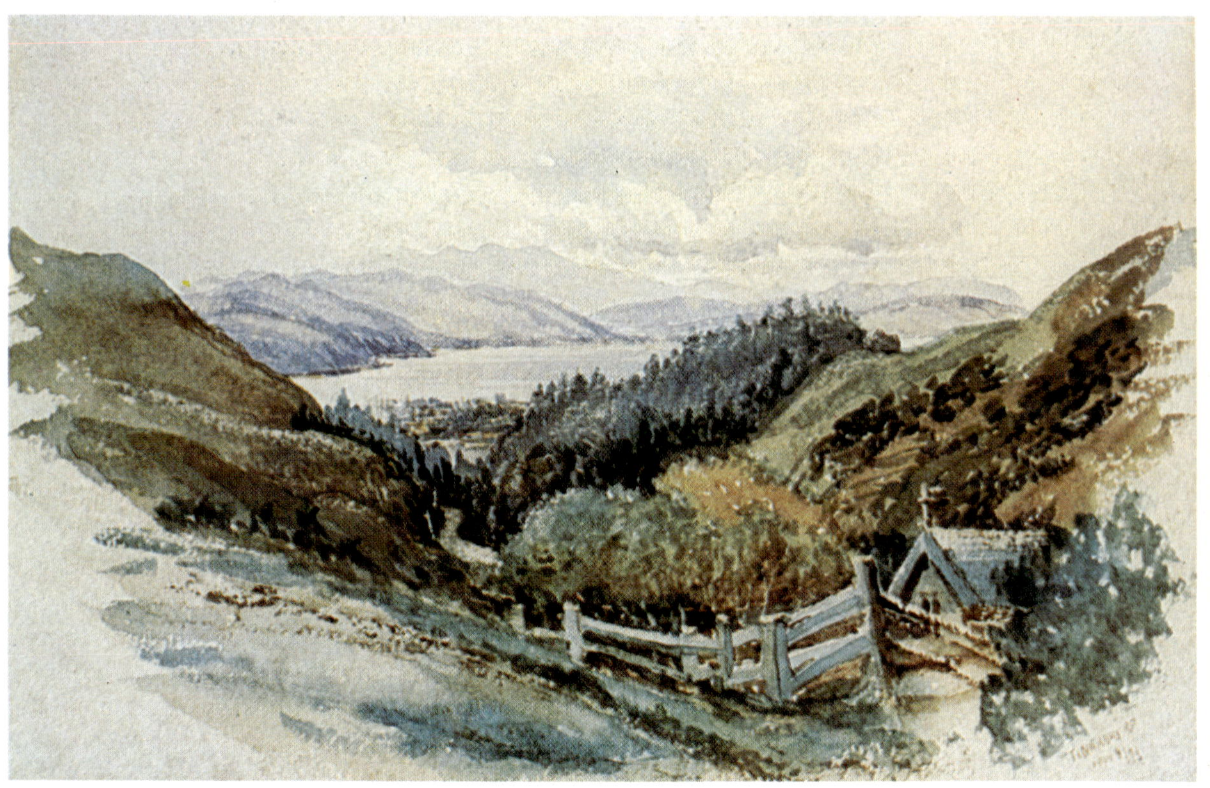

Tinakori Road, Wellington, 1893. Watercolour, 10 × 8 in.

Bessie was thrilled. She had always adored her father, and her earliest memories were of being carried around by him, everywhere he went. In fact, at one public meeting where Charles had been speaking, Bessie had managed to wriggle away from her mother and toddle up to her father on the platform. Charles had quietly picked her up and kept on talking, with the little girl on his hip.

In Wellington, Charles had managed to borrow a very big room in Customhouse Quay for his studio, and there were a couple of smaller rooms at the back to serve as living quarters for himself and Bessie. He planted an indoor garden of native trees and ferns in the studio so that his pupils could paint these 'from Nature' without moving outdoors, and he placed an advertisement in the *Evening Post*:

TO ART STUDENTS
MR CHARLES BLOMFIELD begs to announce
he has made arrangements to hold a series of Art
Classes in Wellington to the practice of Oil Painting,
Sketching from Nature, etc. For particulars apply
at his studio, National Mutual Life Assurance
Buildings, Customhouse Quay.

Bessie was still very young, only twelve, and often grew homesick for her mother and sisters in Auckland. Charles's reaction was typical:

"My dear," he told his little daughter on one occasion, drying her tears with his big white handkerchief, "you are such a comfort to me. I have been so lonely in Australia with no-one with me. But I tell you what I'll do. I'll teach you how to paint, and then when you come home from school, we can do things together."

Bessie cheered up considerably, and the very next afternoon when she returned home from school, Charles picked a white daisy from the garden and showed her how to draw, how to mix up colours, and how to paint, using the right colours to get the shading correct. When Bessie had finished, Charles was so proud of the painting that he had it framed, and hung it on the wall of the studio where he could show it to his pupils and customers.

After a few months, Charles realised that although he had several pupils, his paintings were not selling very well in Wellington, and it was obvious that Ellen did not want to leave Auckland, so he packed up his things and returned to Wood Street. He set up his studio in Karangahape Road, and settled down once again. Then in October 1894, another daughter, Dorothy, was born — an afterthought, and the spoilt darling of the whole family.

Bessie stayed at school until she turned fifteen, when she was allowed to leave school and go to work with her father in the studio. By this time she was painting really well, specialising in flower pictures; and she very soon had her own pupils, and also exhibited in her own right. After a year or two, Charles gave up teaching, and handed all his pupils over to his daughter.

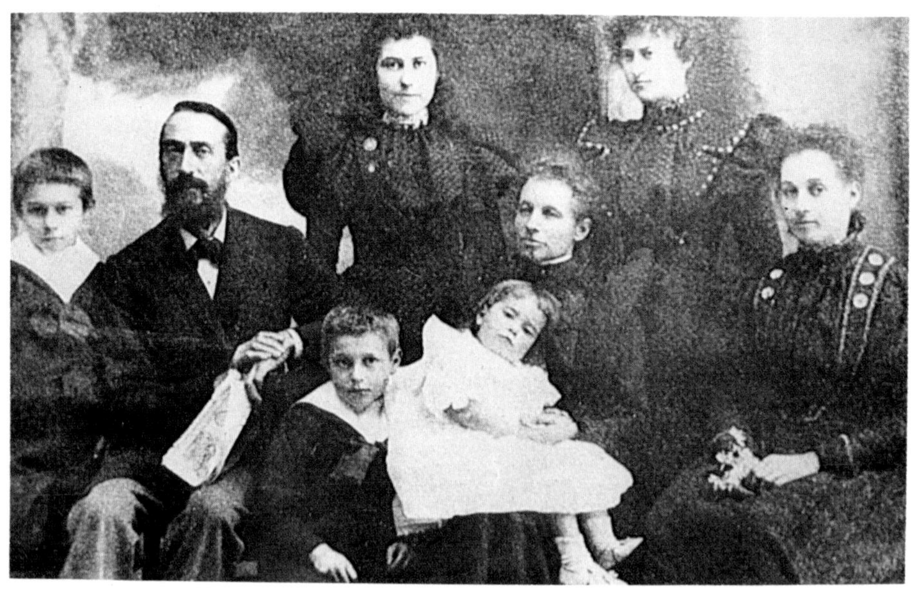

The Blomfield family in 1896.

During the first half of 1897, the whole country was busily engaged in preparations for Queen Victoria's Diamond Jubilee. In Auckland they decorated Queen Street, and Bessie and Charles were commissioned to paint some of the transparencies of the Queen and her late husband, Prince Albert. They used very fine calico, and while Charles painted the background, Bessie would put the finishing touches to the faces, which she found she could do with greater ease than her father. When they were finished, they were hung up in front of the gas lights, so that the light shone through the designs.

The Auckland *Weekly News* described the scene:

The illuminations in themselves were a remarkable proof of deep-rooted loyalty. Never since Auckland has been a city has "the Corinth of the South" presented so magnificent a sight. From the higher levels the view was peculiarly fascinating. A dull glow hung over the city like the reflection of a far-off conflagration.

Standing at the top of Upper Queen Street the *coup d'oeil* was of a matchless and indescribable character. One looked down an avenue of blazing light, while on the heights on either side unusual lights shone high in the night air, the whole presenting a somewhat awe-inspiring and fantastic appearance. Over all, high above the brilliancy below, a haze like thin smoke drifted slowly seaward, completing the suggestion of a city on fire.

Strikingly prominent in this fascinating picture was the imposing illumination, by means of the electric light, of the whole facade of the lofty *Herald* building. As one descended the hill and strolled along Queen Street towards the wharf, the weird picturesqueness of the scene was lost, and its more detailed beauty came into view.

The stillness of the night — a night as perfect as the day had been — enhanced the charm of the scene, and enabled each illumination to be displayed to the utmost advantage, while the graceful and artistic arch at the wharf, with its charming and effective illuminations, brought to a fitting close the long array of dazzling beauty. The scene looking towards the city from the wharf, was also one which will not readily be forgotten; and we may well be forgiven, therefore, if we have lingered over the great event of last night, and endeavoured in the full description which follows below, to impress it in detail upon the minds of our readers;

> Dull would he be of soul who could pass by
> A sight so touching in its majesty;
> This city now doth like a garment wear
> The beauty of the night . . .

Very touching and impressive, too, was the sea of faces in Queen Street as witnessed from the upper windows of the *Herald* building — faces old and young and fair to look upon, types of all sorts and conditions. Yet withal, as we have said, a loyal and joyous multitude, orderly, good-humoured, and patient. And to think of it! When Her Majesty came to the throne, Queen Street was a fern-clad gully, with a Maori whare here and there. The city of Auckland had neither a local habitation nor a name. The tide flowed wheresoever it listed. Primitive nature reigned supreme. What a transformation! Who could have believed, looking down on the brilliant and animated scene on Monday — the blazing lines of variegated lights worked into cunning devices, the multitude of waving flags and Chinese lanterns and graceful greenery, and the dense masses of happy, loyal people moving in the streets in their thousands — that within the reign of one British Sovereign this marvellous change has been effected.

At the relief of Mafeking, three years later, Bessie and her father were again asked to paint transparencies, this time of Lord Kitchener. Bessie realised that she had a certain knack for painting faces, but decided she needed some drawing instruction, so she asked Mr Goldie if he would give her some lessons. He agreed, and taught her drawing for over a year, but she found drawing very difficult. Goldie cheered her up by telling her that he had had to spend six whole years in Paris learning nothing but drawing, and was not allowed to start painting until he had mastered the art of drawing. Bessie felt she could not wait that long, and decided to try painting a portrait by herself.

A Mr Carr had a secondhand bookshop a few doors along from the studio, and Bessie asked him to sit for her. He agreed, and Bessie collected some of his books and placed them on the shelves behind him, and set to work to paint his portrait. When it was finished she took it along to show Goldie.

"You have done very well," was Goldie's comment. "If only you could draw as well as you can paint, there would be no holding you."

She also showed him a painting she had done of red and white roses and of this he said, "You certainly chose the hardest subject to paint, and did it very well."

Bessie was delighted, and exhibited her roses with some other paintings, but she took Mr Carr home and hung him on her wall. She later painted several portraits, but in each case she gave them to the model.

Of the roses, the newspaper critics wrote:

It is with very sincere pleasure that Miss Bessie Blomfield is hereby complimented on two of the finest flower paintings from the brush of this artist the writer remembers to have seen. The most difficult subject, and the one into which every atom of technical skill Miss Blomfield possesses has been lavished, is unquestionably 'Springtime', a wealth of clematis and yellow kowhai painted amidst their natural surroundings in the native bush. It is an amazing piece of work, but whether the choice of the bush as a background, with flowers life-size in the foreground, is a success, is rather a debatable point. In technique, the picture is wonderful, but perhaps on the whole it is more wonderful than beautiful, which is not, one presumes, either the object or the intention of the artist.

'Love's Offering' while showing almost equal technical skill, is altogether and supremely beautiful; therefore, as the poet tells us, 'a joy for ever' to the happy person into whose hands it may fall. The pure white roses are handled with extraordinary delicacy and skill, and the artistic contrast with the rich blood-red blooms with which they are mixed is as striking as it is artistic. A really notable and charming work of art.

Bessie soon became engaged to William Kendon, a serious young man whom she had met at the Baptist Tabernacle. He decided to go to Australia and make his fortune before they were married, so he went to Melbourne until early in 1908, and they made plans for an Easter wedding. But this was not to be!

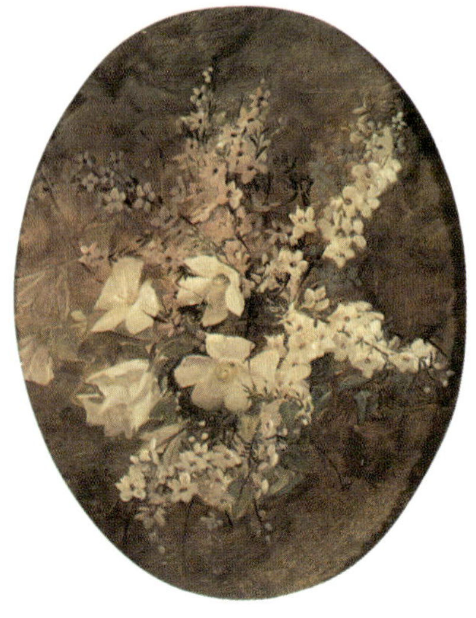

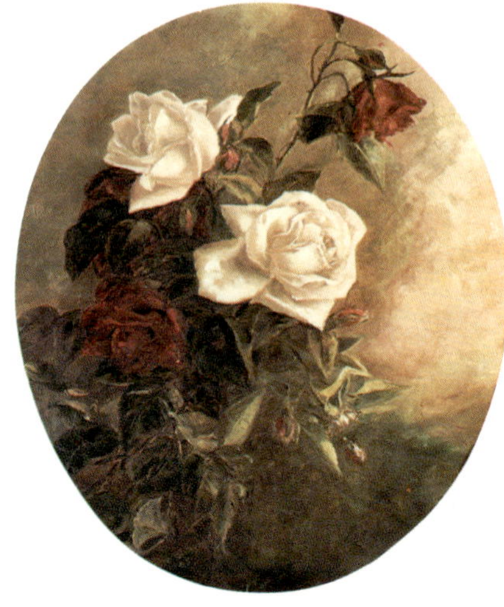

Teatree and native convulvulus by Bessie Kendon (née Blomfield), 1897. Oil on card.

Love's Offering, by Bessie Kendon (née Blomfield), 1905. Oil on canvas.

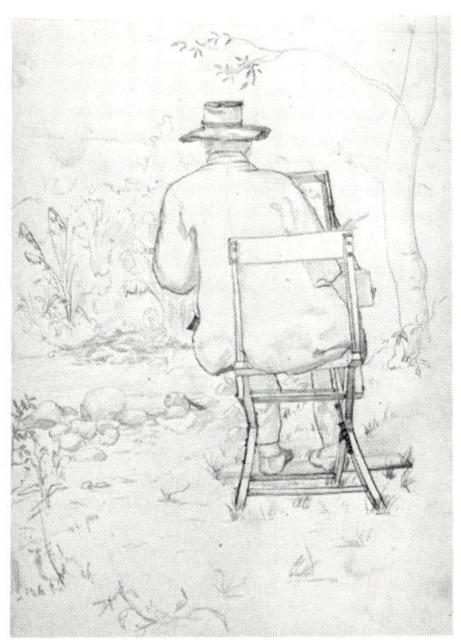

*Sketch of Charles Blomfield,
by his daughter Bessie.*

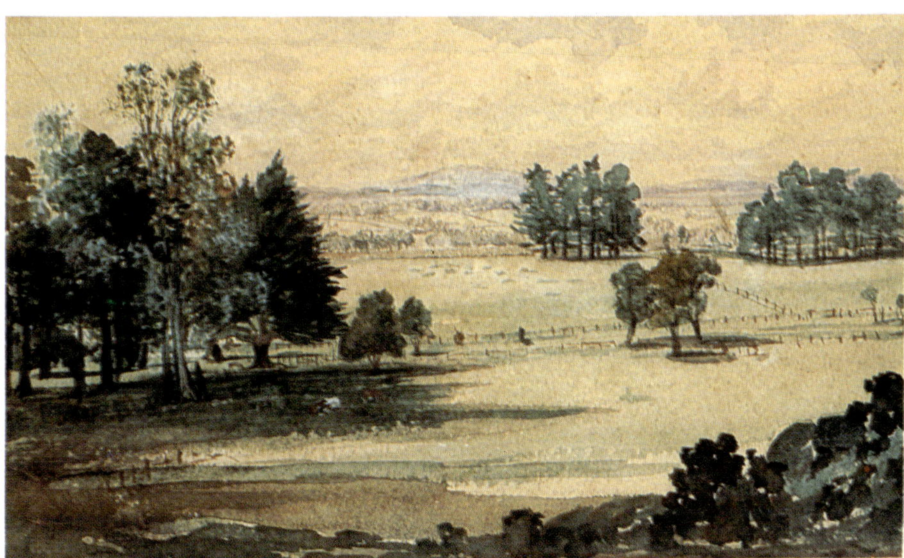

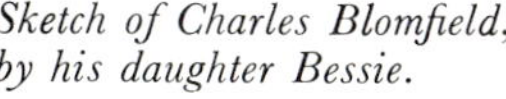

*One Tree Hill, undated.
Watercolour, 10×7 in.*

Bessie was coming home one Saturday evening, walking along Ponsonby Road from the studio, when she heard the fire siren. She hurried along, hoping it was not a neighbour's house on fire — but as she came down Rata Street, she could see smoke pouring out of her own home. When she got closer, there, sure enough, it was her own bedroom on fire. She could see a hole right through the wall, and the smoke and flames billowing out.

Before long, the fire brigade had the fire under control, and when she was allowed inside, she found that it had been confined to her own room. Her trousseau was inside the kauri chest of drawers her Uncle Sam Blomfield had built, and what was not completely ruined, was badly marked with smoke and water. Luckily her wedding dress was being made for her by her next door neighbour, Mrs Urquhart, so it was not in the house at the time, but everything else was either ruined or badly damaged. The pictures on the wall were all burnt, including a painting of Queenstown that Bessie had done on a Sunday, and as it was a cardinal rule of her father's never to paint or travel on a Sunday, Bessie believed that she had brought this calamity upon herself by disobeying this rule. She had felt at the time of painting it that she was tempting fate, but that Sunday had been the only day during her stay at Queenstown when the lake was not obscured by rain. However, never again did Bessie flout the rule; to this day she refuses to paint on a Sunday.

Everyone came to Bessie's aid, making new clothes for her trousseau, and her Aunty Kate took her petticoats home and washed and bleached them until they looked like new again, and were ready to wear for her wedding, which had to be postponed for three months. The house was soon repaired, and the chest of drawers was sanded and repolished, and no one could tell it had ever been through a fire.

At last on July 29th 1908, Bessie walked down the aisle of the Tabernacle on her father's arm, to be married to her beloved Will. She carried a bouquet of roses, and the bridesmaids carried golden daffodils, while Dorothy, the flower girl, had a large bunch of violets. Will was absolutely thrilled! The first time he had ever seen Bessie, she had been wearing a daffodil in her hair, and this was the perfect climax to their engagement. He never forgot, and every year on July 29th, right up until his death in 1966, he brought home a bunch of daffodils and violets for her wedding anniversary.

When her first child, Nancy was born in 1912, Bessie put her paints away, and devoted herself to looking after her home and family. She had six children in all — Nancy, then three boys, Roy, Phil and Murray, and finally two more girls, Muriel and Lois. All went well and happily, as they kept on moving into larger houses, finally settling in a big house on the side of One Tree Hill. But unfortunately, tragedy struck the family in 1923, when little Lois, only twenty months old, died of meningitis.

Bessie was heartbroken, and nothing seemed to cheer her up. Finally, one day, her father arrived on her doorstep, armed with his paint box. He remembered how he had stopped her tears thirty years before, and said again:

"Come on my dear. I'll teach you how to paint again."

"Oh, Father," she cried. "I've forgotten all I used to know."

"Never mind," he replied. "Come on up One Tree Hill with me, and I'll show you all over again. Bring little Muriel with you, and we will have a picnic in the park, and you'll soon find you can paint again."

Off they went up the hill, and in next to no time, Bessie was once again enthralled in her painting. She found that she still remembered how to mix the colours and put them on to the canvas, and her first picture was a real credit to her.

Charles again became a constant visitor to his daughter's home, and off they would go with their paints together. Bessie continued to paint mostly scenery, but a few flower and fruit pictures, and even after her father's death, she carried on on her own, bringing joy not only to herself and her family, but in gifts to many of her friends.

In 1966 her beloved Will died, and she carried on in the big old home by herself for six months, then she too became very ill, and the family sold the house, knowing that she would never be able to look after herself again. But she recovered, and made her home with her daughter in Howick. She had cataracts removed from each of her eyes, and regained enough sight to be able to continue painting, and now at the age of 98, she is still painting almost every day, and still exhibits with the New Zealand Fellowship of Artists. Surely a great memorial to her illustrious father!

16. Nature's Cathedral

Ever since his arrival in New Zealand, Charles loved to wander through the native bush. It was while in the bush at Coromandel that he first began his painting career, and when in Auckland, he often tramped through the Waitakere Ranges, painting his beloved native trees. While in the Waitakeres, he came across the Waitakere Falls, and immediately took a picture, using only his palette knife. Later, when the Cascades were discovered, the newspaper published an article about him:

Some time ago we gave a description of a new waterfall at Waitakere, equal, if not surpassing in attractions, the far-famed Waitakere Falls. Among the first to visit it, was Mr Charles Blomfield, who spent two days sketching, in the early part of last month.

Mr Blomfield describes the scenery on Cascade Creek, as this latest addition to our many fine sights is called, as quite unique in its rugged beauty, and sure to prove a great attraction to visitors and sightseers, especially as the new road from Swanson makes the journey a very easy one. There are many fine views along the creek within the space of a hundred yards or so, and Mr Blomfield obtained the material for several fine paintings. One of these, showing the cascade coming through the chasm with the rocks nearly meeting overhead, is now finished and forms a striking picture. Those who have seen it can scarcely credit that such a fine sight, although not half a mile from a settler's house, should have remained undiscovered until a few weeks ago.

The painting is on view at Mr Blomfield's studio, Victoria Arcade, and we are sure when our fellow citizens have seen the painting they will not rest satisfied until they have seen the original.

It always distressed Charles when he heard of the destruction of the native bush and other beauties of the countryside, and he became one of New Zealand's first conservationists, writing on more than one occasion, begging the authorities to look after their natural heritage.
He wrote from Lake Taupo:
I would call attention to the wanton way in which the waterfall at Waihi and other sights in this fair land are being disfigured or destroyed — sights unequalled in many respects, and which must prove of untold value as years roll on, if by any means they could be preserved. The Maoris have burnt the bush on one side of this fine fall, greatly disfiguring it; the grand scenery of the Aratiatia Falls, on the Waikato River, is being destroyed by the same cause. The Crow's Nest geyser has lost all its curious incrustations; everything worth taking has long since disappeared from Tokaanu; and to come nearer home, even our own Waitakere Falls have suffered by a large fire among the kauris

there last summer. Last year, when I visited Wairakei, I congratulated myself that there at least was one place safe from these acts of vandalism, being off the line of traffic, and in private hands it was then intact, fresh from the hand of nature. But last winter our paternal Government in their wisdom (?) saw fit to make a road right through the geyser valley, and the consequences are most deplorable. Specimens which must have taken hundreds of years to form are now the prey of every passer-by. The curious Eagle's Nest is ruined, nearly all the encrusted sticks are gone, and a fire has made sad havoc among the graceful manuka; the lovely coralline filagree work of the red cascade is being smashed up, and what used to be a most beautiful glen has now a great ugly cutting extending all along its side.

From Queenstown in 1893, he begged:
Lake Wakatipu will always be a popular resort for tourists and sight-seers, and every care should be taken to preserve the natural features of the country, and make the place as attractive as possible. Among the many excursions which may be made from Queenstown, that to Rere Lake will be a favourite one. This charming little lake is entirely surrounded by beautiful native birch trees, and it is the sylvan charm which these graceful trees lend to the lake and its approaches that constitute its chief attraction. And here is a possible danger. On the third instant, one of the party of excursionists fired a tree stump on the lake shore, and the next day, when sketching on the lake, I found the fire still smouldering and endeavoured to put it out, unsuccessfully, I fear, as it had spread underground. Can nothing be done to stop this careless fire raising? If not, I fear it is only a matter of time, and instead of sylvan beauty there will be black desolation. As an artist I have often grieved over the loss of many a fine sight through the same cause. On the Blue Mountains of New South Wales, at Katoomba, Wentworth Falls, Lovett's Leap, etc. — wherever picnic parties resort — a large stone fireplace has been built at each locality, and a notice board warns persons, under various pains and penalties, from lighting a fire any-where else than in the fireplace. I commend the idea to the authorities here.

And from Wanganui:
New Zealand has often been called a show country and certainly the sights and scenes within the length and breadth of our island home are unique and various, and will no doubt attract an ever increasing number of tourists from other parts, and among them all the wild and romantic scenery of the Upper Wanganui must soon take a leading place. In the meantime there is great danger of the best parts being disfigured by the bushman's axe and the settler's fires. I devoutly wish I had to make the laws in New Zealand, when I would pass a law that not a fern or tree should be touched for at least a chain on either side of the Wanganui River.

He was also interested in town planning:

A great deal of interest seems to be centred just now on town planning and beautifying, but the question often occurs to me, have we any real love for the beautiful? Do we really desire our city to present a charming appearance on the eye? Looking around there seems very little evidence of it. We disfigure our streets with hundreds of huge wooden posts that would disgrace the stone age, and spoil the appearance of most of our large buildings by unsightly iron ladders and balconies, affording ready access to the nimble burglar. We place our finest building in a hollow, amid mean and ugly surroundings, and block the entrance to our principal thoroughfare with a tall pile of stonework. In our domains we cut down the beautiful native shrubs, and plant pines and willows. Our native forests are cut down and burnt, and our lovely waterfalls are regarded as so much electric energy going to waste. It seems to me, before we talk about town planning for the future, we have a deal to learn, or unlearn, in the way of making our present city worthy of the magnificent advantages with which nature has endowed it.

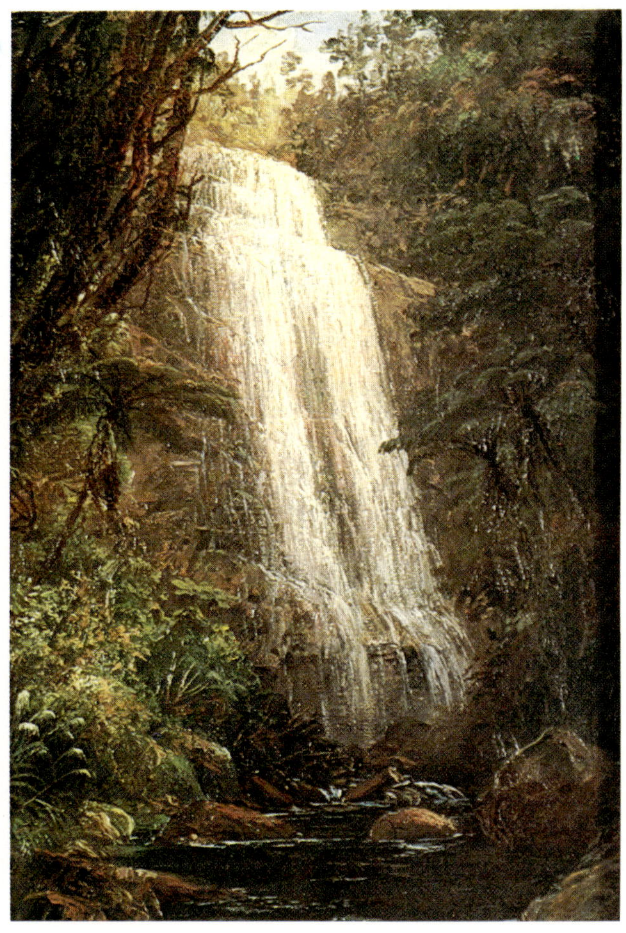

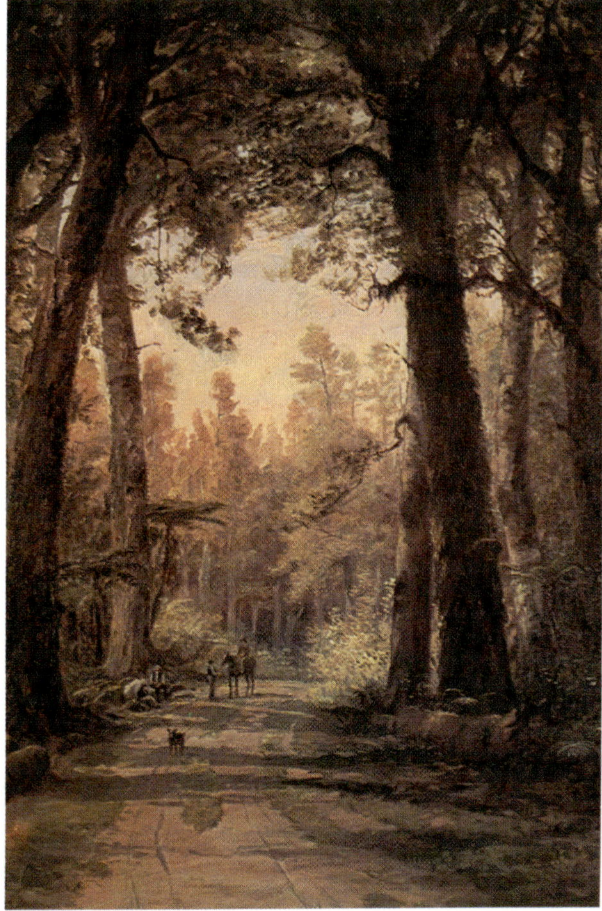

Waitakere Falls, undated. Palette knife and oil on canvas, 12 × 16½ in.

Hongi's Track, undated. Oil on card, 13 × 19 in.

When Tom and Reg were old enough, their father took them with him
on a camping trip on the shores of Lake Rotoehu — a day's journey on
foot from Rotorua, carrying the camping gear. They had the tent and
their blankets, a good stock of simple food, like flour, rice, porridge,
sausages and cocoa, and of course Charles's paints and easel and canvases.

Life was good and the boys loved it. Their father would sit quietly
painting. The days were free to play as they pleased — within reason of
course. Tent living was simple and wholesome — up with the birds, and
to bed with the set of the sun at night. Meals — plenty of whatever there
was, cooked by their father at the proper time, and served on plates and in
cups, that were properly washed up and put away again after meals.

In the evening, when the dishes were done, they sat in the tent doorway
and sang — not just idle light singing, but serious, beautiful part singing,
with Charles singing the deep notes and Reg and Tom taking the air and
accompanying parts in their clear true boys' voices.

One evening as they sang, Charles said in a low voice:

"Don't look both together, but see behind you."

Furtively, in turn, Tom and Reg glanced over their shoulders still
singing. On the shore of the lake, close by, but not too close, a Maori was
crouching, listening to their song.

"Keep singing," murmured their father, as he changed to a new song.
On and on they sang, as if they did not notice their shy listener. He edged
closer and closer along the beach, sitting on his heels, his feet leaving two
long snail trails behind him in the sand. Then the sky began to darken and
next time they looked the Maori had gone.

"Afraid of the dark," said Charles simply. "He'll come again tomorrow
and bring his tribe with him."

Sure enough, the following afternoon, late in the day, the area around
was filled with members of the Maori's family. At a respectful distance
from the tent, and apparently all busy with their own affairs, the whole
tribe seemed to be there, men, women and children. Tom and Reg and
their father serenely ate their tea and washed up their dishes, ignoring
the chattering and movement of the natives nearby. Then Charles produced
his tuning fork and a mouth organ.

"*Ehu*," commanded an elderly woman, and the shouting and calling
of the native children ended abruptly. Everyone settled down at once to
listen. The concert had begun!

Charles and his sons sang and sang, on and on and on, until at last
when the evening had come and the boys' voices were almost cracking
with weariness, their father announced:

"*Waiata pukurau* — song finished."

Grunts and exclamations of wonder and pleasure had accompanied
their songs. Now the Maori folk rose up to go home. Their village was on
the shore of the adjoining Lake Rotoiti, a short distance away, through the
bush by way of Hongi's Track. The crowd melted away quietly into the
darkness, barefooted, accompanied by a loud chorus of horrible haka

shouts and cries, and stamping of the young strong men — frightening
away the spooks and demons who inhabited the dark depths of the forest,
as every Maori well knew.

Then Charles came into the tent and quietly called, "Come."

Trembling the boys arose and followed him into the night, wondering
and afraid. Then they saw what he had led them out to see — indescribably
lovely, gleaming in the soft darkness, under a mossy bank, the starry
brightness of glow worms.

Next day the Maoris welcomed the Blomfield trio to their village, for
a return of hospitality. A true Maori village, unspoiled by European
civilization, but enjoying the amenities of the new culture just the same.
One elderly motherly woman was cooking bread in a camp oven, over a
fire of coals, and from a neat cupboard made from a kerosene box, she
produced a large loaf, cut two huge slices of bread, spread them with jam
and gave them to the boys. It was almost more than they could do to eat it.

All too soon it was time to go, as they had to walk through Hongi's
Track and on to Whakatane. While there Charles was particularly thrilled
with the cloud formation, and later wrote about the glories of cloud
pictures:

Some magnificent cloud effects are to be seen occasionally in New
Zealand; we have seldom a cloudless sky and the cloud forms are varied
and beautiful. At sunrise and sunset the gorgeous colours add additional
charm to the cloud pictures, and where the peaks of high mountains
mingle with the cloud forms the effect is very fine.

I remember standing on the deck of the little steamer plying on Lake
Wanaka with a tourist from England; the glorious colours of evening
were tinting the mountains and clouds, and reflecting in the lake. He
stood entranced, motionless, until the last faint flush of colour had died
out, and then turning to me, he said with great enthusiasm:
"Well, I have seen the Italian lakes, the mountains of Switzerland, and
most of the finest scenery of Europe, but I never saw anything to
equal this."

One of the finest cloud pictures I ever saw was one evening in the
Whakatane Valley. The day had been gloomy, dark clouds hung about,
and towards evening they gathered blackness. One great cloud in the
east, of a remarkable inky blue colour, with its trailing skirts took on
the appearance of a huge waterspout, and as this cloud moved majesti-
cally along with the rising wind, it appeared as though a great curtain
was being drawn aside, and revealed a wonderful scene behind. Far
away beyond a huge mass of cumulus cloud standing out against a
purple sky, a giant castle rose terrace above terrace, battlements and
towers, all tinted rose colour by the sunset glow. This slowly faded to
a ghostly grey, and darkness coming on, the whole scene faded from
view. But now another act in the sky-drama commenced, for suddenly
the fairy castle was lit up by a vivid flash of lightning, then another
answering flash revealed another great mass of cloud on the opposite
side of the valley. For the space of an hour this was kept up, flash

answering flash; sometimes the clouds would be illuminated from outside, sometimes from the inside, outlining every tower and pinnacle in transparent alabaster. As the cloud masses drifted slowly seawards and the distance increased, one could imagine two contending armies engaged in mortal combat, the flash and roar of their artillery growing fainter and fainter, as the pure south wind swept the angry clouds to sea, and the peaceful moon sailed forth in a cloudless sky.

After a trip to the Trounson Kauri Park, Charles commented in the *Herald*:

Auckland is singularly favoured in public benefactors. One valuable gift after another is poured into the lap of the community. Among them all, the latest gift stands out in prominence —- the gift by Mr Trounson of Kauri Park, Kaipara.

I have been camping in this park for the last few weeks, sketching the kauris, and have no hesitation in stating — and I have been through most of the kauri areas — that this bush contains the finest specimens of the kauri in New Zealand, and saying that is equivalent to saying the finest specimens of the kauri in the world. Whether in size, height, variety or environment, there is nothing equal to it anywhere.

Viewed from a neighbouring hill overlooking the park, the forest appears to be all kauri. There is nothing to be seen over the whole expanse of three or four hundred acres, but the tops of kauri trees, and the top is singularly level. No towering tree over-tops its fellows.

But when we enter the forest we find a variety of smaller trees and shrubs adding to the charm of the bush. The taraire is the most plentiful, forming with its handsome foliage and rambling branches, a pleasing contrast to the stately kauri. The graceful tawa, the beautiful kowhai, and the karaka with its large glossy leaves, all grow luxuriantly. Above them the kauri lifts its massive branches, forming an almost continuous canopy.

The first thing that strikes the visitor is the difference in colour. Some trees are grey, inclining to purple, while many are a warm brown, almost a salmon colour. In some the tree casts its bark in large flakes, leaving the surface deeply marked, in others the trunk is beautifully smooth and the bark falls in thin flakes no bigger than an autumn leaf. In some the trunk carries an enormous head of massive branches, giving the tree a top-heavy appearance, and in others the top is very small with scarcely any foliage. While the eye meets at every turn stately specimens of this noble tree, there are several trees that stand out prominently in their size, shape and colour.

The celebration tree, under which the opening ceremony was held, is a huge ungainly giant. It measures thirty-five feet in girth. While it cannot be called a handsome tree, there is a certain rugged picturesque beauty about it that appeals to an artist. Its trunk, gnarled and twisted, and shaggy with loose bark, supports an enormous head, the massive branches crowded with a mass of alien growth. It has the look of a decrepit old man fast hastening to decay.

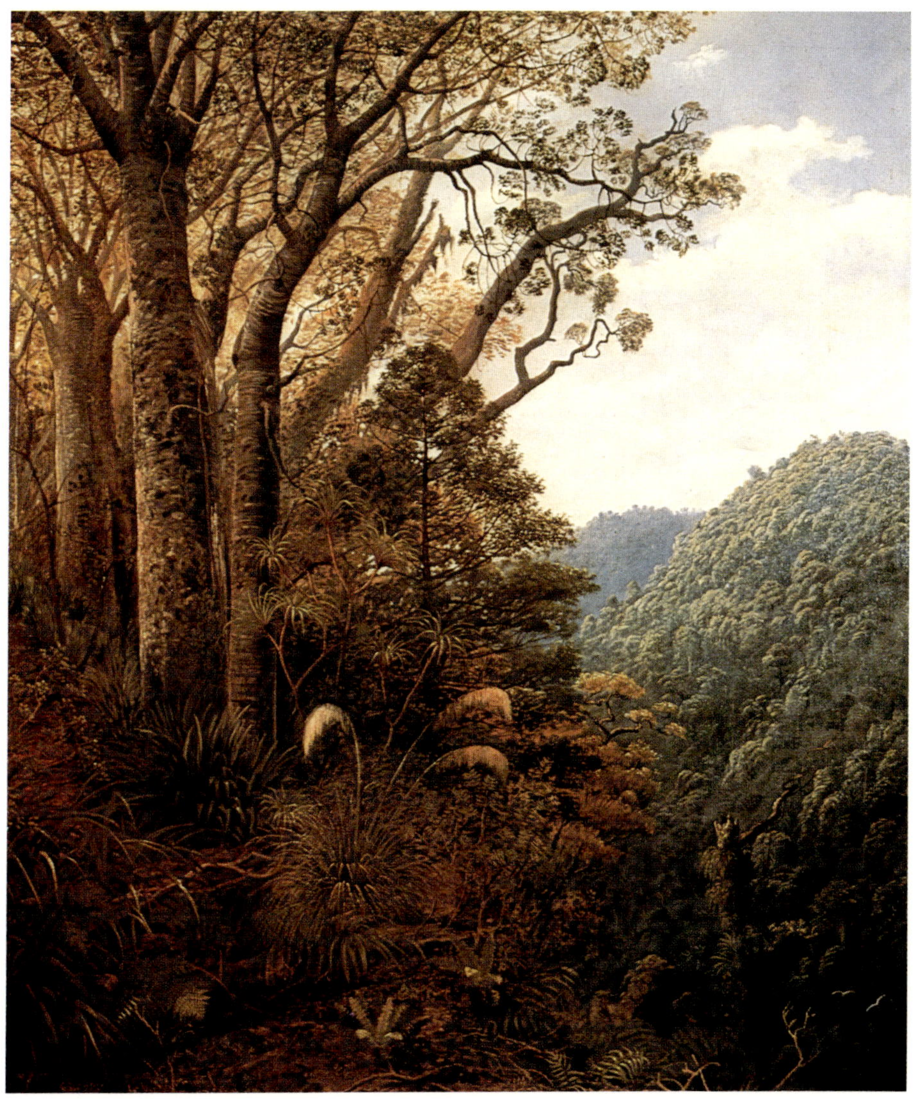

Waitakere Ranges, 1883.
Oil on canvas, 32 × 39 in.

There is another old giant not far away, so old that the centre has completely decayed. A cave-like opening on one side gives access to the interior, where seven or eight persons might stand.

The two finest trees are near the gate, but a little off the track and may easily be missed by the visitor. One of them has a girth of 27 feet and a height of barrel of about 45 feet. The other, a trifle less in girth, has a trunk reaching at least 65 feet to the first branch. There is no sign of decay about these two trees, they are in the stage of vigorous manhood, the very prime of life. The shaft of the taller one towers up straight as a plumb line, its sides are parallel, its bark clean, its beautifully rounded trunk rising 65 feet without a knot or blemish of any kind. You could fancy it the massive column of some great temple. It seems a crime to cut a tree like this down, but the sawmiller has no sentiment. He estimates a tree by the amount of timber it will yield. This tree is calculated to produce 20,000 feet of sawn timber, which at the present price would be worth £300.0.0.

There is no doubt these trees are the finest specimens in the forest, but magnificent trees abound on every hand. Trees six and seven feet through are common. They grow very close, there is not a spot where you have not one or two large kauris in the line of sight, and in some places the eye takes in ten or twelve in one view. Often two are found growing from one root and in one case there is a family of four growing from one stump. These are not very big trees, but they are very tall and straight. One of them towers up over 100 feet without a branch — a splendid spar. One huge tree brings to mind the Siamese twins — two great trees united into one solid trunk threequarters of the way up, and then branching into two separate trees.

A curious freak of nature is to be seen on one of the trees near the entrance, in the shape of a huge growth or carbuncle cropping out of the side, about eight feet from the ground. Looking up from below the likeness to a monstrous face is quite startling. Long protuberances hang down, terminating in rounded nodules. One of these forms the nose, a small one the right eye, others form the ear, and feet with claws. Tufted mosses form the eye-brows, and trailing grasses the hair, and most remarkable of all just where the other eye should be two tiny fern leaves have grown and drying curled up in the shape of an eye. Looking at the creature sideways the profile is perfect; the long nose, the moustache, the mouth, teeth, chin and beard are all there. The colour is a warm brown with deep shadows in the hollows. It was surely some monstrous growth like this that suggested the idea of the satyr and woodland faun, or supplied the old Gothic builders with a model for those grotesque gargoyles they were wont to decorate the tops of their walls with. This curiosity is certainly one of the sights of the forest and ought to be carefully preserved, but alas! every small boy who comes along tries to poke its nose off with a pole.

Some of these trees must be a great age. I counted the annular rings on one recently felled and made the tree to be 360 years old, and this was by no means an old tree. The veterans of the forest must be over 1000 years old. The annular rings tell more than the age of the tree. Its life's history is recorded in those minute lines. That small cluster in the centre represents the tree when it was but a sapling, as the tree develops the rings begin to vary, here they widen out telling of years of plenty and vigorous growth, then comes several years when the growth is slow and the rings close together. Sometimes the lines will close up on one side and widen out on the other, caused probably by prevailing winds. As the tree approaches maturity the growth is slower and the lines so close that in 50 years the increase will be only an inch or two.

It is a thousand pities the Government could not secure the whole of this forest. It has a large State reserve some miles further on, stretching for 14 miles towards Hokianga. This contains several large areas of kauri, but it is too far away for sightseers, while Kauri Park is easy of access and will soon be connected by rail. It would be better for the Government to sell the larger area and secure the whole of this, and so be able to preserve for the public these magnificent samples of the fast disappearing kauri. In any case a caretaker should be appointed without delay. It will be a most difficult job preserving this fine park from fire. It is surrounded by a land from which the kauri has been taken, and which is now covered with tall fern and old stumps. The rotting sap on the stumps is like so much tinder, a spark would set it on fire, and given a high wind and a dry summer, nothing could save the living trees. The settlers all around are burning off every season, so you have every element of danger. Only the other day a bush fire spread to the State forest beyond and destroyed a number of fine trees. Visitors too, will be coming in increasing numbers, lighting fires, and smoking in the bush, digging up the ferns and destroying the lovely undergrowth. It is only a little bit compared with the cleared areas around; let us make every effort to preserve it intact.

Charles had this to say about the New Zealand 'Bush':
I use the term in its original sense. The word is partly losing its meaning. Nowadays we are becoming accustomed to hearing the term applied to any rough country place. A fern hill or even a tract of teatree is called the bush; but by bush I mean the unbroken forest country — the 'Forest Primeval', such as the Thames or Waitakere ranges were in the early days and such as the Urewera country and a few other parts of New Zealand are today.

I have never ceased to be thankful for two things. One is that I was born with an intense love for the beautiful of Nature, and the other that I came to New Zealand before the hand of man had spoiled most of its natural beauty.

Some people dread the bush, they never feel at home in it; the gloom and silence gives them an uncanny feeling, the absence of life fills them with a sense of loneliness, and they feel uncomfortable until they return to the brightness of the outside world. But as for me, I love the bush, I delight to wander through it hour after hour. I never tire of its wonderful charm. I love the glinting sunlight and the mysterious gloom, the sweet smell of moist air and the resinous perfume of the pines.

Many a day I have spent alone exploring its sylvan glades, and I can truly say that never once have I felt lonely or a desire for company. Even the hard rough work of struggling through the maze and tangle of the denser parts is exhilarating. I love to push my way up the spur of some steep bush range or leap from stone to stone travelling up some babbling creek.

There is a wide difference in the character of the bush of the north and the bush of the south, a difference caused in a large measure by the difference in temperature. The rainfall is also a factor in determining

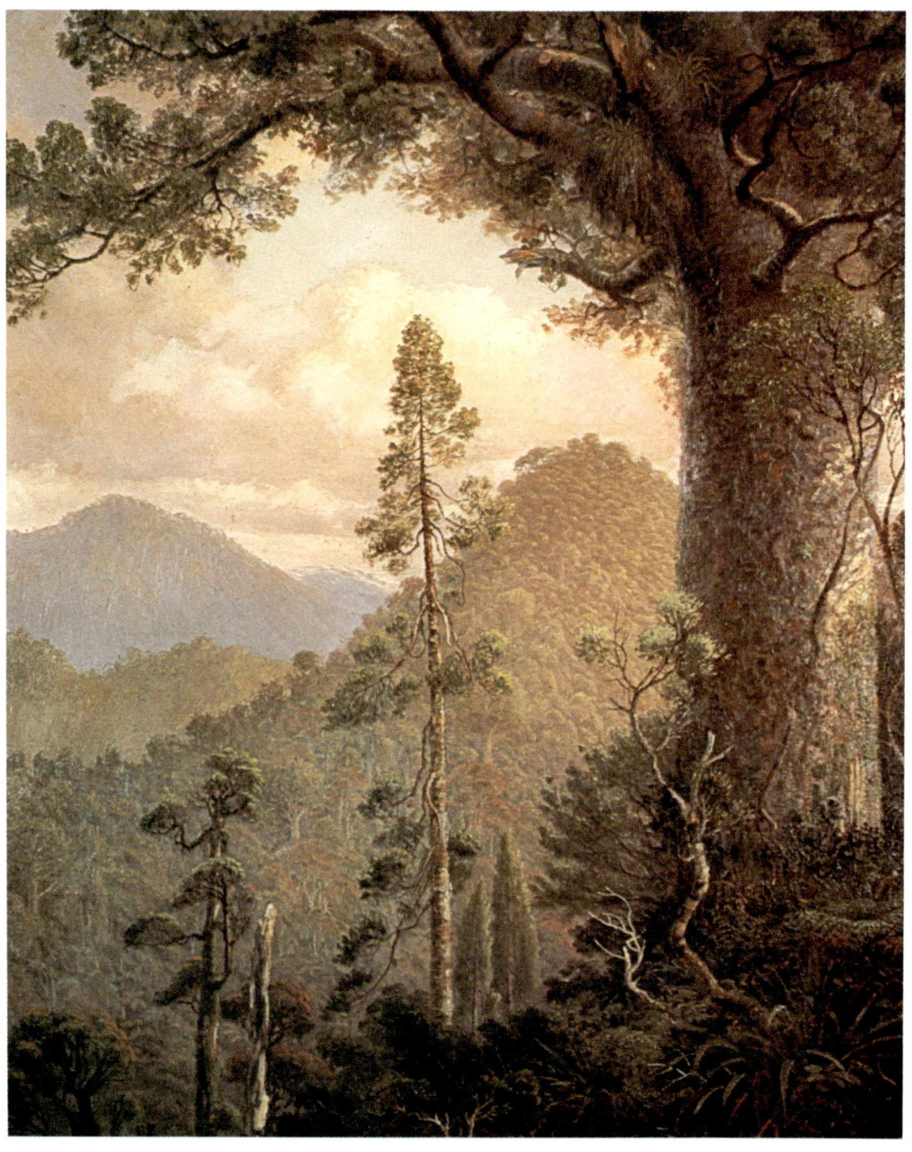

Kauris at Thames, 1915.
Oil on canvas, 28 × 34 in.

the nature of the growth. This is very noticeable in the South Island.
On the western side of the chain of snow mountains, where the rainfall
is abundant, the bush grows rank and dense; but as soon as you cross
the dividing range and descend the drier eastern slopes, the difference
is very noticeable. Forests of black and silver birch clothe the mountain
sides, and the undergrowth is scanty. In the forests round Auckland
where the climate is subtropical and humid, there is a charming variety
of vegetation.

It is said an acre of land will often contain between forty and fifty
different kinds of trees and shrubs — a larger number than can be
found in the whole of Britain.

166

The lordly Kauri, King of the Forest, and his graceful consort the Rimu, hold sway over a numerous court of stately trees. The sturdy Puriri grows side by side with the handsome Tawa, throwing out its dark tapering branches in picturesque abandon; the ornamental Puketea with its buttressed root and the Kohekohe with its broad canopy of large delicate leaves; the Kahikatea and the Matai struggle upwards to get a glimpse of sun and air, while the Hinau, close attendant on the king, is content to dwell in the shade. The court jester is not wanting, for just look at that giant Rata, its uncouth form leaving under it a mass of creepers and parasites that completely hides its shaggy trunk, while the forest vines like ropes and cordage, wanton from tree to tree hang in graceful festoons gently swaying in the summer breeze. The court ladies are there too; here, there, and everywhere the tall tree ferns lift their feathery fronds, their slender shafts decorated with an exquisite mantle of moss and lichen; and the little ones gambol about the feet of their elders while the floor is carpeted with the softest of moss.

The New Zealand bush has no colour you say. Just watch that ray of sunshine which, penetrating the dense canopy above it, descends like a fairy's wand transforming whatever it touches — that leafy branch above stands out against the gloom in brightest green, and here where the pencil of light falls on this mossy trunk, it changes the sombre tints to gold and emerald, rich brown and amber; and there, where it has caught a mass of hymenophyllum on that old stump the exquisite forms stand out like the finest lace. Wherever the eye rests, from the tall tree tops to the lowly ferns and mosses at our feet, there is a wealth of beauty which bewilders us — infinite in variety, exquisite in design, overwhelming in its riotous exuberance.

Strange thoughts sometimes haunt the mind when travelling through the bush. Here is all this beauty, multiplied a million times all around us, and existing and being reproduced for ages before the advent of man. Why is all this waste of beauty? Does the creator bring it into being for his own gratification, or are there other intelligences unknown to us, who are endowed like us with a sense of beauty, perhaps to a higher degree than ourselves, whose admiration and praise are welcome to the Great Designer?

The bush has its drawbacks as well as its beauties. It is not an easy road to travel through. When camping at the Thames in the early days, three of us went exploring in the bush — prospecting was what we called it, but I think the love of adventure had more to do with it than the love of gold. We packed a week's provisions of flour and biscuits on our backs and struck a bee line for the back country. Steering by compass we went straight ahead, up hills and across gullies, building a little shelter of Nikau to sleep under at night.

The beginning was mostly uphill. There was no track — no cattle had cleared the way — we were pioneers. It was a constant struggle through a tangle of undergrowth, sometimes you would reach a spot where progress seemed impossible. You searched all round for something like an opening, but in vain — there was nothing for it but to push ahead;

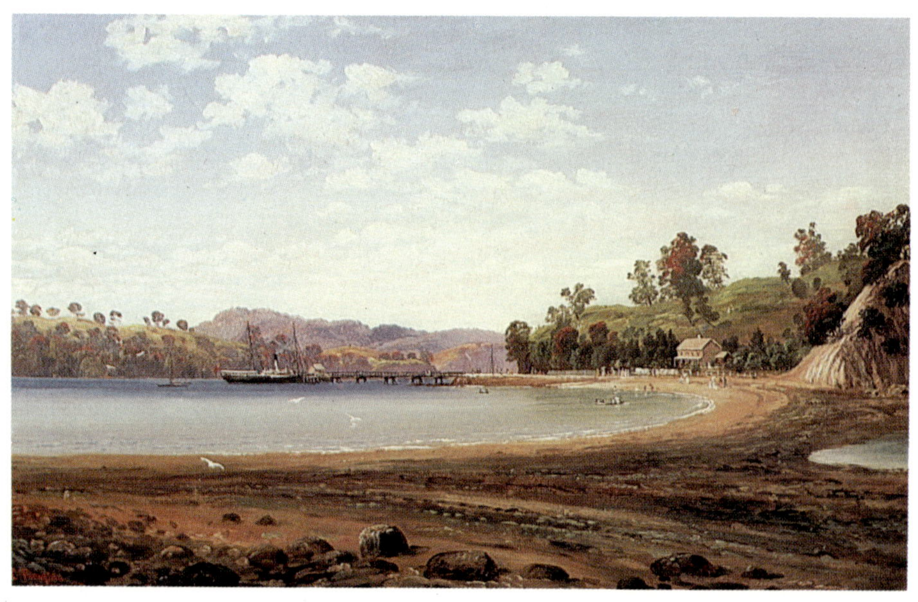

Scotts Bay, c. 1900.

so taking comfort in the thought that it was better before, you lower your head and charge. Your hands are busy dividing the branches whilst a thousand tiny claws are tugging at your raiment; you free one leg and make a plunge forward but find the other leg imprisoned; you stop to free that one and your hat falls off. You think at last you have advanced a step, when the swag at your back gets entangled in a supplejack. When at last you emerge, it is with a multitude of ventilating holes in your nether garments, which the persistent mosquitoes call attention to at every halting place.

As we rise in elevation, the scented Taneakea becomes more plentiful. Tall young Kauris rise like masts on the hillside, and a few Totara appear. We leave the troublesome supplejack behind us; kidney ferns mingle with the mosses on the rotten stumps; and the cutty grass becomes more plentiful. Crossing the top of the spur the ground becomes more level, and we presently come upon a grove of noble Kauri trees. Here the undergrowth is comparatively open, giving a magnificent view of these monarchs of the forest. Side by side they rise, their tall straight shafts the columns, the interlacing branches the gothic arches, of some vast cathedral; the softened light falling in delicate tracery on the bare trunks as from some mullioned window.

Now we cross a deep ravine where the graceful Nikau mingles with tall tree ferns. In these sheltered gullies the Nikau palm is seen at its best, its long feathery leaves bending over with exquisite symmetry, a shapely vase poised on its slender stem. The supplejack tangles the ground or trails in twisted cords from branch to branch — its scarlet berries like bunches of red currants making a charming bit of colour.

It seems nothing short of a crime to destroy so much beauty, but the bushman's axe and settlers' fires are playing havoc with the finest parts

168

of it. The settler regards the bush as so much waste land. He is ever thinking of how much grass or turnips he could grow there; his cattle are free to roam and trample the mossy carpet and break down the ferns.

Fortunately there are exceptions, men who love the natural beauty amid which they are placed, and make an effort to preserve it. A notable example is Mr Edward Morrison of the Red Bluff orchard at Mahurangi, who at considerable personal sacrifice has reserved 80 acres of very fine mixed bush on his property. He has carefully fenced it in from the inroads of cattle and pigs, and formed a winding footpath over two miles in length, giving access to the finest trees. May his example soon be followed by many others.

In 1921, the Auckland Society of Arts was to hold its Jubilee Exhibition, and entries were invited for the Picture of the Year award. The best picture would be purchased by the City Council and hung in the Art Gallery. Charles decided to paint his own masterpiece. He would portray his own love of the bush in a huge canvas, which would give pleasure to all the people of Auckland.

He chose a canvas almost four feet wide by five feet tall, and started to copy the best pieces of several of his smaller pictures of the forest. Each morning, he would set up his easel on the back verandah of his Wood Street home, painting kauri after kauri standing erect, with their branches intertwining overhead, the light peeping through the leaves on to the straight trunks below. Then he added the undergrowth, tree ferns and nikaus, lichen and mosses, until at last he was satisfied. The canvas was too large for him or his brother Fred to frame, and young Tom was called in to do this for him. At last he took it to the Exhibition, sure that it would be chosen as the Picture of the Year, and all who loved nature would be able to see it in the Art Gallery! He called it *The Vaulted Aisles of Nature's Cathedral* and whereas his other paintings were usually priced at about £10.10.0, he put a price tag on this one of £120.0.0.

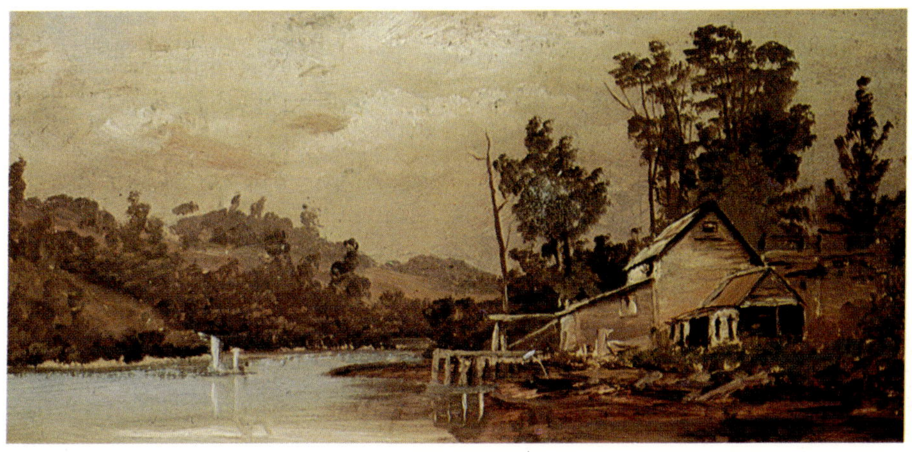

Southgate's Lime Works, undated. Oil on card, 12 × 5½ in.

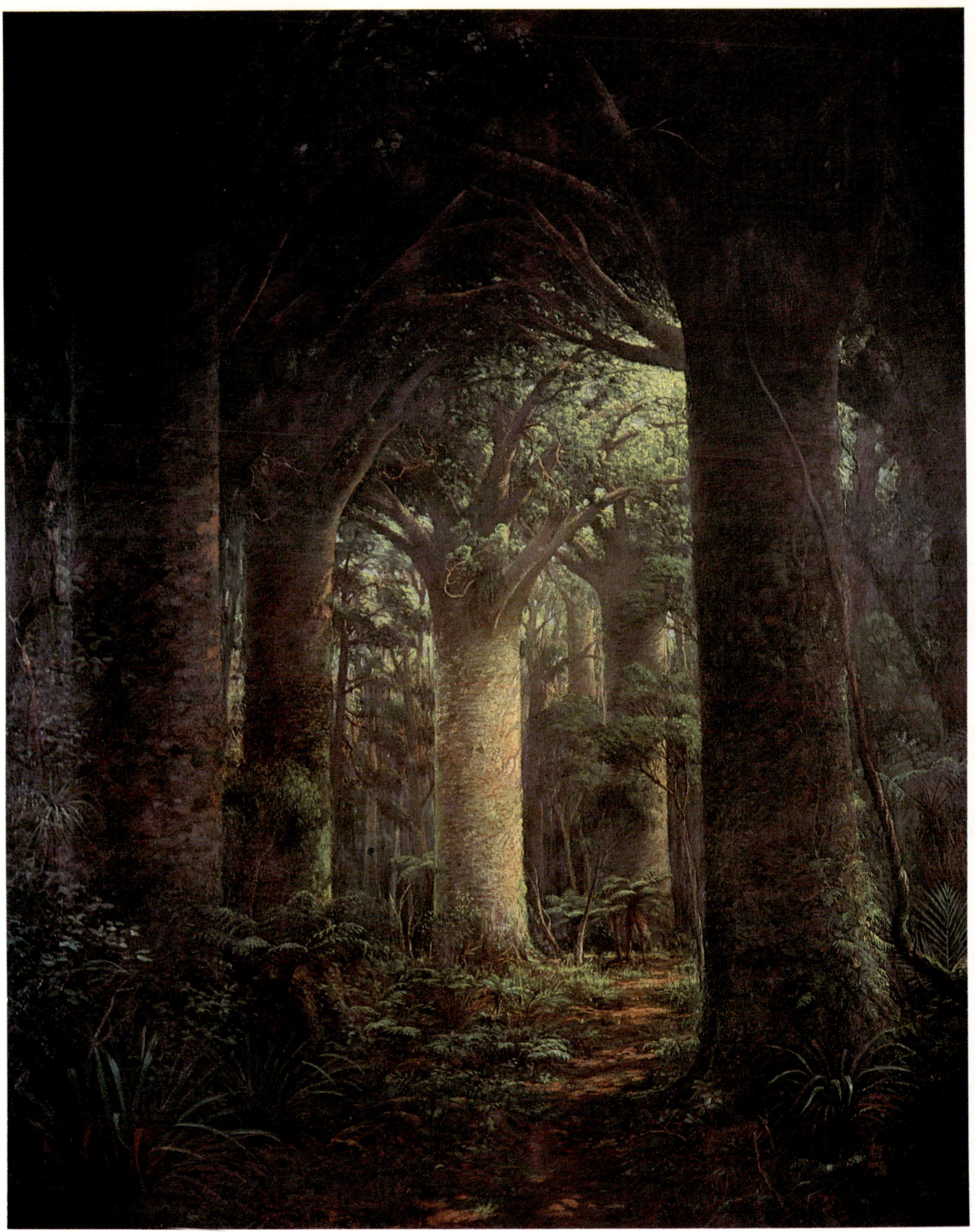

17. Heartbreak

But Charles was to be disappointed. Each person who visited the Exhibition was given a voting paper on which to name the picture which he considered the best in the contest. Charles was led to believe that he had more votes than the others put together, but when the awards were announced, he was only given third place. The report in the paper didn't even mention his work, but stated:

> While the general standard of the work exhibited is high, there is nothing specially ambitious in the work of local artists. The most conspicuous feature of the display is the exhibit sent from America by an Aucklander who has travelled far in the world of art since the days of his early studies with Messrs Steele and Goldie. His painting is an interesting example of a class of work to which this country has not yet grown quite accustomed, but which in England is rapidly taking the place of the older school in which attention to detail and a careful adherence to orthodox methods of treatment were the leading features.

Charles asked the leaders of the Society why he had not won, and they replied:

"We've got plenty of Blomfields in the Art Gallery. We wanted to give a newcomer a chance."

Charles could not believe that his beloved Art Society had accepted the modern trend. "How could you do this to me?" he asked over and over again. Mary Ann went down and gave them all a piece of her mind, but all to no avail. His painting was not purchased for the Art Gallery.

Sadly he brought it home, and hung it in the front hall at the foot of the stairs, where it hung for over twenty years. All his family, grandchildren and friends loved it. They felt as though they could walk right into the forest, the painting was so big and so lifelike. At last in 1944, Ellen presented it to the Auckland Museum, where it is still displayed in the Kauri Section on the first floor.

After this Charles's heart and spirit were broken.

"I paint nature as I see it," he would say. "Surely there is some virtue in that."

But he continued to paint, although he did not travel again. He was all the more determined to give careful attention to detail and his intricate work became better than it had ever been before.

Charles also spent a lot of time meditating on the beauties of nature and sound, and the wonderful scientific discoveries which had been made

'Nature's Cathedral', 1921. Oil on canvas, 48×60 in. (Courtesy of Auckland Institute and Museum.)

during his lifetime, and wrote about the rainbow to the *Herald Supplement*, heading it:

MUSIC AND COLOUR
AN INTERESTING THEORY

What eye has not been charmed at the sight of the glorious rainbow. Produced by a myriad tiny prisms, it appears with a brilliancy so startling that it is hard to realise it is only a vision. It has no reality. It is not a picture painted on the background of the storm. It requires no background. It may appear equally across the pure blue sky or even over distant hills and buildings. Even its position depends on the observer. He has only to move and the bow moves with him. Every observer sees a rainbow of his own and no two are exactly similar.

If we pass a ray of sunshine through a piece of triangular glass we can produce the rainbow artificially, a fact utilised by modern science in vastly increasing our knowledge of the heavenly bodies. But whether produced by the rain cloud, the spray of a waterfall or a piece of glass, the colour spectrum is invariably composed of the same seven colours in precisely the same order. It is evident this fairy-like object, so ethereal and so fleeting yet obeys some common law.

There is a wonderful analogy between colour and music. If we study the structure of the musical scale we find it is composed of seven notes, each note having its own particular character and expression. No matter what sound we take for the foundation, high or low, the moment that sound is chosen the same seven notes spring up in attendance upon it, in exactly the same order and with the same character.

These notes we find are not all equally important. Three of them stand out bolder than the rest, as the strong pillars of the scale, the first, third, and fifth.

In the colour scale there are also three main colours, the primaries (red, yellow, blue) occupying in the spectrum exactly the same position as the leading notes of the scale, the first, third, and fifth. The other colours are secondary and dependent upon the three primaries formed, in fact, by blending two of the primaries together.

It is well known that both sound and light are produced by vibration, sound by the vibration of the air acting on the delicate membrane of the ear, while light is the vibration of the ether acting on the retina of the eye. That this is true is proved by what is designated 'Professor Dove's experiment'. He says: "Imagine a thin bar of steel, fixed at one end and made to oscillate backwards and forwards by some mechanical means, slowly at first, but with an ever-increasing speed. We see it moving and for a time can count the beats, but soon the momentum becomes too great for the eye to follow and now the ear detects a low hum, the deepest bass note. This gradually rises in pitch until an octave is reached. The speed still increasing, the sound mounts higher and higher; another octave and still another, until we reach the pitch of an ordinary tuning fork C, when the steel bar will be vibrating at the rate of 512 beats to the second. There is no pause, the speed increases, the

number of beats doubling with every octave until the shrillest audible
note is reached and silence reigns. Not because the vibrations have
ceased, but because the sense of hearing is too coarse to receive them.
What takes place in this silence gap we know not, but presently as the
rate of movement accelerates we feel a gentle heat and a faint red glow
appears. The vibrations have now reached such a rate of rapidity that
they appeal to another sense, the sense of sight. As we watch, the dull
glow brightens into brilliant red, the red into orange, the orange into
yellow, green, blue, indigo, and violet, and having run up the whole
octave of colour the vibrations pass out of the realm of sight into the
realm of chemical change.''

We have said the seven notes of the scale have each a different
character and effect. If it were not so the art of music would be impossible. It is by bringing the mental effects of these seven notes into play,
either alone or in combination, that music is capable of expressing all
the varied emotions of the human soul.

These facts may be modified to a very large extent by pitch, rate of
movement, accent and association, but when sung slowly while the ear
is filled with the key, their effects may be stated to be the following.
We will set them down in order, placing the corresponding colours by
their side.

Violet,	te:	The sensitive or piercing tone
Indigo,	la:	The weeping or sorrowful tone
Blue,	soh:	The grand or clear tone
Green,	fa:	The desolate or awe inspiring tone
Yellow,	me:	The steady or calm tone
Orange,	re:	The hopeful or rousing tone
Red,	doh:	The strong or firm tone.

If we study the works of the great masters, we find abundant illus-
trations of how a particular note is employed to produce a particular
effect. Thus Handel when he wishes to emphasise the Christian's firm
trust in his Saviour, in the air, 'I Know that My Redeemer Liveth',
places the word 'know' with a strong accent on the doh, the strong firm
note, the solid foundation tone of the scale. When he wishes to impress
upon the mind a sense of desolation and the abandonment of grief in
'He Was Despised' that most pathetic of songs, he uses the desolate fa
on the middle syllables of 'despised', 'rejected'. The same note is used
with marked effect in 'The Heavens are Telling' in Hadyn's 'Creation'.
Who has not felt a thrill of awe at those grand ascending passages in the
bass, leading up to the long-sustained fa? The sad effect of la is so
marked that it forms the keynote of a scale of its own called the minor
mode. The calm, prayerful character of the mediant me is very noticeable in Mendelssohn's 'O Rest in the Lord'.

The dominant soh, the clarion note, is indispensable in martial music;
take the soh away from any of the bugle calls and the warlike character
disappears. The predominance of the leading notes, doh, me, soh, in a
chorus gives strength and brilliance, as is seen in the 'Hallelujah
Chorus'. While, where the notes la, fa, me and te predominate, the

music has a softer, sadder feeling. 'Behold the Lamb of God' is a typical instance.

Turn now to the colour scale and we are struck with a strange resemblance. The strong doh becomes the stately red. The grand clear dominant soh becomes the pure clear blue, emblem of truth. The calm me becomes the soft yellow, the rousing re the exciting orange, while the weeping la is represented by the quaker colour of the scale, the indigo. The resemblance is so marked that if we print two tunes in the colour scale, one bright and joyful and the other mournful, say 'Silchester' and 'St. Brides' we see at a glance the difference in character, the predominance of the primary colours in the one giving it a joyous brilliance, which is lacking in the sombre tones of the other.

When we come to the subject of harmony, we find the relation of the two scales with each other closer than ever. The notes that harmonise in music or colour are absolutely identical. What satisfies the ear in music, satisfies the eye in colour, and the same with discords.

Just as a great painter uses a certain colour scheme to convey his impressions, so a great musician uses particular notes to influence his hearers. And just as a musician introduces dissonances into his score in order to produce a certain effect or enhance the emphasis of a particular chord, so an artist uses discords and broken colours to increase the force or beauty of his colour harmonies.

Thus we see another instance of the unity of Nature and the all-embracing influence of one Master Mind.

In October 1925 Charles wrote his final article to the *Herald*:

WHAT IS ART?

The controversy over the Art Gallery pictures has done good in one way. It has set people thinking; they are asking themselves the question "What is Art?" Each answers the question in his own manner, the answers differing widely one from another according to the standing and intelligence of the inquirer, or his peculiar training and environment.

There is one answer alone which includes and embraces them all. Art is the power to feel intensely and to be able, through various channels, to make others feel the same. We are asked, "Is a certain picture good or bad art?" What a foolish question! There is no such thing as bad art. If it is bad it is not art at all.

Art is not the technique or method of painting. It is the power of the picture to call forth happy feelings, to give the beholder higher and nobler thoughts; to give him some conception of past times and customs; to reveal the beauties of nature, and to elevate and strengthen his soul for the battle of life. If it does this it is good art, no matter how it is painted.

Take that favourite picture, for instance, "The School Mistress' Birthday" by John Morgan. Can anyone look at that picture without feeling the influence of the innocent pleasure of the school children trooping in in breezy haste to present their simple gifts to their beloved

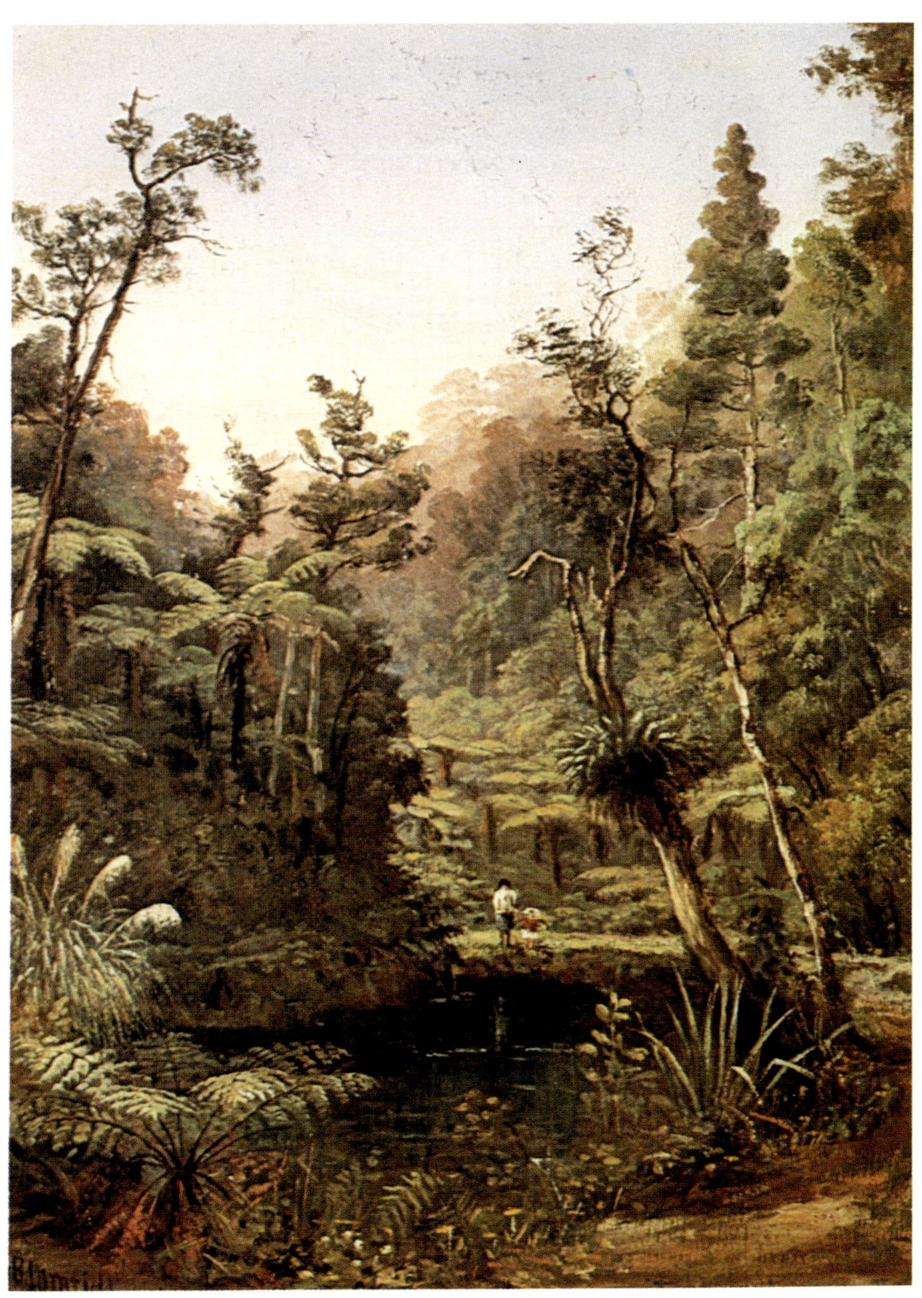

Le Roys Bush, Birkenhead, 1925. Oil on canvas, 14 × 18 in.

teacher on her birthday? How the happiness of the occasion is radiated through the beholder's soul! It is as good as the finest tonic.

Take the painting by Blair Leighton, "In Time of Peril"; a picture objected to by these extremists because it tells a story. How it carries the mind back to the troublesome times of the Crusaders, the armed knight fleeing with his wife and children from a sudden raid, seeking sanctuary by night at the back door of the monastery. The half-scared monks roused from their beds by the untimely summons. The anxiety of the beautiful wife, the wonder of the lovely boy, the peaceful comfort of the sleeping babe, the huddled burden of rich treasures gathered in haste by the strong, faithful retainer at the oars. How the story develops as we gaze! The exquisite workmanship of the painting, the careful detail, the pains taken to include everything that will help the appeal, make the story more convincing and life-like.

Does this picture lose anything by being "old-fashioned" as they call it? Take Melton Fisher's "Sleeping Lady". Who can resist the infinite grace and beauty in the reclining figure?

It is just the same with literature. It is the masterminds whose genius has produced work which stirs the passions, inspires the will, and calls forth our love, whose names are a household word. They felt deeply, suffered keenly, and loved intensely, and by their writings have passed their feelings on. What matters it that the handwriting was wretched and the spelling faulty? It is the inner spirit which counts. When Shakespeare wrote:

> How sweet the moon-beams sleep on yonder bank,
> Here will we sit and let the sounds of music
> Creep in our ears; soft stillness and the night
> Become the touches of sweet harmony.
> Sit Jessica. Look how the floor of heaven
> Is thick inlaid with patines of bright gold:
> There's not the smallest orb that thou beholdest,
> But in its motion like an angel sings,
> Still quiring to the young-eyed cherubim;
> Such harmony is in immortal souls;
> But while this muddy vesture of decay
> Doth grossly close it in, we cannot hear it . . .

he wrote something which will give joy to thousands as long as civilisation lasts.

It matters not that Bobbie Burns was a very indifferent character, and wrote most of his inimitable verse in a beer house. We feel the eternal truth of words like these:

> But pleasures are like poppies spread.
> You pluck the flower, the bloom is shed.
> Or like the snowflake on the river
> A moment white — then gone for ever.
> Or like the borealis race
> That flits ere you can mark its place.
> Or like the rainbow's lovely form
> Evanishing amid the storm.

The same truth is illustrated in music. Our feelings are played on as on an instrument. We laugh or cry, dance or mourn as the master wishes. Our souls are lifted up to Heaven's gates by the glorious 'Halleluia' or saddened to tears by the plaintive tones of 'He was despised'. We feel the solemn awe and grandeur of 'The Heavens are

Telling', and are delighted by the sweet cooing of the gentle dove and charmed by the haunting notes of the nightingale.

It is all the same. Just the same simple fact. Painting, poetry, music, drama, architecture — it is the soul that counts; the form is nothing.

The other night I listened to the playing of Chopin's 'Nocturne in E Flat'. It was played with skill and feeling. I was weary for want of sleep and ill with worry, but the moment the music of the great master filled the room my mind was carried away with the most beautiful thoughts and images.

It was a march. The march of a mighty host through the sky! Oh! the magic of it! In a moment my ills were healed. With measured tread, without noise or bustle, the mighty host went on. Inscrutable! Stupendous! With the tramp of arrayed hosts was mingled the patter of children's feet, and the sound of a thousand tongues.

Sometimes there would be a digression, minor armies roving hither and thither, discords in the harmony, but nothing could stay the mighty impulse. It was the march of mankind through the ages, gathering in every wanderer, overcoming every obstacle, every discord resolved in a finer harmony. It was the march of eternity, the very footsteps of God. And so it went on, higher and higher, further and further, until, far away up in the ethereal depths of space, it vanished in a final quiver of celestial beauty.

Oh, the power of such mighty genius, such supreme art, to lift the very soul above itself and enchant it with such magnificent imagery!

Yes, Art is more than mechanism; it is more than method; it is more than outward show or fashion; it is independent of times and seasons; it is the power to influence the souls of others, to cause them to glow with love or burn with passion. It is the power to create that intense longing for something better and nobler, that mysterious, ineffable something which is the most sublime attribute of the human soul.

But the disappointments and heartbreaks that Charles had received, by his work being rejected as old-fashioned, preyed on his mind until he had a mental breakdown. Tom and Reg realised that for their mother's sake he needed to go to hospital, and one night, they drove him in Tom's car to the Avondale Asylum. Tom dipped his lights as they entered the gates, but their father looked up and recognised the building.

"You're surely not taking me to the Mental Hospital are you?" he cried. "I didn't think you'd ever do this to me."

Tom and Reg shepherded their father into the capable hands of the Matron, signed the necessary papers, and fled, both of them heartbroken.

Some time later, when Bessie called to visit her father, he was having one of his lucid periods. Turning his sad eyes on her he cried:

"I didn't think you'd let them do this to your father, Bessie."

Bessie ran from the hospital and arrived home in tears.

"I'm going to get him out of that place," she said. As good as her word, she went to the minister of the Tabernacle, Rev. J. W. Kemp, and begged him to help her. He called on the hospital officials and found that Charles was much better mentally, but weaker physically. They considered he

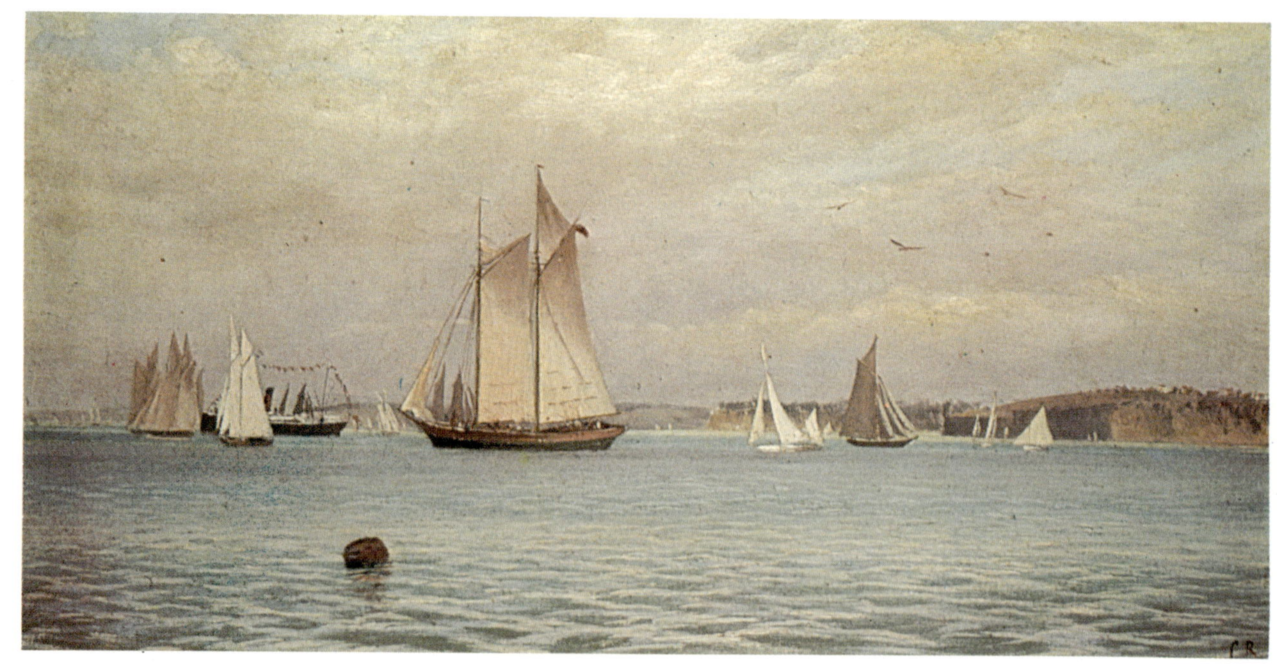

*Auckland Regatta Day un-
dated. Oil on card, 21 ×
12 in.*

was well enough to be looked after at home, so gratefully Mr Kemp
brought Charles back to Wood Street.

After this, Charles tried to paint, but not only was he too weak, but his
ability had deserted him. He ruined some of his good pictures by daubing
over them, and his attempts at drawing were strange. One day his doctor
came to visit him, and asked if he could buy a Terrace picture.

"But you haven't signed it, Mr Blomfield," he said.

"I'm too weak and tired to do it," replied Charles. So the doctor gave
him an injection, helped him to sit up, and handed him a brush. Very
carefully Charles signed "C. Blom————" and dropped the brush —
probably the last thing he ever painted.

18. Obituary

Sunday March 7th, 1926 was a cold wet miserable day, but Charles called to his wife, Ellen, "I want to go to Bessie's this afternoon and see her children."

"Are you sure you're well enough?" she asked.

"Yes, I'm sure, and I feel I must go today," he replied.

"Very well, I'll get Tom to pick you up in his car," said Ellen, and she sent Dossie next door to use the telephone and call Tom. Sure enough, Tom and his family called around during the afternoon and Tom helped his father into the old Ford Beauty, wrapping him carefully in blankets so he would not catch a chill. Then he discovered he had a flat tyre.

"Father," he cried. "You'll have to go back inside. I've got a puncture."

"No," said Charles. "If I once go back inside the house, your mother will never let me out again. I'll just stay here while you fix the tyre."

So Tom had to jack up the car with his father still inside. Then when he took off the wheel, he had to mend the puncture before he could put it back on again; and all the while Charles sat very still to make sure the car did not fall off the jack.

At Bessie's house in One Tree Hill, Charles called all the children around him.

"I have something to tell you," he said. "I am going on a journey and I won't be coming back. I don't know just when I am going, but it won't be long now. But I am not afraid, as Jesus will be with me, and if you children want to see me again, be good and trust in Jesus, and you will come to me in the sweet bye and bye."

After this he was exhausted. "I'm tired, Ellen," he said. "You can take me home now."

On Monday March 15th, a week later, Bessie called at her parents' home, as they were all going to see Mr Kemp off to England. She went into her father's room to say goodbye, but noticed a change in him, and decided to stay.

He held her hand and whispered, "Give us a kiss, dear."

She bent down to kiss him, and noticed his breath as sweet as a baby's. He looked up and smiled, and said, "I'm floating on the ocean of God's love."

Then he closed his eyes, and in a few minutes he had passed away.

His death notice told its own story of his life:

BLOMFIELD — on March 15, at his residence, 40 Wood Street, Ponsonby. Charles Blomfield, artist. Dearly-loved husband of Ellen Blomfield.

'Blessed are the pure in heart'.

Funeral will leave above address at 2 p.m. to-day (Wednesday) for Hillsborough. Service at the house at 1.40 p.m. No mourning by the request of the deceased.

He was buried on the hillside at Hillsborough Cemetery overlooking Manukau Harbour, next to Bessie's baby daughter Lois, and had to wait almost twenty years before he was rejoined with his dear wife, Ellen.

Bessie's husband, William Kendon (the founder of the firm of Kendon, Mills, Muldoon & Brown), wrote this obituary to his father-in-law:

Many people have admired and revered Charles Blomfield as an artist, who have not had the opportunity of knowing him as a friend. Having been admitted by marriage into his home circle a good many years ago, and having been privileged to enjoy his friendship ever since, I feel to some extent qualified to speak of his personal characteristics for the benefit of those who care to learn more about him now that he is no longer with us in the flesh.

Looking back over the period of my acquaintance with him, I am most of all impressed by his simplicity of character. Alike in his personal tastes, his habits of living, his choice of food, his social intercourse, his methods of work, as well as in his artistic ideals and achievements, he was distinguished by a charming and ingenuous simplicity. Into simple pleasures, such as entertaining children with stories, or watching the lambs skipping and playing on the hillside, or tracing imaginary pictures in the glowing embers, or reading aloud to the domestic circle, he would enter with zest. Always an early riser, he would be up and about his self-allotted task for the day, whether painting pictures, or working in his garden, or whatever it might be, long before the other members of the household were astir.

In this way he used to get through a surprising amount of artistic work, and many of his best pictures were painted in the early hours of the day when he found his brain and hand were at their best. In many respects he was quite unconventional, and went his own way regardless of custom. Thus he would eat only if he were hungry, and only what he liked; if he were weary he would retire to rest no matter what the hour or who was of the company; and he liked to come and go as the spirit moved him. It seems quite fitting to apply the well-known words of Tennyson to him, for he was truly

    . . . as the greatest only are,
      In his simplicity sublime.

In intercourse with other men, he bore himself with a certain natural dignity, and would meet those who might think themselves his social superiors, on an equality of footing which he seemed to claim unconsciously as an undisputed right.

This simplicity of character, which was perhaps partly inherited from his mother — who was of the best pioneer type — was no doubt largely derived from and fostered by his love of nature. In him, love of nature was in no sense a pose or an affectation; it was a lifelong, genuine and instinctive affinity for that creative and upholding Power which he believed to be immanent in the visible universe. That it was genuine must be apparent to all who know his paintings, with their wonderful power of conveying to the beholder the very atmosphere of New Zealand scenery; that it was lifelong is evident from a brief autobiographical fragment written not long ago, in which he says that when travelling to this country on the ship *Gertrude* as a lad of fifteen more than sixty years ago, the sight of the ocean with its vastness and resistless might produced in his breast feelings of awe and reverence for the great Creator.

Even in those early years these feelings were struggling for expression; and when, a few years later, he was encamped in the bush in the Thames district and supposed to be looking for gold, he received such an inspiration through his meditation upon the glories of nature by which he was surrounded that he was impelled to try his 'prentice hand at transferring the beauty to canvas. When we reflect that he was without any knowledge of art, and was ignorant of its most elementary principles, and moreover that there were no facilities at hand for learning, his later achievements are seen to be really remarkable.

His close contact for many years with natural objects, bred in him wonderful powers of observation, and he was as expert in his knowledge of the trees and birds of the native bush as if he were a naturalist by profession. He delighted to impart his knowledge to any who might be interested, and a day in the bush in his company was a liberal education.

All things sublime and beautiful evoked his admiration, as will be realised by those who have studied his paintings of the Southern Alps and the glaciers. Amongst other matters, he had a quite considerable knowledge of the difficult science of astronomy. He made it a constant practice to observe for himself the motions of the heavenly bodies, and he supplemented his own observations with a close study of the works of authorities like Sir Robert Ball, R.A. Proctor and others. As a consequence, he was able to discourse most interestingly about the various planets, fixed stars and constellations, while he was quite an authority in his way, on such celestial phenomena as comets, meteors and the various eclipses of the sun and moon.

Other branches of science also came within his ken, and he made a point of keeping abreast of the times, in matters scientific. To any one displaying an interest in such topics, he seemed always equipped for a conversational discussion, on subjects ranging from aviation and wireless telephony to the nebular theory or the evolutionary hypothesis.

Of course in these days there is nothing very startling in a person having a more or less discursive knowledge of various sciences; but in him the fact seemed noteworthy, first because of his lack of educational advantages in his youth, and second because his main concern was with his art, and the practice of art does not usually go hand in hand with the study of science.

In addition to all this, though he did not claim to be a scholar, he had a decided taste for general literature, and was familiar with the principal writers of English poetry and prose. As might be expected, Ruskin was one of his favourite authors and exerted a considerable influence upon him. Of the poets he was familiar with Tennyson and Wordsworth, Milton and Shakespeare, the first-named being probably his first choice.

But a mere catalogue of authors would give no true idea of his extensive acquaintance with general literature — an acquaintance gained largely by the use of his spare moments for reading. This love of reading was a source of great solace to him in his later years, when by reason of his deafness he was to a considerable extent debarred from the social pleasures of conversation.

A curious instance of the breadth of his literary sympathies was his liking for books like the Koran, the Tahmed, and the Apocrypha. With the literature of the Bible he was closely acquainted, particularly the poetical books; Job, the Psalms, and the Song of Songs. To the Psalms he turned instinctively in times of sorrow and adversity.

Of his religion this is not the place to speak, but this much should be said: he translated his Christianity into everyday deeds, and perhaps there is no keener test of a man's genuine worth than that.

With all the varied interests of his life, however, it was with his art, as I have already said, that he was chiefly concerned. He had in large measure the artistic temperament, though not in the sense in which that term is sometimes understood. Of the Bohemian, velvet-jacketed, beer-drinking type of artist there was absolutely nothing in his make-up. But he liked to feel free to take up his palette or put it down as he chose. He could not work at his best unless he had the inspiration upon him; then he would turn out first-class pictures, rapidly and easily. He took his art seriously; to him it was more than a profession, it was a vocation — a means of expressing himself and glorifying God. In his view, the proper function of pictorial art was to faithfully portray Nature, in all her infinite variety, for the pleasure and elevation of the beholder. As is fairly well-known, he had no sympathy with the modern school of impressionists, and looked upon their particular cult as a mere temporary phase through which Art was passing.

By standing up for his own artistic ideals, not only with his brush, but with his pen — and he could wield the pen trenchantly on occasion — he believed he was doing a service to the cause of true Art which would some day be recognised. The seeming triumph of opposing ideals during the past few years did much to darken the latter part of his life.

New Zealand has lost one of the most characteristic, if not one of the greatest, of her sons in the passing of Charles Blomfield. If it were possible to gather together in one gallery some hundreds of his greatest pictures — as was done recently in London with the paintings of the late John Sargent, R.A., what a revelation of our beloved land to its citizens it would afford! For he has painted his country from north to south, in all her beauty and with all her changing moods. The magic colouring of the Wanganui, the serene splendour of Mt. Egmont, the dazzling glory of Mt. Cook, the charm of her countryside, the magnificence of her sea coast, and, above all, the witchery and wonder of her forests — all these and much more than these have been flung onto canvas by a master-hand.

By this means he has identified himself in a peculiarly fitting way with his country, and has left a noble heritage for his fellow citizens. That heritage will, I believe, be better appreciated twenty or thirty years hence than it is today. Meanwhile, I crave this opportunity of paying thus publicly a brief and imperfect, but thoroughly sincere tribute to a genuine, simple, modest and kind-hearted gentleman.

Index

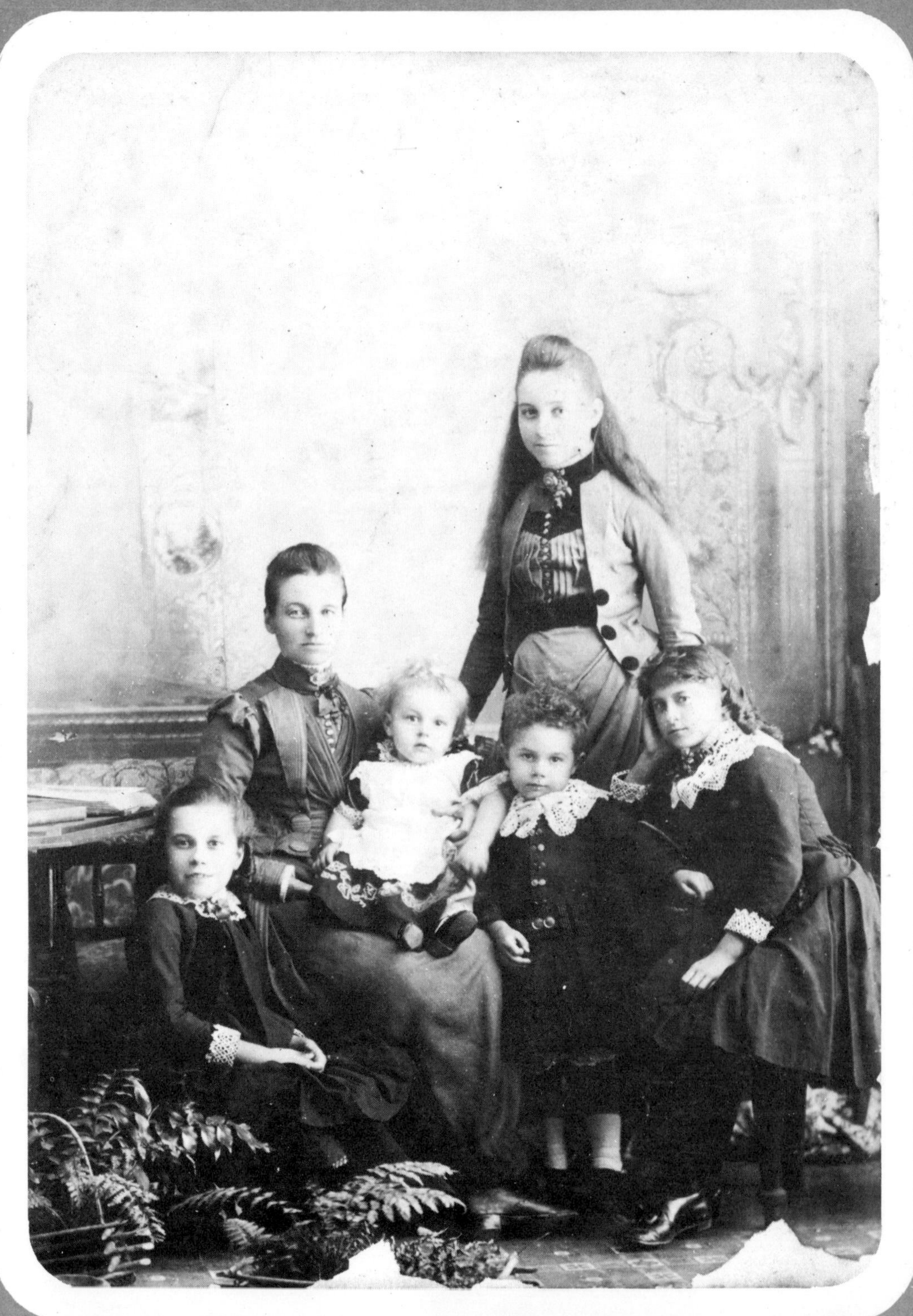